Designing and Building
Outdoor
Furniture
with 47 Projects
2nd Edition

Percy W. Blandford

TAB FURNITURE WOODSHOP SERIES

TAB **TAB BOOKS Inc.**

Blue Ridge Summit, PA

SECOND EDITION
FIRST PRINTING

Copyright © 1988 by TAB BOOKS Inc.
First edition copyright © 1983 by TAB BOOKS Inc.
Printed in the United States of America

Library of Congress Cataloging in Publication Data

Blandford, Percy W.
Designing and building outdoor furniture, with 47 projects / by
Percy W. Blandford. — 2nd ed.
p.   cm.
Rev. ed. of: Constructing outdoor furniture, with 99 projects, 1st
ed. c1983.
Includes index.
ISBN 0-8306-0184-8   ISBN 0-8306-2984-X (pbk.)
1. Outdoor furniture. I. Blandford, Percy W. Constructing
outdoor furniture, with 99 projects. II. Title.
TT197.5.09B58   1988   88-11762
684.1'8—dc19   CIP

Questions regarding the content of this book
should be addressed to:

Reader Inquiry Branch
TAB BOOKS Inc.
Blue Ridge Summit, PA 17294-0214

Edited by Suzanne L. Cheatle
Designed by Jaclyn Saunders

Contents

Introduction

IF THE CLIMATE WHERE YOU LIVE allows you to spend time outdoors for worthwhile periods, you need furniture intended for use in the open air. It might be possible to improvise or occasionally use indoor furniture, but it is always better to have furniture especially intended for outdoor use.

Wooden furniture blends well into natural surroundings. If the woods and construction techniques are carefully chosen, wooden outdoor furniture can be expected to have a long life. With some woods, appearance improves with age. Another attraction of wood is that it can be worked with simple or elaborate equipment.

Outdoor furniture is a specialized subject. It is not really an extension of indoor furniture. The wood used for outdoor furniture is usually of larger sections than that used for indoor furniture. Joints are often simple, but they are strong. Frequent use is made of nails and screws (with bolts where needed). At one time, glue was rarely used in furniture making, but with modern, fully waterproof glues available, extra strength comes from using glue with metal fastenings.

Seating can range from a simple plank bench, suitable for a brief rest, to something with all the upholstery needed for comfort and positions that allow for sitting upright or anywhere between that and reclining fully. Chairs can have backs and legs in a basically similar configuration to indoor chairs, or there can be some arrangements not seen indoors. There can be provisions for removable arms and cushions.

Tables might not seem to have so many variations, but there are a great many ways of achieving the desired result of a level flat surface at a suitable height. Tables can be combined with seating, as in the almost universal picnic table. Tables and chairs can be made to fold for storage or transport. Making combined furniture or folding furniture requires more thought and attention to detail, but the skill required should be within the capabilities of most amateur craftsmen.

For most projects, there are working drawings drawn to scale, giving one or two elevations and a plan. There can be slight variations when drawings are reduced for reproduction, but for sizes that are not immediately obvious, you can compare with something on the same view that is dimensioned. Unless otherwise marked, all sizes are in inches. Where a view is symmetrical and only part of it is shown, the centerline is indicated by the draftsman's broken line of long and short dashes.

For information on using a lathe, see *The Woodturner's Bible-2nd Edition* (TAB #1954).

1

Design

FURNITURE FOR OUTDOOR USE serves many of the same purposes as furniture for indoor use but presents several special considerations as well. It might occasionally be possible to use indoor furniture outdoors, but you will soon discover that it is not the best for the purpose. Outdoor furniture tends to get rough treatment. Quality indoor furniture would suffer if used very much outdoors. Indoor furniture is not usually designed to withstand dampness and dirt. Excessive sunlight will damage its finish and upholstery. The finish put on indoor furniture will not always stand up to outdoor conditions and the glue used might soon deteriorate.

Outdoor furniture should be specially designed. There might be a few items that you could take indoors for use, but it is better to regard open air as outdoor furniture's normal environment. That does not mean outdoor furniture should be massive and crude, however. Some of it fits that description, but other items qualify as fine specimens of furniture making as much as indoor furniture.

Outdoor furniture does not need to be uncomfortable. Some of it can be simple and rather basic, but if its proportions are right, it will give all the comfort you need. Attached upholstery cannot be used on furniture that will stay outdoors in rain, but much can be done with cushions that can be taken indoors.

SIZES AND PROPORTIONS

Sizes and proportions of furniture need to be correct so the furniture can be used by the people for which it is intended. Fortunately, most of us are near an average size, and a furniture size that is right for the majority will suit us. One advantage of making your own furniture is that you can alter sizes to suit individuals. If you have someone very tall or very short in the family, you can alter the dimensions to afford them the same comfort that the average person gets with average equipment.

For sitting upright, the support should be around 16 inches from the floor. You might reduce this amount to as low as 12 inches or go up an inch or so, but the height is about right when your thighs are horizontal. For something like fishing or tending a camp fire—where you must lean forward or reach the ground—the height can come down to perhaps 10 inches, but that is not the height you want to sit at for long periods. Remember to allow for the thickness of a cushion, if one is to be used, but it is the compressed thickness that counts. Even quite a thick cushion goes down to about 1 inch under body weight.

If you are to sit upright for eating or working at a table, the seat should be wide enough. At the front it can be 16 inches wide or more, and about the same back to front, but it could be an inch or two narrower at the rear (FIG. 1-1A). If you measure several of your indoor chairs, you will find that the proportions are much the same.

It is possible to manage with a smaller seat, but you will not want to sit on it too long. Stools should have tops no more than 10 × 6 inches, particularly if they are intended to fold very compactly. Such a support could be valued as an alternative to standing or sitting on the ground, but it is a compromise (FIG. 1-1B).

If it is a rigid seat, you can allow for some padding. If it is a slung seat, made of canvas or other flexible material, the important height is near the point of greatest sag (FIG. 1-1C). The sling must support you under and around those two bits of hard bone in your posterior. It is surprising how little area of seat is needed.

Most people want support for their backs if they are to sit for long. Stools or other backless seats are unsuitable for long use. You could have a chair back reaching high enough to support your shoulder blades, but for most outdoor furniture support at the small of your back is sufficient. Thus, the top should be about 15 inches above the seat (FIG. 1-1D). Then you have to consider its angle. A level seat and an upright back would not be comfortable. It is the angle of the part that fits into your back that counts. The arrangement of its support is not so important, providing it is clear of your back. The part you rest against needs to slope back slightly; 10 degrees past vertical is about right (FIG. 1-1E).

With that sort of upright chair, there will be a matching table. For a comfortable working or eating height, it will be somewhere between 27 and 30 inches from the floor (FIG. 1-1F). This height will be just below the level of your elbows, when sitting, so you can reach comfortably over the table.

There are variations for tables. If you make small folding stools and want a folding table to use with them, it will need to be low to match their heights. You can bring it down to as low as 20 inches, particularly if compactness of folding is important.

The table area will be determined by your needs, but it should not be too small in relation to its height if it is to be free standing; otherwise it will be unstable. If it is to be attached to the ground, that problem does not arise. For a free standing table, particularly of lightweight construction, you should make its top sizes no less than the table height. In other words, the minimum size occupies a cube.

LOUNGING SEATS

Much sitting in the open air can be described as lounging. If you do not want to sit at a table, the requirements of seating are very different. You do not need to sit as high and you will want to lean back. It is the angle of your thighs that is crucial for comfort. The front edge can be nearly as high as for an upright seat, but your thighs slope back. How much of a slope depends on the degree of lounging. Back to front can be up to about 20 inches (or more) if there are cushions. Ideally, the slope of the back of the chair should be adjustable. In the most upright position, the back should be 10 degrees or so more than a right angle to the seat (FIG. 1-2A). Further angular positions can go back some way, depending on how near a horizontal position you want to reach, but 45 degrees past perpendicular to the seat is a reasonable limit (FIG. 1-2B). If it is a fixed back, you will need to settle for a compromise position.

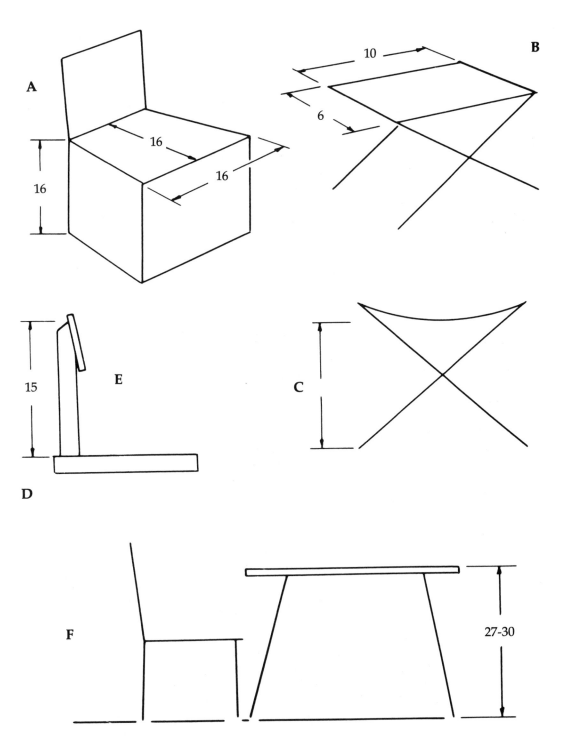

Fig. 1-1. Suggested average dimensions for various types of furniture.

Fig. 1-2. An armchair can have different back angles and the legs can slope to give stability. The seat of an armchair is usually bigger than that of a chair without arms.

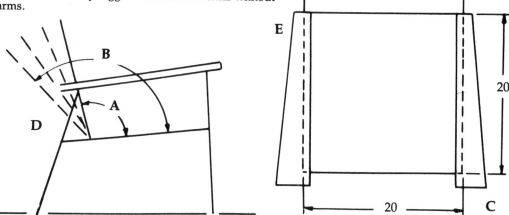

There are lounging chairs without arms, but if you want to lean back and read or sew there is an advantage in having a chair with arms. The area contained in the arms and back needs to be large enough to allow body movement. If someone wants to curl up with their legs under them, there should be room. In any case, you do not want anything like a form-fitting chair. If the seat is 20 inches square, that is about right, but it could be a few inches wider (FIG. 1-2C).

Usually the seat is parallel, but it could be slightly narrower at the back. The arms can be about 10 inches above the seat and can be slightly nearer it at the back (FIG. 1-2D). Many chairs have seat and arms parallel in side view. The arms should not restrict the seat, so they are usually parallel with it on their inner edges. For the sake of appearance, they can taper back on the outer edges. (FIG. 1-2E).

BENCHES

Wider seats for two or three people have much in common with armchairs or lounging seats, but they are usually arranged rather more upright. They are not, however, as upright as chairs used with tables—unless that is their purpose. The seat height is comparatively low, say 14 to 16 inches, and deeper back to front than some chairs (probably 18 to 20 inches). The back is given a comfortable slope and can go higher than a simple chair (FIG. 1-3A).

Comfort in a seat can be increased by giving it a curve. Some plastics are molded almost to figure form, but it is impractical to make a double curvature in wood. Instead, there can be a curve back to front, which is usually made up with laths (FIG. 1-3B). Back supports usually are made of slats straight across (FIG. 1-3C). Shoulders accept straight support, where a posterior is better fitted with a curve. There can be a curve across a back if slats are vertical on hollowed supports (FIG. 1-3D).

Arms to not need to be straight. Some shaping in side view improves appearance and actually conforms better to your arm resting with the elbow in the hollow and your wrists and hands over the curve. The amount of shaping depends on the available equipment for cutting curves in fairly thick wood (FIG. 1-3E).

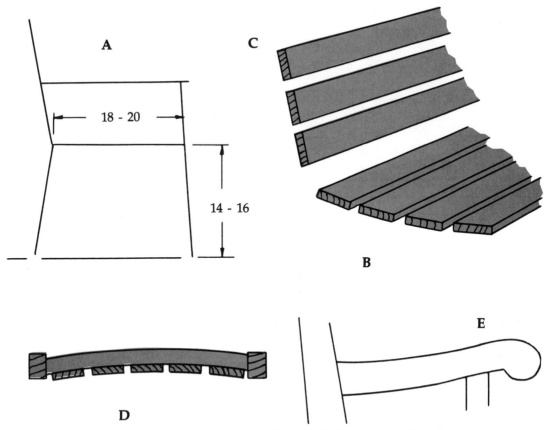

Fig. 1-3. The general sizes of a chair can be developed to allow for
a curved seat, a slat back, and curves in the back and arms.

STABILITY

A chair, table, lounger, or other piece of furniture that will not stand steadily could be just an inconvenience or a definite danger. The design must always have regard for stability. If you are making things that will be attached to the ground, they will not fall over, but the items could still be so fragile that they collapse.

On the whole, it is safe to assume that the supports of anything should cover at least the same floor area as the top. Unfortunately, furniture users do not just sit with their weight thrusting downward. Furniture must be designed so it will stand up to just about whatever the user does. Leaning back heavily in a chair is usual. Tilting a seat on two legs is common. Leaning or sitting on a table must be expected.

Examination of chairs in your home will show how they are designed to remain steady. Front legs need not be quite as far forward as the front of the seat (FIG. 1-4A). People do not tend to tilt chairs forward. Rear legs should go farther back (FIG. 1-4B). The higher the chair back, the more leverage is applied by anyone leaning back heavily, and the farther back the legs should go to resist this. Obviously, there are limits and excessive leg projection must be avoided. Even then, some outdoor chairs have their rear legs much farther back than would be

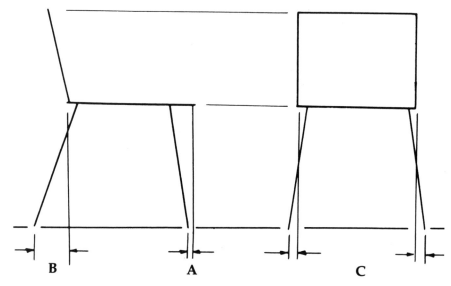

Fig. 1-4. The seat of a chair is arranged for convenience, but the legs splay outward
to give stability.

usual indoors. This applies to all kinds of seating that is not held down. Several
people pressing back together on an unsecured bench will put on a considerable
tilting strain.

When viewed from the front, there is less need for a great spread of legs
because there is less tendency for a user to put on sideways loads. Nevertheless,
it helps to have the spread of feet greater than the seat (FIG. 1-4C), particularly
if the seat is not very wide. A broad-armed chair is more stable because of its width.

Table supports should spread to come under the corners of the top, or very
near that, whether there are separate corner legs, slab ends, or some other means
of support. Much depends on size. A large tabletop will be tolerant of feet farther
in from the corners than would a small table, which needs all the spread for
stability it can be given.

Weight affects rigidity and stability. A massively constructed piece of furniture
gains stability by its sheer weight, providing it is of reasonable proportion. An
example is a picnic table with bench seats included alongside (all supported on
heavy crossed legs). Some picnic tables almost require a crane to move them.

RIGIDITY

Rigidity is the resistance of a structure to fold or collapse unintentionally. *Stability*
is the resistance to tipping over. These terms are related, but rigidity is more the
consideration of producing a structure where the parts provide mutual support,
without necessarily being heavy—unless that is a requirement.

Resistance to deflection comes from triangulating. If you have a three-sided
frame with loose joints (FIG. 1-5A), you cannot push it out of shape. If you have
four pieces similarly joined, you can alter the shape easily (FIG. 1-5B). If you make
the shape into two triangles by adding a diagonal, its shape cannot be altered
(FIG. 1-5C). This principle also applies to items standing on uneven ground. A

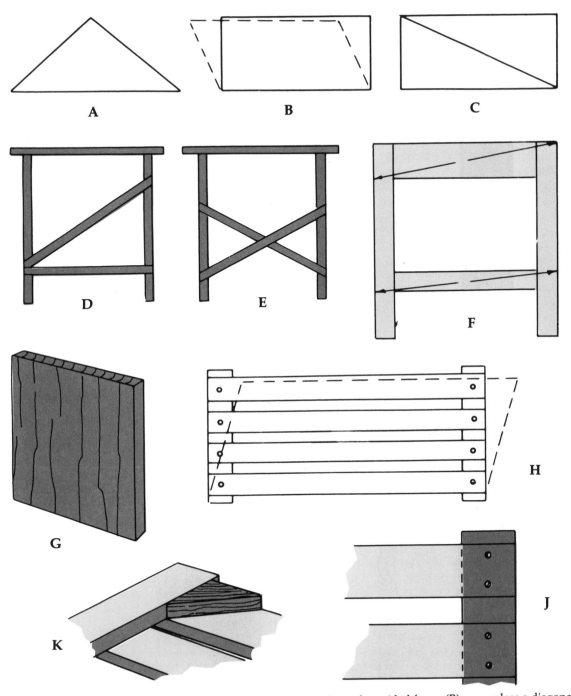

Fig. 1-5. A triangular frame (A) cannot be pushed out of shape, but a four-sided frame (B) can, unless a diagonal divides it into triangles (C). Framing (D, E) can provide an outside triangulation. Construction can provide an internal triangulation (F,G,K), or you can use the arrangement of nails or screws for that purpose.

tripod will stand without wobbling. Four or more legs will not always stand firm with equal load on all legs. Tables and chairs do not lend themselves to three-legged construction, but three-legged stools are possibilities, and a round table tabletop can have three legs.

Light frames can be held in shape with diagonal braces. A pair of legs can have one brace straight across near the feet and a diagonal above the brace (FIG. 1-5D). A diagonal at about 45 degrees provides the best bracing, but this is not always possible. A better bracing has two diagonal strips (FIG. 1-5E).

Some assemblies will appear to have four-sided frames, so there is no apparent triangulation, but that is not so if the joints are rigid. There is the effect of triangulation in the rails (FIG. 1-5F). The deeper a rail and its joints, the more the triangulating effect. There is usually more than one rail, so triangulating occurs at both levels.

If the whole panel is solid wood, it obviously cannot be pushed out of shape (FIG. 1-5G). In effect, it is multiple triangulation. If a seat is made with many slats, each held by a single screw, the assembly could be pushed out of shape (FIG. 1-5H). If the joints are glued and two screws are spread at each joint (FIG. 1-5J), the assembly has a good resistance to distortion. A diagonal brace below would have a similar effect, but that might not be practical. Corner blocks (FIG. 1-5K) also would resist distortion.

Crossed legs have a triangulating effect in themselves (FIG. 1-6A). Under a table, they can be symmetrical, but they also can be altered to get better stability under a chair (FIG. 1-6B), with the rear foot coming farther back.

If rails are added to an assembly, their stiffening effect can be judged. Suppose a lower rail or stretcher is to come low down between the ends of a table or bench. It could be put flat or on edge. In resistance to distorting the assembly lengthwise, it would be better on edge (FIG. 1-6C), where the triangulating effect would be wider. A flat rail would have negligible resistance (FIG. 1-6D).

CONVENIENCE

A piece of outdoor furniture might look good and be well made, yet not fulfill its purpose because it is impossible or inconvenient to use. Lower rails are necessary in many assemblies to give rigidity. On a chair, rails between front and back legs are not in the way of a sitter's legs, at whatever level they are put (FIG. 1-7A). Neither would a back rail be, but a low front rail—particularly in a chair used for upright seating—would be a nuisance. A front rail could be high (FIG. 1-7B). The top rail could be deep to give stiffness without the need for a lower one (FIG. 1-7C). Another arrangement has a crosswise rail between the side rails instead of the front legs (FIG. 1-7D) so that it is far enough back not to interfere with swinging legs.

A similar problem occurs with table rails. With slab ends, all the necessary bracing can come from a central stretcher (FIG. 1-7E), leaving clearance for sitters' feet at each side. The crossed-leg sawbuck arrangement also can get all the stiffness needed from a central rail (FIG. 1-7F).

With corner table legs, it is possible to stiffen with deep top rails only and dispense with lower rails. Then there is another problem, however. A sitter might not be able to get his knees under a deep rail. With the usual chairs and normal tables, you cannot have top rails deeper than about 5 inches without encountering this problem.

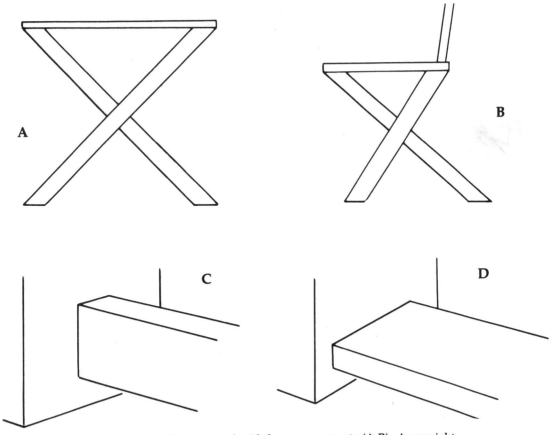

Fig. 1-6. Rigidity is varied with leg arrangements (A,B). An upright stretcher (C) stiffens a table better than a flat one (D).

Diagonal lower rails are kept away from feet (FIG. 1-7G), but then there are problems of strength on the crossing and the joints to the legs. Otherwise there can be a similar arrangement to the chair, with the rail one way between the rails the other way, or even double rails (FIG. 1-7H). That still leaves rails far enough out to interfere with the feet of anyone sitting at the ends.

APPEARANCE

Fitness for purpose is the main consideration in making outdoor furniture. Fortunately, if an item is functional and looks right, you can consider its appearance to be acceptable. In making furniture for use in the garden or yard, there is certainly no need to decorate for the sake of decoration.

There are some design considerations. A square is not considered as attractive as a rectangle. If you are making something that has a boxlike configuration, it looks better if all of its surfaces are longer one way than the other and if at no angle of viewing does the outline appear to be a square. You might not consider attractiveness important in a functional piece of furniture, but if you will get your

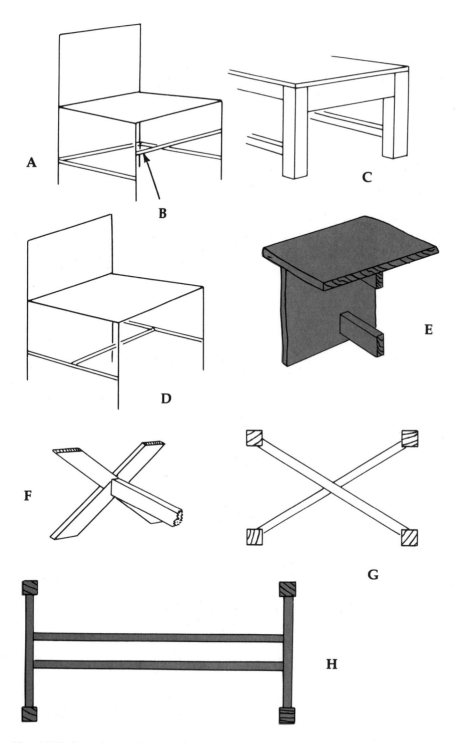

Fig. 1-7 Rails and stretchers can be arranged in many ways to provide stiffness in the underframing of tables and chairs.

results just as well with a rectangle as with a square, chose to make the item rectangular.

Curves are considered better looking than straight lines. You will need to include many straight lines—wood construction is more easily done with straight pieces of wood—but consider adding curves. The arms of a chair can include curves. Because they are the most prominent feature, the curves will have a softening effect on the whole design. If the top of a chair back is cut with a curve, it will look better than with a straight edge.

It is possible to cut curves into straight edges. This choice can also be functional, such as at the bottom of a bench end, where the curve produces feet at the corners. A rectangular cutout would be less pleasing.

Color also has a place in design. Do you want to draw attention to the piece of furniture, or would you rather it was inconspicuous? Most hardwoods left untreated will soon weather so they blend into their surroundings. At the other extreme, you might want to paint the wood in bright colors. Against the mainly green background of foliage, red and yellow are the colors that stand out. Paint your work bright red if you want to shout "Look, I made it!" Such a color might match the paintwork of an adjoining building and be justified.

More usual colors for furniture in a formal or cultivated garden or on a well-kept lawn are white and green. White looks attractive and inviting, but it needs to be kept clean and you will need to touch up the paint frequently. Fortunately, there is no problem in matching that color. Green can be more of a problem for touching up. Supposedly, there are more shades of green than of any other color.

You can use treatments such as linseed and other oils to preserve the wood, as well as give it a mellow appearance. However, oil takes some time to dry, and you will not be thanked if someone gets it on their clothes. Varnish is another finish that lets you see the wood grain, but it must be the best quality outdoor varnish; that is, boat varnish. Then give the wood at least three coats. Be prepared to touch up as necessary, or the wood rubbed bare will stain and you cannot put that right.

FOLDING

You must keep all of the design considerations affecting rigid furniture in mind when you are planning take-apart or folding furniture. Usually folding furniture must be light for portability. Select wood with reasonably straight grain and without flaws. There will be little margin to take care of weak parts.

The important thing concerning folding furniture is that there must be no fear of it folding or collapsing in use. When you are using it, you should be able to treat it in the same way as rigid furniture. Whatever locks the parts in place must always do so. Ideally, there should be no loose parts because loose pegs and other things can be lost and then the assembly cannot be put together. Worse are nuts and bolts that must be taken out and that require wrenches to tighten them.

Some people never disassemble their folding furniture. Before making anything with the inherent complication of folding, consider if a rigid item might serve just as well.

PRACTICALITY

Designs in this book cover all types of construction. If you do not think your skill is up to a particular construction technique, you might find a simpler one for something serving the same purpose. When you design something yourself, think through all the steps in construction. Much of the skill in making anything is in anticipating the move after the next. Will you have all the tools needed for what you want to do? If not, you might be able to buy wood already machined to suit or you might need to pay someone to do work for you. Will that be worthwhile or is there some way of achieving the same ends with your own tools and skills?

It is very easy to come up with a design that requires a different section of wood for almost every part. If you have your own circular saw and jointer, that might not matter, but if you must pay for wood to be machined to many sizes it will be expensive. It is better to discover what stock sizes your supplier can provide and design at least most of the project around those sizes. Remember that bought planed wood is usually about ⅛ inch under the specified size. It will not matter, for instance, if wood is 2⅞ inch or 3 inch wide, but if you insist on a finished size of 3 inches, you will pay much more for it.

Do not underrate your own skill. If you have the tools necessary, tackle work you have not done before. It will take much longer for you to cut a particular joint than it would take an expert, but having plenty of time is an advantage for an amateur. You will experience a greater sense of achievement if you are able to look at a piece of craftsmanship that incorporates a new skill than if you accepted some simpler alternative.

2

Tools and Materials

THE MAKING OF OUTDOOR FURNITURE is a branch of woodworking that embraces a large range of construction methods. There are considerable variations in the skills needed, as well as in the equipment required. There are opportunities for using woods that would not be suitable for use indoors. It is possible to use wood almost straight from the tree. At the other extreme are pieces of outdoor furniture made of woods that might also be used for indoor furniture. Some of the first woods can be made into crude, but satisfactory, furniture with very few tools and little precision. These tools and techniques would not be suitable for high-class work done with lumber that has been seasoned, planed, and made with cabinetwork joints.

No one tool kit is recommended to anyone planning to make outdoor furniture. You must consider what sort of work you intend to do.

In general, you will do better work with a small collection of good tools than you will with a larger number of inferior ones. This is also a consideration when there is a choice of tool for the same purpose. For instance, you can buy a pump-action screwdriver that certainly puts screws in quickly. For the same price, however, you could buy several plain screwdrivers of different sizes that would be of more use to you.

SAWS

You will do most of the cutting to size by hand. A circular saw, either a portable one or one mounted in a saw bench, will be useful, but it would not be a first priority in buying. Instead a good *handsaw* or *panel saw* about 20 inches long and with about 8 teeth per inch will do most cutting (FIG. 2-1A). Notice that the teeth are set in alternate directions so the groove they cut is wider than the metal from which the saw is made. This *kerf* prevents the saw from binding in a deep cut, and it is particularly important if there is still sap, in the wood.

Normal teeth are a diamond shape and they are designed for cutting across the grain. There are *ripsaws* that look the same, but their teeth are more upright on their leading edges so they cut more efficiently along the grain. It should not be necessary to buy a ripsaw. The small amount of cutting along the grain can be done with cross-grained teeth.

For finer work there is a *backsaw*, 10 or 12 inches long, with a stiffening piece along the back. Teeth can be as fine as 16 per inch. One type of backsaw is the

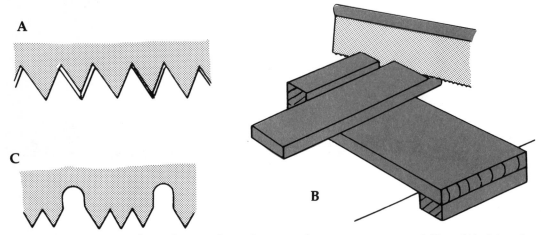

Fig. 2-1. Crosscut saw teeth are sharpened to points opposite ways to sever wood fibers (A). A bench hook is convenient for sawing small parts (B). Saws for greenwood can have gullets between groups of teeth to clear sawdust (C).

bench saw. It does not tear the grain much. If you want to cut grooves across wood or make mortise-and-tenon joints, you must have a backsaw.

A panel saw is best used with the wood supported at about knee height. You can make a trestle or use an old chair. Then you can hold the wood with one knee while making cuts downward. Some sawing with the panel saw is better done with the wood upright in a vise.

Joint cutting with a backsaw can be done with the wood in a vise or held against a bench hook (FIG. 2-1B), which is easily made. A bench with a good vise helps in doing accurate work. Any table-sized structure will do. What you need is rigidity and a front edge stiff enough and strong enough to stand up to hammering and planing.

If you want to make furniture from natural wood—either slabs cut from logs or pieces of poles—the wood probably will still have sap in it, and a saw suitable for dry, seasoned wood would not cut far without binding and coming to a halt. The saw teeth must be fairly coarse and be given more set than the other saws so that they make a wider kerf as they progress through the wood. It is also best to provide deep gullets at intervals to clear any sawdust (FIG. 2-1C). Saws are made with these teeth that look like panel saws, but it is more usual to have the blade narrow and tensioned in a tubular frame.

CHISELS AND KNIVES

For any sort of furniture you will need edge-cutting tools. In most situations, the tool most easily controlled to do what you want is a chisel. They are available in many widths. The general-purpose ones can be described as *firmer chisels*. Long, thin ones are *paring chisels*; they are not meant to be hit and you are unlikely to need them. If you are buying new chisels, start with ½ and 1-inch-wide chisels. The simplest chisels have square edges; others have wide bevel edges. (See FIG. 2-2A.) If there is little difference in price, get bevel-edged chisels because they will do all that the square-edged ones will and get closer into corners which are less than square.

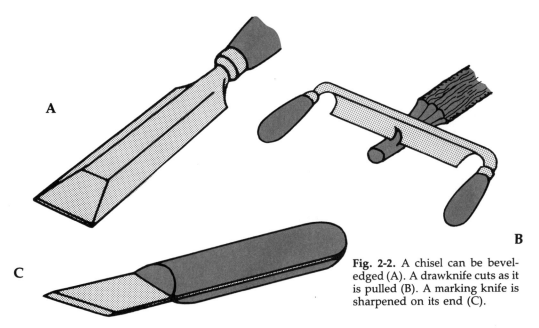

A

C

B

Fig. 2-2. A chisel can be bevel-edged (A). A drawknife cuts as it is pulled (B). A marking knife is sharpened on its end (C).

If you will be cutting mortise-and-tenon joints, it is helpful to have chisels the same width as the mortises. Usually, mortises are one-third the width of the wood. Much of your wood will be between 2 and 3 inches wide. There will be uses for ⅝- and ¾-inch chisels. A very wide chisel is useful for paring broad surfaces, and you might want one that is 1½ inches wide.

Modern chisels mostly have plastic handles that can be hit with a hammer without much risk of damage. Wood handles are better hit with a wooden mallet. In any case, a mallet has uses during assembly of many structures. The mallet can be quite crude and it can be homemade.

A tool dealer has many different types of chisels. You will probably never need most of the special ones. A chisel curved in cross section is called a *gouge*. Delay buying one until you find a definite need for it. If it is sharpened on the inside of the curve, it is called *in-canelled* and is used for paring concave edges. If it is sharpened on the outside it is *out-canelled* and is used for removing waste from hollows.

There are uses for a good knife. It might be a hunting knife or a clasp knife; the important thing is that it can be kept sharp enough for whittling cuts. If you want to do upholstery with foam filling, a carving knife is the tool for cutting that material.

In some types of outdoor furniture, natural poles must be tapered to go into holes to make something like a dowel joint. The traditional tool for tapering the ends is a *drawknife*. You must use a vise to hold the wood then use the tool in both hands to make cuts toward you (FIG. 2-2B). The edge of the drawknife is beveled on one side, like a chisel. If you use it with the bevel downward, you can regulate the depth of cut by altering the angle of the handles.

If that is not the type of woodwork you want to do, but would prefer the cutting of joints in prepared wood, you will find a use for a *marking knife*. It has its cutting edge at the end and could be made from a broken table knife (FIG. 2-2C). This is used, instead of a pencil, when marking a part of a joint that must be sawn across the grain. As the knife severs the grain fibers it will leave a much cleaner edge if you arrange the saw kerf against the waste side of the line.

PLANES

Whether you need many planes or not depends on the types of furniture you want to make and in what state you obtain the wood. If you have a jointer or other power planer, you can deal with wood bought from the saw. You could buy your wood already planed. If you only want to make rustic furniture from poles, you will not need a plane. Even then, though, you will find uses for it.

Machine-planed wood has a series of tiny ridges across the grain. The size of the ridges depends on the coarseness of cut and how fast the wood was passed over the cutters. For much furniture, that sort of finish is all that is needed. If you want a better surface, you will need to hand-plane the power plane marks away.

The most commonly used hand plane is the Stanley or Record *smoothing plane* (described as 4 inches, or 4½ inches for a wider one). That should be the first plane you buy. It is intended for planing along the grain with fine cuts, but you can use it for trimming across the grain. If you adjust its mouth wide, you can set it coarse to take off thick shavings.

If you want to plane surfaces and edges straight, the plane should have a longer sole to span inequalities. A very long plane is called a *fore plane* or *jointer*, but your second plane could be the intermediate size called a *jack plane*. There will be occasions when you need to straighten edges. That is easier to do with a long plane than with the shorter smoothing plane.

Another useful plane is the little *block plane*. There are several versions, but all are intended to be used in one hand. The block plane is used for dealing with a ragged end or to take the sharpness off the angle between two surfaces. You often will find yourself picking it up for small cuts.

A *spokeshave* is something like a plane. Its blade is in a narrow surface controlled by a handle at each side. It is the tool for following curves, such as the shaped edge of a board. The modern metal version works like a plane, but an older type has a blade something like a small drawknife and makes more of a slicing cut.

SHARPENING

Everyone who has cutting tools should have the means and knowledge to sharpen them. A skilled man will pause for sharpening much more frequently.

Most edge tools of the plane and chisel type will have two bevels (FIG. 2-3A). The long bevel is put there by grinding. The short bevel is made on an *oilstone* or *whetstone*. The edge can be revived a great many times on the oilstone, but when its bevel gets very long the tool must be ground again. Therefore, you start with just a narrow bevel again on the oilstone.

You can grind on a high-speed electric stone, but you must use care to avoid overheating and to keep the bevel true. Dip frequently in water to cool the steel. If rainbow colors appear on the steel, that is a sign of overheating which has drawn the temper (softened the steel). Professional grinding is done on a slower, larger stone that is kept wet. The need for grinding is so infrequent that you might prefer to pay for it and only sharpen on the oilstone yourself.

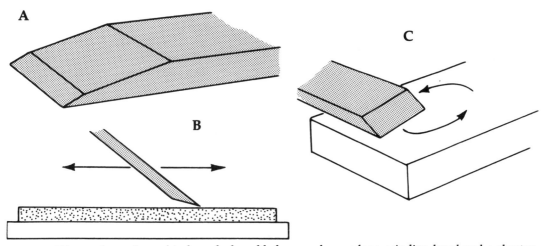

Fig. 2-3. Edge tools, such as chisels and plane blades, can have a long grinding bevel and a shorter sharpening bevel (A). The latter is maintained on an oilstone (B), and any wire edge is removed by rubbing the tool flat against a stone (C).

Plane blades and chisels are only sharpened on one side. The other side should be kept flat. The usual sharpening stone for these tools is a block about 8 × 2 × 1 inches, and it can be mounted in a wood case. Various degrees of coarseness are obtainable. A coarse stone cuts quickly, but the edge given to the tool reflects the size of the grit and would appear to be like a saw edge under a lens. That sort of edge would be good enough for some rough work, but it is better to follow with a finer stone. It is possible to get combination stones, with fine and coarse grits on opposite sides, but most craftsmen prefer separate stones.

Most coarser stones are manufactured grits, but the finest stones are natural (such as Washita and Arkansas). For most outdoor furniture planing, there is no need to go down to the finest stones, where are more appropriate to edges for finishing quality hardwoods in cabinetwork.

To sharpen a chisel or plane blade, have a thin oil on the stone. Light lubricating oil or kerosene is better than motor oil, which would make a barrier between the steel and the stone. Have the bevel angled downward with one hand holding higher up and the fingers of the other hand applying pressure (FIG. 2-3B). Rub the tool at a constant angle along and about the surface of the stone. The stone, as well as the steel, wears away. So keep it level and rub it all over the surface of the steel. The greatest difficulty, at first, is maintaining a steady angle along the length of the stone, but that comes with practice.

Wipe the oil off the stone and feel the edge on the flat side. If there is a roughness there, that is a *wire edge*. This is a tiny sliver of steel rubbed off the sharp edge, but still clinging to it. It indicates that the edge is sharp. Put the flat of the steel on the stone (FIG. 2-3C) and give it a few circular rubs. That should remove the wire edge. If it does not, slice the edge across a piece of scrap wood.

If you used a coarse stone for that sharpening and you want to follow with a finer stone, make sure the edge is clean. Then repeat all the sharpening on the fine stone. You only need to rub long enough to remove the scratches from the coarse stone.

To sharpen a knife, note the angle toward the edge at each side and hold the blade at that angle on the stone. Again control with one hand while the other puts on pressure. Move about if it is a curved edge, but maintain the angle. After rubbing well on one side, turn the knife over and do the same on the other side. Continue until you can feel a wire edge and then slice across a piece of scrap wood to remove it.

MARKING OUT

You will need to mark squarely at right angles. A try square that you can push against a straightedge while you mark along its blade is the standard tool, but there is a limit to its size. Several other tools can be used.

You can use an adjustable square with a pencil for marking lines parallel with an edge. Its blade is adjusted to the distance and a pencil held against the end is pulled along with it. The tool made specially for this purpose is a *marking gauge*, with a steel spur projecting to scratch from the stem. For mortise-and-tenon joints, there are *mortise gauges* with two adjustable spurs to mark both lines at the same time. One of these will be worth having if you plan to make many of these joints.

If you are planing wood true and to width and thickness, the first side is called the *face side* and the first edge, square to it, is the *face edge*. In subsequent marking out, you should work from these surfaces. There are conventional marks to pencil on them to indicate what they are (FIG. 2-4).

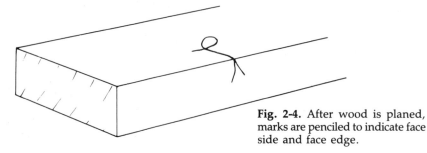

Fig. 2-4. After wood is planed, marks are penciled to indicate face side and face edge.

HOLES

If you have only one power tool, it should be an electric drill. This tool will not do all your drilling, however. For holes up to about ⅜ inch for screws and bolts, you can use drills originally intended for metal. Above that it is better to use drills designed for wood. Some will fit the electric drill, but you will reach a stage where you must use a brace to drill by hand. If you buy a brace, it is worthwhile paying a little more for a ratchet brace. It will allow you to work in a restricted space where you cannot sweep a complete circle with the handle. In addition to making holes, the brace can be used with a screwdriver bit for the many large screws used in outdoor furniture. It also will countersink holes for screw heads or just to take off roughness.

A particularly useful tool for the holes needed in rural construction using natural poles is an *auger*. This is a bit extended to have its own lever handle. The working end is like a woodworking twist bit, but it is usually longer so it can be used for deeper holes. It is not an essential tool, but if you can find one, it is useful.

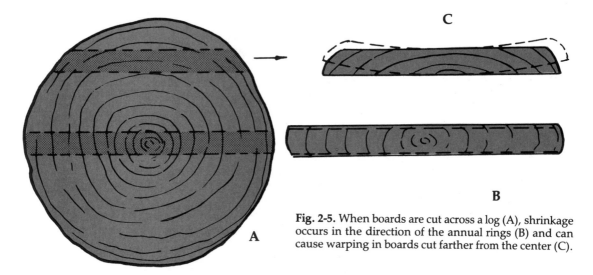

Fig. 2-5. When boards are cut across a log (A), shrinkage occurs in the direction of the annual rings (B) and can cause warping in boards cut farther from the center (C).

WOOD

As a tree grows, it increases in girth with the production of annual rings (FIG. 2-5A). As the tree gets older, the inner part becomes more compacted, and that is the *heartwood*. The outer part, with the rings, is the *sapwood*. The heartwood is stronger and more durable. Some woods can show little difference between sapwood and heartwood. Where there is any choice, use the heartwood for outdoor furniture.

As wood is dried, it shrinks. For practical purposes, shrinking can be regarded as mostly in the direction of the annual rings. Therefore, a board cut radially will get thinner, but remain flat (FIG. 2-5B). One cut farther out will warp because shrinking is around the curve of the rings. (See FIG. 2-5C.) Controlled seasoning minimizes the problem, but looking at the end of a board allows you to estimate what will happen to it with changes in moisture content.

NAILS AND SCREWS

Many joints in outdoor furniture are made with nails, screws, or bolts. You must consider the effects of corrosion. Pure iron has a good resistance to corrosion. Its initial light coating of rust resists further rusting. Very little pure iron is available now. What we loosely call "iron" is actually mild steel. This is iron with a small amount of carbon in it. Rust on mild steel is an ongoing thing. Unprotected mild steel in damp conditions will eventually rust away.

Copper has a good resistance to corrosion, but it is soft and therefore not of much use. It can be alloyed with zinc to make brass or with tin to make bronze. Both of these alloys have a good resistance to the effects of moisture. Aluminum also resists moisture, but in its pure state it is soft. Other metals alloyed with it give hardness, but sometimes with reduced corrosion resistance. So-called stainless steel is not immune to all kinds of attack, but it can be alloyed to resist certain liquids. The usual variety should be satisfactory in normal weather.

Mild steel can be protected by plating. There is no need for some of the expensive plated finishes for outdoor furniture, but zinc gives fairly inexpensive protection. One such treatment is called *galvanizing*. Mild steel bolts buried in wood can have a long enough life, particularly if their exposed ends are painted. You can use rust-inhibiting fluids on steel fastenings before driving them and before painting.

Nails are described by their length. For most furniture, you will need fairly large nails with standard heads. Diameters vary with length and you will not have any choice. Nails of other sections and with different heads are meant for other purposes and are not for your sort of woodworking.

Barbed ring nails have teeth cut around them that resist pulling out (FIG. 2-6A). They are available in mild steel, possibly galvanized, but they are also made in bronze for boatbuilding. Both types are useful where you need a firm attachment but not much depth for holding or space for many nails.

Screws are made in many lengths and in thicknesses described by a gauge number (the higher the number, the thicker the screw). Sizes start with tiny screws, smaller than you will need, and go up to quite large ones. The usual screw has a flat or countersunk head (FIG. 2-6B). You might sometimes need round-head screws (FIG. 2-6C), but for most purposes flat heads are all you will require.

Screw length varies with the wood surface. Within each length, there will be at least three gauge thicknesses available. In general, you want the thicker ones. In any case, avoid slender screws that will shear off when being driven. Typical useful sizes are 8 gauge by 1½ inches, 10 or 12 gauge by 2 inches, and 12 or 14 gauge by 3 inches. In longer screws, you will not usually need very much larger than 14 gauge. Brass screws are not as strong as steel ones. Therefore, you will need thicker ones, or you could drive a steel screw first, withdraw it, and then replace it with the brass screw.

In heavy construction, the best fastening method is to bolt right through. A *bolt* is a fastening with a screw thread only a short distance from the end. If the

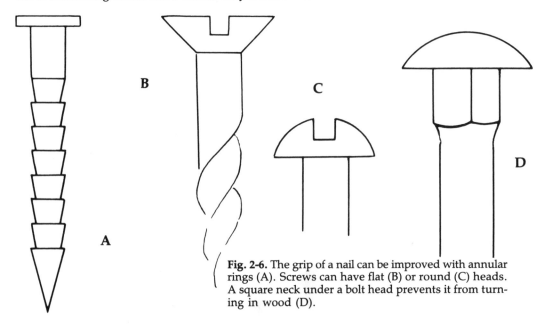

Fig. 2-6. The grip of a nail can be improved with annular rings (A). Screws can have flat (B) or round (C) heads. A square neck under a bolt head prevents it from turning in wood (D).

thread goes for nearly all the length, it is an *engineering screw*. To avoid confusion, the screws for driving into wood can be called *wood screws*.

Quoted lengths are from the surface, which would be under a hexagonal or square head, but from the top of a countersunk one. A *coach bolt* is particularly intended for woodwork. It has a shallow "snap" head and a square neck under it (FIG. 2-6D). The square pulls into the top of the drilled hole and resists turning when the nut is tightened on the other end. Normal bolts require a wrench at both ends. When choosing bolts, it is usually better to have one large bolt through a joint than several smaller ones. Quoted diameters are fractional. You will not usually need 1/4-inch bolts. The general sizes are 3/8 or 1/2, but for large work you will need larger bolts.

GLUE

Not so long ago, the use of glue on outdoor woodwork would not have been considered. Many modern glues are unsuitable even though claims for some of them might imply otherwise. Nevertheless, there are glues developed particularly for boatbuilding that can be used on outdoor woodwork.

In most constructions that will be left outside, it is still common to have metal fastenings, as well as glue. In tenoned construction, glue alone will provide security. It is where parts merely overlap that there should be screws or bolts through, but you can put glue between the parts as well.

It is not always easy to identify a fully waterproof glue because it might only be described by a trade name. If the glue is in two parts to mix before use or apply to meeting surfaces, it is almost certainly waterproof. This is particularly true if it is described as for boatbuilding. A powerful waterproof glue (in two parts) is resorcinol. It leaves a red glue line that normally will not matter for this type of furniture. The strongest of these glues is epoxy. In addition to joining wood to wood, it also will join many other materials to themselves and to wood.

Most glues require the surfaces to be in reasonably close contact. If you try to fill a gap with glue, it will not provide any strength. In that case, you can mix sawdust with the glue. This method bonds the glue and particles to the surfaces to make a stronger joint. Do not tighten a close-fitting joint so much that most of the glue is squeezed out. There must be enough glue left to make a bond.

There is not much need for stoppings in outdoor woodwork. Make sure you do buy an exterior stopping, however; some are only intended for indoor use. For filling holes over punched nails, there are stoppings to press in and sand level. They appear to set hard, but actually they remain slightly flexible. They can be used in cracks, but larger gaps are better filled with a more flexible stopping sold for the purpose. These synthetic stoppings are superior to any you might mix yourself.

FINISHES

Some woods can be left untreated, and they have sufficient resistance to rot to last a long time. They will take on a weathered appearance that you might want. For other woods or appearances, you must apply a finish.

Wood preservatives are available. For them to be most effective, the wood must be soaked. You can, however, obtain some protection by brushing on the preservative. Some preservatives are clear. Others are colored, often green, but that is translucent and it fades fairly rapidly. It is unwise to rely on the preservative to contribute much to appearance. Most preservatives can be followed by paint, but check the directions on the can. Some take a long time to dry before the furniture can be used or paint can be applied.

Most paints now available are synthetic. They are superior in durability and quality of finish to the older paints made from natural materials. Read the instructions on the can. There might be a limit to the amount of brushing advised. Too much will alter appearance by causing air bubbles. Most paints must dry between coats, but on some a further coat must be put on before the earlier one is fully dry. There might be a maximum or a minimum time between coats.

The best protection comes with a gloss finish. The effectiveness of the finish depends on what is applied underneath, as much as on the quality of the final coat.

The first coat on bare or preserved wood must make a bond with the wood grain. This is a *primer* that is thin so it penetrates. Its color is not important, but is usually white or pink. There might have to be a second coat of primer. This is followed by an undercoat that is a matt finish of a color compatible with the *top coat*. It is better if it is not exactly the same shade as the top coat. Then you can see how you are progressing on the final coat.

It is the undercoat that provides the body in the paint system. You might need to apply two coats of undercoat because this is where thickness is made, not at the final stage. In some paint systems, the primer is the same as the undercoat—probably thinned. Get thinners recommended by the paint manufacturers and use them sparingly.

If the undercoat is not as smooth as you prefer, use wet-and-dry, medium abrasive paper with water. The top gloss coat is a once-only coat. You will actually need to buy more undercoat than top coat. If you apply a second top coat, it tends to run on the earlier gloss and finish unevenly.

It is inadvisable to mix different makes of paints. Most paint manufacturers recommend complete systems of finishes. Have one and follow it through.

Check that the paint offered is intended for exterior use. The most durable paint is produced for boats and it can be used on furniture. Check that it is intended for use on wood and not fiberglass. Some boat paints, supplied in two parts, must be mixed before use. There is no need to use them on furniture.

Paint obscures the grain of the wood. If you want to protect the wood but still see the grain details, the usual finish is varnish. Be careful what you use. Avoid anything with shellac in it because it will not stand up to even slight dampness. Like paints, most varnishes are now synthetic. Not only has this given them better protection, but it makes application easier.

A varnish described as "exterior" might be satisfactory, but a boat varnish should be even better. Some of it is described as "spar varnish." That has good weather resistance. There are no primers or undercoats for varnish. The first coat should be thinned, using the thinners recommended by the makers, but further coats are applied with the varnish as supplied.

3

Basic Techniques

THE MOST BASIC FURNITURE is formed from natural poles or slabs of wood. Often the bark is left on and the parts are either nailed or assembled with a simple peg arrangement. Little regard is provided for the niceties of squaring and exact size. Other furniture is comparatively massive and made of wood that has been sawn to squared sections, but not finished in a way that would make it suitable for indoor furniture. Sometimes the wood is used almost directly from the tree and it does not season until after it has been made into furniture. In other situations, the furniture is made of planed, seasoned wood and it would be acceptable to use the items inside the home, as well as outside.

There is room in the making of outdoor furniture for a wide range of skills. It is possible to make satisfactory furniture if all you can do is saw wood to length and nail parts together. For that work, the range of tools needed is also slight. With more skill and more tools, it is possible to produce more advanced furniture. Anyone experienced in making indoor furniture of good quality will probably feel happier producing outdoor furniture of almost cabinetmaking quality.

The items described in this book cover the whole range of construction and skills. Most workers can do better than they think if they try. In any case, there are some basic techniques that ought to be mastered, and it is worthwhile learning them before you start on your projects.

NAILING

Most people believe they already know how to nail and can hit the nail on its head with a hammer more than they hit their hand. There is more to it than that, however. Most nails used in outdoor furniture are fairly large. You must take into consideration other things than being able to hit the nail every time.

If the wood is not very hard and the nail not too large, you could just position the nail and drive it. If it is near an edge, you might split the wood. Usually, if you are dealing with nails 3 inches long or more, it is better to drill a starter hole for each nail. If you are nailing two pieces of wood together, it is the grip of the nail in the lower piece clamping the upper piece to it under the nail head that counts (FIG. 3-1A). You do not gain anything by having a nail tight in the top piece (as it would be if you nailed without drilling).

For much nailing, you can drill an undersize hole through the top piece and partly into the bottom piece. How much undersize and how far depends on the

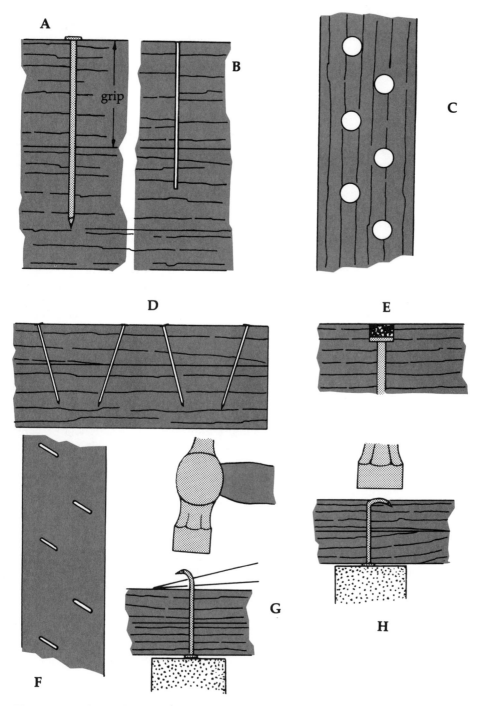

Fig. 3-1. A nail grips between its head and the lower part (A). A hole will be needed (B). Staggering nails reduces splitting and adds strength (C); so does toenailing (D). A nail set below the surface can be covered with stopping (E). Nails can be taken through and clenched (F-H).

size of the nail and the wood. If it is very hard wood, the hole in the top piece can be the same size as the nail, and you can use a smaller drill to continue into the bottom piece. Usually one drill size will do (FIG. 3-2B). Even in very hard wood, it is best to stop the drill short so the nail makes its own way into the last short distance. Even if you are dealing with an assembly where you can drive nails without drilling, you should drill nail holes near the edge of the board so that there is less risk of splitting.

It is not easy to decide on the length of nails and spacing. It is largely a matter of experience. Remember, it is the length of nail in the lower piece of wood that provides the grip. About three-fourths of the way through the average board will be about right. About twice the depth of the upper piece of wood is another guide for thinner parts. As for the number of nails, too many is better than too few. Do not drive nails wastefully, however. Use a minimum of three nails in any joint, but in many furniture constructions a 2-inch spacing is about right. Try to avoid driving nails close by in the same line of grain. That encourages splitting. If there is space, a zigzag line (FIG. 3-1C) makes a stronger joint and spreads the nails in the grain. If the lower part of a nail is going into end grain, it should go about twice as far into it as it would in side grain, if possible, or there will need to be more nails going to a lesser depth.

If you must drive nails in a row, there is a gain in strength if you drive them at alternate angles, called *toenailing* (FIG. 3-1D). The slope used need not be much. If you are aiming at equal spacing, remember it is the spacing where the boards meet, rather than at the heads, that is important.

Nail heads normally finish level with the surface. For neatness, you can punch the heads below the surface and then fill the hole with a stopping material (FIG. 3-1E). If you are making furniture with wood that has not been fully seasoned, you should assume that a board will probably get thinner as it dries out. In that case, it is advisable to punch nail heads below the surface so that they are not left standing and liable to snag clothing as the wood surface shrinks. For large nails, use a very large punch. You can use a piece of iron rod, 1/2 inch or more thick, filed at one end to about the diameter of the nail head.

In some places, the greatest strength will come from taking the nail right through and turning over the point. This is particularly true where the wood is thin and where there would not be much grip with normal nailing. This *clench nailing* is not just a matter of hitting over the projecting nail end. The neatest way to bury the point is along the grain, but it is stronger to go squarely or diagonally across the lines of grain (FIG. 3-1F).

It is better to bury the point than to merely turn it over. Burying the point is stronger and prevents the point from scratching anyone or tearing clothing. This method is best done in stages. Drive the nail through, then support the head with an iron block or a heavy hammer. Put a spike beside the projecting nail point and hammer the end to a curve over it (FIG. 3-1G). Pull out the spike and hammer the nail point into the wood (FIG. 3-1H).

SCREWS

Compared with nailing, screwing parts together has the advantage of exerting a clamping action. The force of hammering at one place can cause nails to loosen at another place. That problem does not occur with screws. It is possible to pull parts together progressively by going back over screws for further tightening. If you expect that parts will be disassembled later you can withdraw screws without damaging the wood. With nails there would be damage even if you could pull them out.

For better class work, screws are always preferable to nails. As with nails, the choice of screw size is largely a matter of experience. Screws have parallel unscrewed necks. The longer the screw, the longer this neck. Usually the plain neck goes into the top piece and the screwed part goes into the lower part. It is only the screwed part in the lower piece of wood that provides the grip. There is nothing to be gained by having it cut a thread in the upper piece. In fact, that could prevent the screw from pulling the upper piece tight to the other piece.

For each length of screw, several gauge thicknesses are available. For most outdoor work, you should choose the thicker screws because they are stronger and they grip better. They need not be spaced as closely as thinner screws. As with nails, avoid getting close screws in the same line of grain (because of the risk of splitting). You can use a zigzag arrangement.

Screws in the sizes used in building furniture must have starter holes drilled. The clearance hole in the top piece of wood should allow the screw to pass easily and be drilled right through, even if part of the screw thread will come within it (FIG. 3-2A). The size and length of hole to drill in the lower piece depends on the screw and the wood. In soft wood, the hole can be quite small in relation to the screw and only be taken about half as far as the screw will go (FIG. 3-2B). In hard wood, it should be bigger and be taken deeper (FIG. 2-3C). Even then, however, leave a short distance for the screw to make its own way.

Large screws are difficult to drive tightly. It helps to rub wax or a candle on a screw before driving it. That method is cleaner than using lubricating oil or grease. Even with a large screwdriver, it might be difficult to exert enough torque. In any case, make sure the end of the screwdriver matches the screw head. You will waste a lot of energy if the driver does not match. The best way to get a large screw fully tightened is to use a screwdriver bit in a brace (FIG. 3-2D).

If you are using countersunk screw heads that are to finish flush with the surface, drive one screw as an experiment. In many woods, it will pull its head in without any preparation of the top of the hole. If it does not, use a countersink bit to recess the hole. Do not recess the hole as deeply as the size of the screw head is. Allow for some pulling in (FIG. 3-2E). If you use round-head screws, put a washer under each head (FIG. 3-2F). Otherwise the head will partly pull in and it will look untidy.

The neatest finish comes from *counterboring*. With this technique, the screw heads are far enough below the surface for a wood plug to go over each of them (FIG. 3-2G). Because the wood is usually quite thick, there is plenty of depth to allow the heads to be sunk without loss of strength. The size of the counterbored hole depends on the size of plug. The best plugs are cut across the grain with a plug cutter that fits in a drill chuck, which can be used in a drill press or with an electric drill mounted on a stand. You also can use a piece of dowel rod as a plug.

Sink the screw head about the same depth as the diameter of the plug. After that, drill for the screw in the usual way. Make sure the screw is fully tightened because you will not be able to get at it later. Let the plug stand high so that you can plane it level after the glue has set. If you use a plug cutter on a piece of the same wood used to make the furniture, then put the plug in with its grain the same way as that surrounding it. It will be inconspicuous in the finished work.

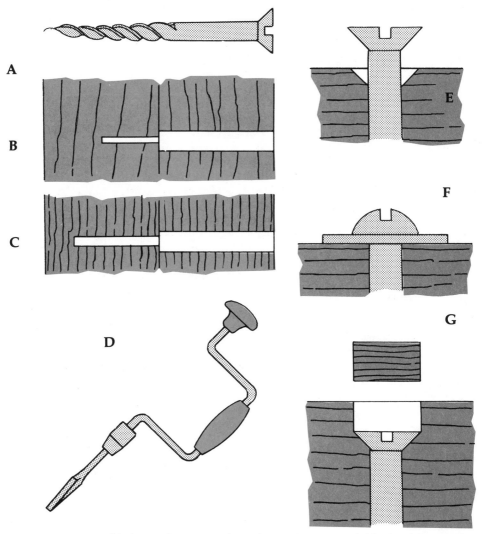

Fig. 3-2. Screws need holes (A-C). A screwdriver bit in a brace is useful for large screws (D). A hole can be countersunk (E). A washer spreads pressure (F). A plug in a counterbored hole hides a screw head (G).

RIVETS

In building outdoor furniture, you will not find many uses for rivets. Nevertheless, where wood is too thin to provide much grip for screw and where bolts would be inappropriate, a rivet is the answer. Where parts of folding furniture need to pivot, a rivet is preferable to a bolt for the wood parts to turn on.

The method or riveting used for joining pieces of wood is based on a technique used in boatbuilding. Choose a nail that will go through the project a short distance (FIG. 3-3A). Drive a small washer over the nail. Ideally, it should have a hole that needs forcing on the nail. Therefore, you need a hollow punch (FIG. 3-3B). Hold the nail head with an iron block. Then cut off the end of the nail a short distance above the washer (FIG. 3-3C). You must judge the amount left as enough for hammering onto the washer. Use a small *ball peen* or *cross peen* hammer to spread the end tightly on to the washer (FIG. 3-3D). Aim to form a rounded head by hammering around the end, rather than on top only to get a broad flatter head.

In boatbuilding, that kind of riveting is done with copper nails; copper is a metal that spreads easily. Because copper resists weathering, it would be very suitable for joints in trellis or any furniture that must be left outdoors.

For furniture pivots, the diameter needs to be ¼ inch or more. Therefore, nails cannot be used. Some rivets come with round (FIG. 3-3E) or countersunk heads (FIG. 3-3F) already made on one end. You can usually arrange for the manufactured head to come on the more prominent side; the head you make need not have such a good finish. Never have a rivet head directly on the wood; it will pull in. Always use washers. Try to avoid any slackness at the washer hole. If you try to spread a rivet head over a loose-fitting washer, much of your effort will go into spreading the neck of the rivet to the washer hole size.

Normally, there will be washers each side of and between the moving parts (FIG. 3-3G). Cut the end of the rivet to allow enough for forming the second head. There are tools called rivet *setts* or *snaps* that are like punches with hollowed ends to match rivet heads. If you have one of them available, you can support the manufactured head in it while you form the other end (FIG. 3-3H). Otherwise, you can use a lead block to hold the rivet against hammering so you don't damage the head. Hammer all around the projecting end to make the new head. For any riveting through wood, do not hammer too hard or you will bend the rivet in the wood. Try to make a head that matches the one on the other side. If you can hammer it approximately to shape, you can round it by hitting a rivet snap on it (FIG. 3-3J).

BOLTS

Many parts of outdoor furniture are held together with bolts. If you use bolts with hexagonal or square heads and nuts to match, have washers under the heads and nuts (FIG. 3-4A). If the threaded part extends some way through the nut, it looks better if it is sawn off fairly close in. If the bolt is through moving parts, there is a risk of the nut working loose. The traditional way of locking it is with a *locknut*, which is a second, thinner nut (FIG. 3-4B). Do not merely tighten one on top of the other, but hold the lower nut with a wrench while you tighten the other. Then turn the wrenches toward each other so that the nuts jam.

There are alternatives to locknuts. It is possible to get nuts with a friction arrangement built in; these are sometimes called *stiffnuts*. They lock well enough without further action (FIG. 3-4C). A simple method of securing is to hammer over the end of the bolt so that the nut cannot come off (FIG. 3-4D). There are epoxy glues intended for locking nuts to threads. The glue is smeared on and left to set.

Coach bolts are popular for outdoor furniture. The shallow, round head of a coach bolt does not project much and the square neck under it pulls into the wood to prevent the bolt from turning as the nut is tightened (FIG. 3-4E). For these and other bolts, drill a hole the same size as the bolt diameter. The square neck will pull in as the nut is tightened.

For some assemblies, you will want a bolt action, but the length will be more than a normal bolt will reach. In that case, you can use a rod screwed at both ends with nuts and washers attached (FIG. 3-4F). If you have screwing tackle

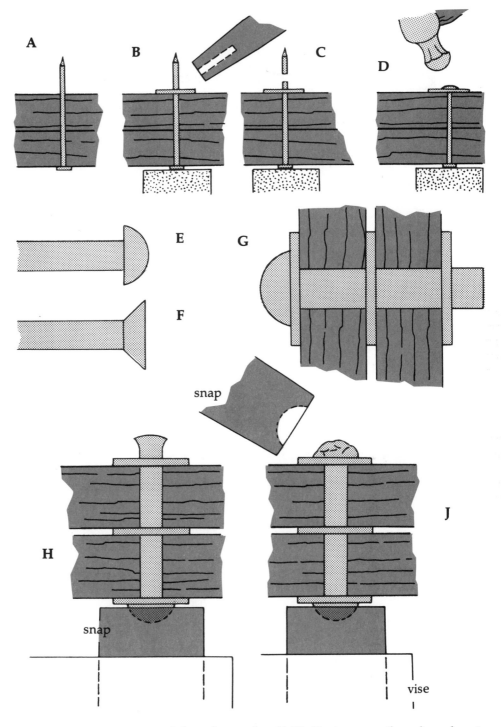

Fig. 3-3. A nail can be riveted through a washer (A-D). Rivets can go through washers to make pivots for moving parts (E-J).

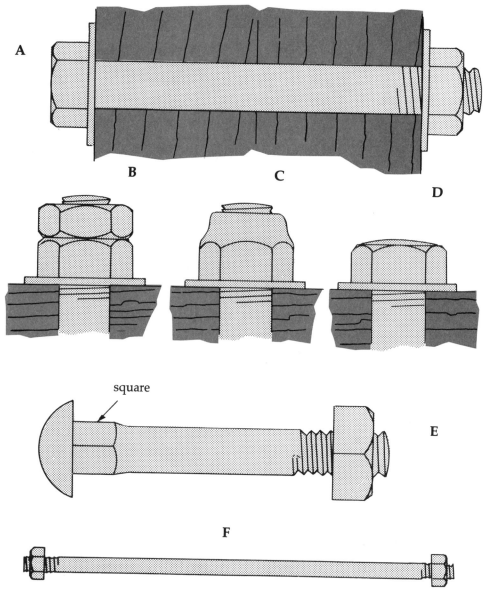

Fig. 3-4. Bolts through wood need washers (A). Nuts can be locked in several ways (B-D). A square neck prevents a bolt from turning (E). Threaded rod can be used instead of long bolts (F).

available, you can make such a rod when required. Otherwise a craftsman could easily make up what you need.

NOTCHED JOINTS

In most outdoor furniture, the joints are not complicated and not many pieces require the careful fitted work of indoor furniture. Although securing parts that cross by resting surfaces against each other and fastening through will be all that is needed in many places, there are some situations where something more is required to resist movement of one piece over another. The solution often is *notching*.

If the load on one piece will tend to make it slip on another, a notch can resist this tendency much better than any other method of fastening. If a horizontal member will come under load—as it would if supporting a seat—a notch in a vertical or inclined member will hold it (FIG. 3-5A). The notch does not need to be very deep, and there can be a bolt to hold the horizontal piece into it. If there is a possibility of movement in both directions, you can notch the other part as well (FIG. 3-5B). Notching deeply would weaken the wood. Notches should be no deeper than necessary (for example, ½ inch deep in 2-inch wood).

In some constructions, the crossing parts must be brought to the same level. In such a case, half would need to be cut out of pieces of the same thickness (FIG. 3-5C). That is what a cabinetmaker calls a *half-lap joint*. If the pieces that cross are not the same thickness, but one surface must come to the same level, the joint is stronger if less is cut from the thinner piece (FIG. 3-5D). Of course, all crossings are not square and joints must be cut accordingly, but the principle is the same.

Another place for halving joints is at corners. If two meeting members must come in the same plane, whether they meet squarely or not, you can cut half from each and use one or more bolts or dowels through them (FIG. 3-5E). You also can arrange a similar joint partway along one piece (FIG. 3-5F).

If the crossing parts do not need to be in the same plane but notching is required to resist sliding, the notching need not be as deep (FIG. 3-5G). In that case, the resistance to sliding is in the direction square to the longer piece, but there is no resistance in the direction away from it (except that provided by bolts). If the joint is to resist pulling apart, you can cut the end as a dovetail (FIG. 3-5H). The slope of the dovetail does not need to be steep; about 1 in 7 or 8 will do. For example, in the width of a 4-inch board, the taper could be ½ inches.

To do their job properly, notches should make a reasonably close fit on the other part. Mark the width from the other part; don't rely on the measurement that it ought to be. Square down the edges and gauge the depth of cut on both sides (FIG. 3-6A). Saw on the waste side of the lines. To be certain of following the lines at both sides, tilt the saw while cutting from one side (FIG. 3-6B). Then go to the other side, saw back, and finally saw straight through. Chop away the waste with a chisel (FIG. 3-6C). If you cut diagonally in a wide notch, it will pare more cleanly. First slope up from both sides, until you have cut almost to the lines (FIG. 3-6D), and then chisel straight across. Ideally, you will get the bottom of the notches exactly level.

Check with a straightedge laid across. Having the center high would interfere with getting the other part bedded down properly. Making it slightly hollow would be better. The best joint will go together with just a little help from a mallet or hammer. Put a piece of scrap wood over the joint and hit on it to prevent marking the wood and to spread the force of each blow.

A less common notched joint in outdoor furniture is where the end of a piece goes into a notch. For indoor furniture, this joint would be used to hold a shelf into an upright and is called a *housing* or *dado joint*. For outdoor furniture, the parts are not usually as wide as a shelf, but there are occasions where the most convenient joint for a particular purpose is this form (FIG. 3-7A). Make the notch as previously described. Cut the end of the other piece squarely.

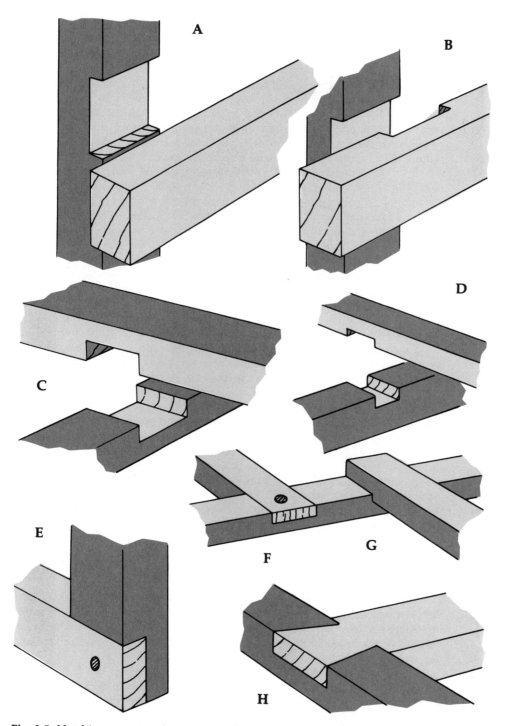

Fig. 3-5. Notching parts together prevents them from sliding over each other and can bring them to the same level (A-D). They can be secured by dowels (E-G) or dovetailing (H).

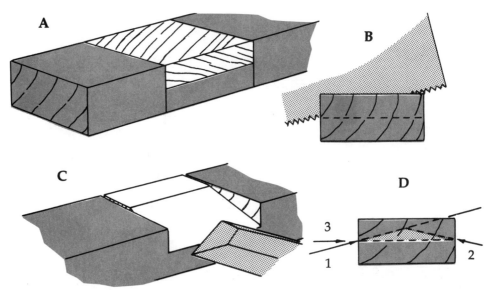

Fig. 3-6. Notches are marked out (A), then cut by sawing and chiseling from opposite sides (B-D).

You can use a simpler version, if you prefer (FIG. 3-7B). This has the advantage of having all the cuts made by sawing. In both cases, you could drive a nail or screw diagonally upward (FIG. 3-7C) as a stronger alternative to one driven into the end (FIG. 3-7D).

The parts do not necessarily have to be planed squared wood. You can use similar joints with natural round rods (FIG. 3-7E), or you can notch a top crossbar and nail it downward (FIG. 3-7F).

MORTISE-AND-TENON JOINTS

In just about all branches of woodwork, the most commonly used joints are mortises and tenons. They are not quite so common in outdoor furniture. A *mortise* is a rectangular hole into which the projecting *tenon* on the other part fits. If the parts are the same thickness, the tenon is about one-third the thickness (FIG. 3-8A). In the simplest form the tenon goes through. If it stops inside the mortised part, it is called a *stopped tenon* or *stub tenon* (FIG. 3-8B).

As with other joints, mark the sizes of one piece on the other directly from the wood, rather than by measuring, whenever possible. Mark all around the wood (FIG. 3-8C). For the finest work, cuts across the grain are marked with a knife and the width of tenon and mortise are marked with a mortise gauge (which has two adjustable spurs). You could manage with an ordinary marking gauge or a rule and pencil.

You can saw the shoulder and sides of the tenon, preferably with a fine backsaw. Most of the waste in the mortise is best removed by drilling. Usually this is done partly from each side if it is a through mortise. Then the shape is trued with chisels, cutting across the grain first.

Although you should use waterproof glue, it is advisable to further strengthen mortise-and-tenon joints that are to remain outdoors exposed to all weathers. You

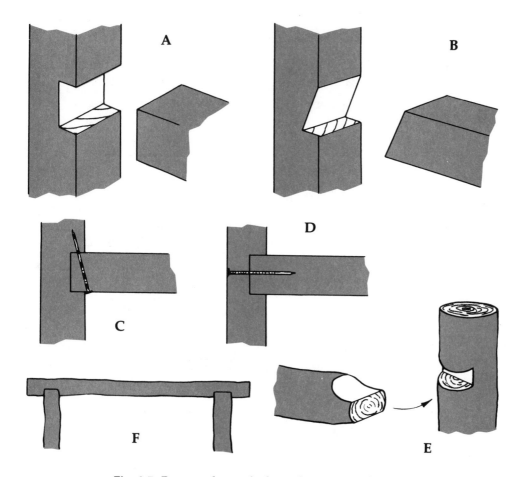

Fig. 3-7. Parts can be notched together in several ways.

can cut a mortise slightly wider so you can drive wedges at the ends of the tenons (FIG. 3-8D). Probably a better way of wedging is to make saw cuts across the end of the tenon before assembly, and then drive in wedges (FIG. 3-8E). Glue the wedges and the joint. Then plane the ends level after the glue has set.

Tenons can also be held in by dowels, usually one at each joint. Drill across after assembly and drive a dowel through (FIG. 3-8F). It is often difficult to clamp the large structures involved in outdoor woodwork, and there is a method of using dowels or pegs that will pull joints together. Before assembly, mark and drill through the mortise and tenon. Locate the hole in the tenon slightly closer to its shoulder so that when the joint goes together the holes do not quite match (FIG. 3-8G). Taper the end of an overlong piece of dowel rod or made a similar peg. Drive it in and the tenon will be drawn tighter.

There are many variations on the mortise-and-tenon joint that are mostly applicable to indoor furniture. In this book, variations are given as they occur in projects.

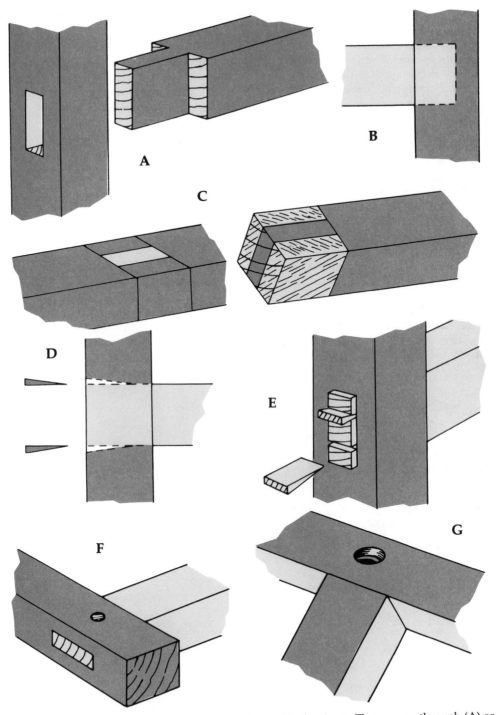

Fig. 3-8. Mortise-and-tenon joints are commonly used in furniture. They can go through (A) or be stopped (B), and the tenon is often one-third the thickness of the wood (C). Wedges or dowels hold and pull the joints together (D-G).

DOWELING

In the manufacture of indoor furniture, there is much use of dowel joints—usually in places where the older hand craftsman used mortise-and-tenon joints—because doweling lends itself better to quantity production. There are fewer uses of dowels in outdoor furniture, but on some occasions dowels make the best joint. You should use prepared dowel rods. They are made of hardwood and are available in many diameters. For most outdoor furniture, the dowels should be fairly thick. Usually they are near half the thickness of the wood being joined. The use of dowels in securing tenons was described earlier, but there are joints where dowels themselves form the joints.

The typical joint comes where dowels are used instead of tenons (FIG. 3-9A). When you are planning this sort of joint, make sure the dowels provide about the same glue area that would be given by a tenon. There should never be less than two dowels in any joint. How deep to take them depends on the wood. Approximately two to three times their diameter is about right, but they could go deeper into end grain.

Always allow for the holes being rather deeper than the dowels will go. A dowel acts like a piston and you must allow air and surplus glue to escape; otherwise the wood will burst or crack. Taper the dowel ends and saw a groove lengthwise for the air to escape (FIG. 3-9B). Careful marking out is important. There are jigs available for getting holes to match, but they are mostly intended for wood of the smaller sections used in indoor furniture.

There are places in outdoor furniture where you can use dowels instead of screws or bolts, with holes drilled right through (FIG. 3-9C). You can make saw

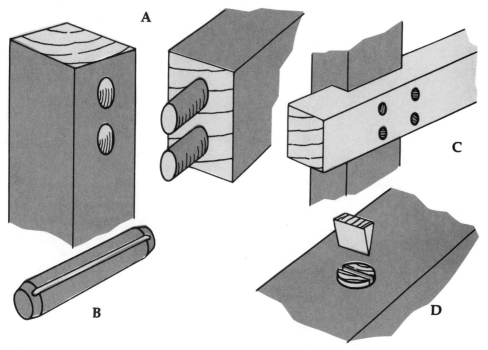

Fig. 3-9. Glued dowels are alternatives to tenons (A,B,D). They also can be used to strengthen other joints (C).

cuts across the ends to drive wedges in, in the same way as suggested for tenons (FIG. 3-9D). Arrange the wedges across the direction of the grain in the surrounding wood.

CLAMPING

Although there will be uses for ordinary C-clamps, bar clamps, or other versions of clamps to fit on pipes or the edges of boards, much of the assembly work in outdoor furniture is outside the reach of these devices.

Wedges have some uses. If you have a rigid board longer than the parts to be clamped, you can nail or screw on blocks, then drive wedges at one or both ends to tighten the joints (FIG. 3-10A). A similar idea employs two long boards and bolts. Drive the wedges against the bolts (FIG. 3-10B).

Single wedges do not put on direct pressure and driving them will tend to move the parts. It is better to use pairs of similar wedges called *folding wedges* (FIG. 3-10C). By driving them alternately against each other, you apply a parallel thrust (FIG. 3-10D).

Instead of wood you can use rope. There can be a tight lashing around the work over scrap wood. Then you drive wedges under the wood (FIG. 3-10E).

Another way of using rope is as a *Spanish windlass*. Use one turn of thick rope or many turns of thinner rope with the ends tied together. Put a rod through the rope loops and twist (FIG. 3-10F). This method places a considerable load both on the parts being clamped and on the rope. Make sure the rope is strong enough. Stop the rod against an adjacent part (FIG. 3-10G) or by tying it to the turns (FIG. 3-10H) to keep on the pressure. The Spanish windlass could go around the four sides of an assembly, such as a seat, as well as be used across a flat frame.

You might need to use several clamping arrangements together to get all parts tight. At the same time, you will have to watch squareness.

SQUARING

Absolute squareness of all parts of a piece of outdoor furniture might not seem as important as when indoor furniture is being assembled, but it is surprising how lack of true in some part will become rather obvious. It is worthwhile checking squareness of most things as you assemble them. If possible, work on a flat floor even if the furniture eventually will be used on uneven ground. You then can check that such things as seats and tabletops are parallel with the floor when the legs are standing level. In the final situation, you will know that leveling will bring these important parts true. Without the initial test, you do not have a basis for comparison.

A spirit level is a useful tool. Try it in all directions on a tabletop or anything else that should be level. If it seems to show a persistant error, turn it end for end in case the fault is in the level. The longer the level, the more accurate your result will be, particularly if you are dealing with a surface that is something less than flat. If you use a small level, put it on a straightedge that will bridge over unevenness.

Where possible, check squareness with a try square. There is, however, a limit because of its size. If you try to extend the blade of a 12-inch try square with a straightedge, a negligible error at its tip becomes a large one at 48 inches, for instance. You can assume that corners of sheets of plywood and other manufactured boards are square, and you can use one of these sheets to check squareness within its limits of size.

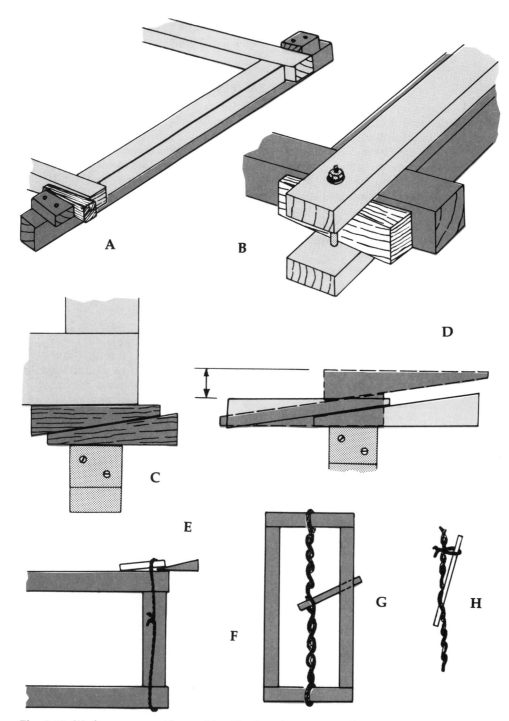

Fig. 3-10. Wedges can provide considerable clamping pressure (A-E). A Spanish windlass made from rope also will serve as a clamp (F-H).

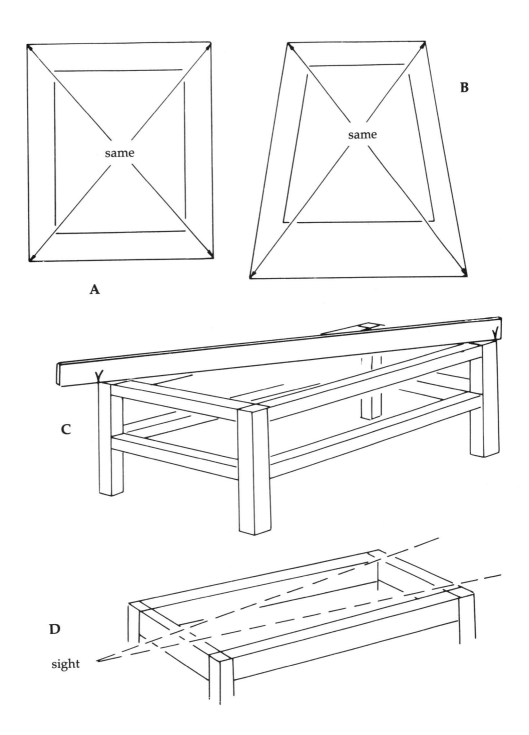

Fig. 3-11. Squareness or symmetry can be checked by comparing diagonals (A-C). Twisting or winding can be checked by sighting across (D).

Most assemblies are rectangular. If they are not rectangular, they are usually symmetrical. In this case, it is easier to check squareness by comparing diagonals. If you have a four-sided frame that should be square, measure corner to corner or between matching points (FIG. 3-11A). When the frame is square, these measurements will be the same. This method also applies to a symmetrical shape. The item is true about its centerline when diagonals are the same (FIG. 3-11B).

You can measure diagonally with an expanding rule or tape measure, but it is safer to mark a board. Make *peck marks* on the edge (FIG. 3-11C) and compare the two directions. In this way, you avoid the possible error of misreading rule divisions or confusing them.

In many assemblies, there are opposite parts that must match, usually as a pair. Normally, it is best to make one part and check its accuracy. Then true the other part by putting it over the first part in the correct relative position (inside to inside). When you have an assembly to make up, it is nearly always best to take two opposite sides with more parts than the other way. Get them together and matching before bringing in the parts the other way.

As you progress with assembly, check diagonals as often as the opportunity occurs. For instance, you make up two end leg assemblies for a table and then you must add a top built up of strips. Check the diagonals of the top assembly as it is added. Then check that the legs are perpendicular to the top by measuring from their feet diagonally to the corners of the top at each side. You probably will be adding bracing to hold the legs, but do not secure any brace until you have checked the squareness of whatever it is to hold.

For a chair, you can make up opposite sides with arms and seat rails. You know that they match, but as you join them with crosswise parts, check diagonals across the back legs and the front legs. Finally, check squareness as viewed from above by measuring diagonals across the seat. Then stand back and look for twists that are not apparent when squaring.

You usually can see twists if you view the assembly from a distance and in several directions. It does help to view across things that should be parallel. If you sight one thing across its partner opposite (FIG. 3-11D), any variation will be obvious. This also applies when looking through a table or chair to see if the legs match. If the assembly is glued, do all this checking before the glue has started to set. Then you can usually pull the parts true. If they still try to spring to the incorrect positions, put a weight on top or clamp diagonally in the direction that will pull the shape right. You will need to overcorrect slightly to allow for springing back.

4

Simple Seats

SEATS ARE THE MOST NEEDED TYPE of outdoor furniture. They do not need to be anything elaborate. There are places and circumstances where a top firmly supported at the right height is all that is needed, particularly in the natural surroundings of trees, bushes, and paths where there is a need for an occasional place to rest. The sort of chair or lounger that would be right on a patio or in a formal garden would not look right in that setting, particularly if it had brightly colored cushions.

There are other situations where simple seating is all that is required. Examples are in a play area or where the seats are likely to get rough use or suffer from neglect. You can leave a simple bench or stool out in all types of weather. Something more elaborate and valuable would need to be put under cover or taken indoors when not in use.

From the practical point of view, simple seating is easier to make. The structures are rather basic. The joints are simple. Usually it is not necessary to be precise. Many simple seats can be made with only a few simple tools.

Many simple seats can be made with wood that might not be suitable for anything more advanced nor for making indoor furniture. Much wood is sound and durable but is normally discarded when converting lumber to standard-size boards. This wood is available for little or no money. Some of it has the waney edges of the outside of the tree where it has been cut right through the log. This design feature can be kept for a seat to be positioned among natural surroundings.

RUSTIC BENCH

You can make a freestanding bench seat in a size to suit its surroundings and the available materials. It uses wood in as near its natural state as needed. You can position the bench in a field or woodland where it will match surroundings. You can use almost any wood, but for the strongest and longest lasting seat, it should be a hardwood free from large knots. If you use softwood, sections should be thicker and you should not expect a very long life. Treating the wood with a preservative will lengthen life. If the wood has been recently felled, allow the sap to dry before you apply preservative.

When a log is prepared for cutting into boards, it is first cut to approximately square section (FIG. 4-1A). The curved pieces removed are usually discarded, but many of them are suitable for seat tops. The same is true for the first board cut if it has a wandering waney edge, which would make it uneconomical to convert to a parallel board (FIG. 4-1B). Both of these offcuts can be suitable as bench tops.

Remove any bark that remains. The traditional tool for doing this is called a *spud*. It was a long-handled tool—something like a broad chisel—with a thin, but not sharp, cutting edge. You can manage with an ax or a large chisel.

Except for removing bark, keep the waney edge. Level sharp edges or exceptionally projecting parts.

Make the top surface reasonably flat, but the perfection of surface required for indoor furniture is unnecessary. A coarsely set plane, used diagonally to the grain, usually will level unseasoned wood. Remove any sharpness around the edges, but otherwise leave the natural appearance.

The legs are also natural pieces of wood that are cut from poles. Their size depends on the overall sizes of the bench, but a diameter of about 2 inches should suit most constructions. Remove any bark. You can plane level the knots left by small branches, but do not use pieces with large knots. Have the legs too long at this stage, and bring them to matching lengths after assembly.

The legs fit into holes in the top. The size of holes will depend on available equipment, but they should be at least 1 inch and preferably up to 1½ inches.

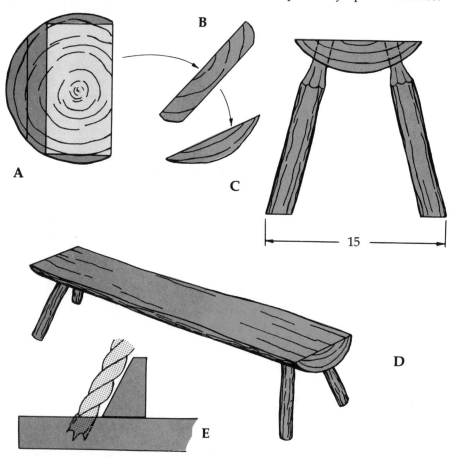

Fig. 4-1. Parts of logs and branches can be made into stools and benches.

The way you arrange the holes depends on the shape of the board section. If it is a parallel thickness, you can mark out a regular arrangement. If you are dealing with an irregular shape, such as the outside curved section, the holes do not need to be arranged squarely or in line. Try to spread the feet at least as wide as the board. If the board is narrow, let them be about 15 inches apart on the ground (FIG. 4-1C) when you have cut them to the correct height. At the ends of the bench, the feet should not be very far in from the end of the seat; otherwise someone sitting on the end could tip the bench (FIG. 4-1D).

Drill from the top diagonally outward. You might be able to estimate the angle—particularly since each leg can slope differently on an odd-shaped piece—or you could cut a scrap-wood template as a guide (FIG. 4-1E). If the grain breaks out as the drill goes through the underside, that should not matter.

Taper the end of each leg to drive into its hole (FIG. 4-2A). It will be stronger if you taper gradually on a long slope than if you have a more abrupt change of section. The traditional way of tapering is to use a drawknife (FIG. 4-2B), while the wood is held diagonally in a vise, but you can get a similar effect with a broad chisel used with its bevel downward. It will help to draw a circle of the right size on the end. Have a piece of scrap wood with a hole of the right size drilled in it to slide over the end so you can see that it is down to size for a sufficient length

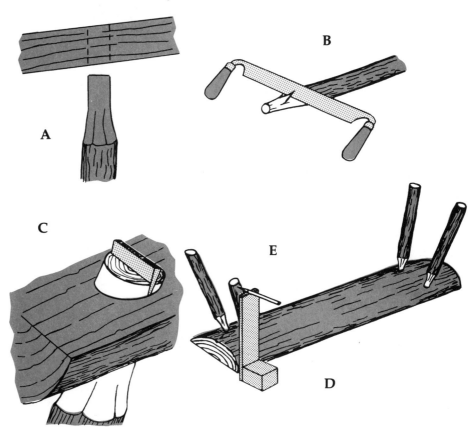

Fig. 4-2. Tapered ends can be driven into holes and wedges (A-C), then legs cut to length (D,E).

to go through the seat. There is no need for absolute precision, but try to get a reasonable drive fit.

Make a saw cut in the end to take a wedge. Assemble the joint with the cut across the seat grain. Let the leg end project slightly, then drive in the wedge (FIG. 4-2C). Decide if you want to use glue. If you do, it must be a waterproof type (preferably a boat-building grade). If you know the wood is still green or only partly seasoned, it is best to assemble each joint dry. Wedging will tighten it, and the shrinkage that occurs as the wood dries should further tighten it. Wood that is still wet with sap does not bond well with any glue.

With all four legs in place and their tops planed level, invert the bench so you can mark the leg lengths. Make a simple gauge with a strip of the right height attached to a base block (FIG. 4-2D). Use this gauge with a pencil on the end to mark as far around each leg as you can (FIG. 4-2E) as a guide to sawing off. Take off any raggedness from the end and bevel all around so the risk of splitting, if the bench is dragged over concrete or stones, is reduced.

RUSTIC STOOL

A long bench will find its own level when standing on four feet, but as you bring the legs closer together it gets increasingly difficult to make them stand level on uneven ground. As a result, stools and small seats were once made with three legs. A tripod arrangement will stand without wobbling on any surface. In the old days of earth floors in the home, and particularly in the milking shed, three-legged stools were standard. Stools made in this way will produce individual seats to match the rustic bench.

The top can be a piece of waney-edged wood that is cut to about the same length as its width and with the corners trimmed off (FIG. 4-3A). You could cut the ends at two angles so that the final shape is approximately hexagonal (FIG. 4-3B). This would match the three-legged arrangement.

The holes for the legs do not need to be equally spaced, but they should not be too far out. What is more important is reasonably equal spacing on the ground. If you are dealing with an awkwardly shaped top, you might need to alter the angle of a leg to fit it into the top shape, yet bring it to part of a regular pattern at the floor. A top in its natural form will be more interesting than a piece of wood that fits into a symmetrical shape.

The way to get even spacing is to draw a circle and step off the radius around the circumference. The radius will go around the circumference six times so legs come at alternate marks (FIG. 4-3C). Fit and level the legs in the same way as for the bench. Try to finish with the top level and the bottoms of the legs fairly close to the area covered by the top (FIG. 4-3D) for reasonable stability if the user leans or tries to tilt his seat.

FIXED BENCH

Alongside woodland paths there might be a need for simple seats that are secured to the ground. A simple bench top can have vertical end legs that are held down in some way (FIG. 4-4A). The top should be hardwood about 2 inches thick. It can have waney edges or be trimmed parallel. Its top should be level and reasonably smooth, but the underside can be rough. It needs no special preparation except for the removal of sharp edges all around.

One way of making the bench is to let the legs into the ground by digging holes and compacting the soil firmly, then cut the tops of the legs level and nail

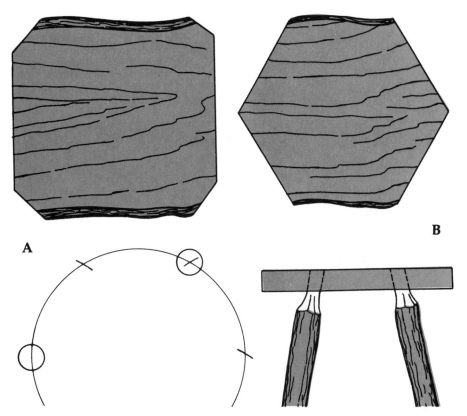

Fig. 4-3. Waney-edged wood can have its ends shaped to make a stool (A,B). Three legs stand better than four on uneven ground (C). Legs should be splayed at least to the limits of the top (D).

on the seat. A firmer support can be obtained from using concrete instead of compacted soil around the legs. There is a snag to either arrangement. Buried wood will rot, and sometimes quite rapidly. Some woods, such as oak, will withstand burial longer, and you can soak the wood in preservative first, but it is better to keep the wood above ground.

To keep the wood above ground, make the bench as an above-ground assembly and hold it down in some way. The simplest assembly is nailed. If the underside of the top is uneven, make a groove across parallel with the top surface for the leg to fit into (FIG. 4-4B). Usually the leg is the same thickness as the top, but if you have thicker wood you can use it as is. Drill the top for the nails to reduce the risk of splitting. The hole should be the same size as its nail or only very slightly smaller. Because you will be driving into end grain in the legs, you need not drill them. Ideally, use nails protected by galvanizing or other means. Plain iron nails should provide a reasonable life.

A better way is to tenon the legs into the top (FIG. 4-4C). Two square tenons should be enough unless it is a very wide seat. Remove the waste from the mortises by drilling and chopping out with a chisel. Make the tenons slightly too long. Cut them for wedges that can come across the grain or be arranged diagonally (FIG. 4-4D). As with the rustic bench, you can assemble the joints dry, particularly if you are working with greenwood. If you prefer, you can use a waterproof glue.

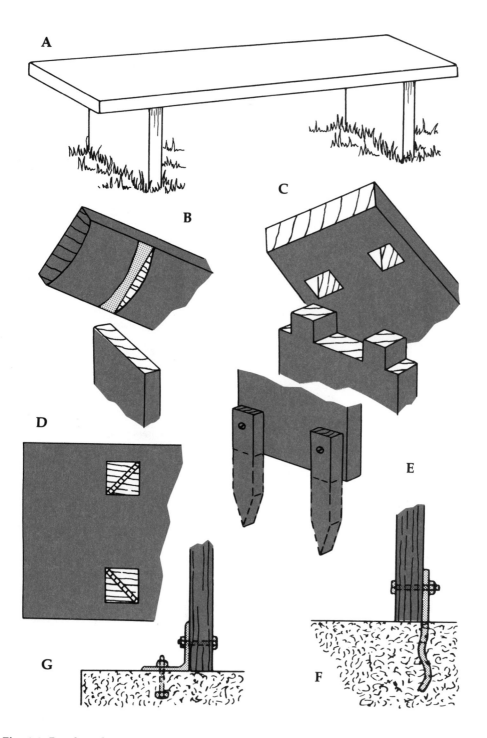

Fig. 4-4. Bench ends can enter the ground (A). Their tops can be notched (B) or tenoned (C,D). Feet can be pegged (E) or bolted down (F,G).

There are many ways of attaching the legs to the ground. If the ground is level and suitable for driving pegs into it, use oak or other hardwood pieces driven in as far as possible. Then screw or bolt through (FIG. 4-4E). If these pieces rot after several years, you can replace them. You will still have the bench intact.

It might be better to put down a concrete base. You might want to concrete over the area where users' feet will come, or it might be sufficient to just have concrete blocks under the bench legs.

You can let strips of metal into the concrete with holes for screws into the wood (FIG. 4-4F). Bend the metal or chop teeth into it with a cold chisel to help it hold in the concrete. Alternatively, put pieces of angle iron on top. Hold them down with the special bolts intended for concrete work or with ordinary bolts buried in the concrete (FIG. 4-4G). In both cases, have holes ready for screws driven into the bench legs.

If you make the bench of hardwood, it probably will look best if untreated and left to weather to a natural appearance. You can make the bench of softwood, but then it would be better to treat it with preservative and paint it. Dark green is the usual paint color for a natural environment. Periodic repainting would be necessary to protect the wood.

SLAB BENCH

A freestanding seat made from quite thick wood will be fairly heavy, but that could be an advantage if it is to spend most of the summer outside standing on concrete, wood, or level ground. The weight makes for steadiness and discourages users from tipping the seat or moving it from the place you prefer to leave it.

For stability, it is better to let the legs slope out slightly, to give a broad base (FIG. 4-5A) with the minimum risk of tipping. If the wood is at least 2 inches thick, mortise-and-tenon joints between the parts should give all the strength needed, without additional bracing.

Set out one end, showing the angle the leg is to come (FIG. 4-5B), and arrange its foot almost as far as the overhanging top. Set an adjustable bevel to the angle and use it for marking out the joint and the foot of each leg (FIG. 4-5C). Mark out the outline of each leg, but cut the joints before cutting the outsides to shape. The tenons and the spaces between them should be about the same, but you will need to adjust this according to the width of wood you are using.

Keep the tenons and mortises on both sides of the wood. Watch the lines on both sides when cutting the tenons. Drill out some of the waste from the mortises, but chop to the outlines from both sides with a chisel. Use the adjustable bevel as a guide to the angle you hold the chisel and saw.

Cut the tapers on the sides of the legs and the V out of the bottom (FIG. 4-5D). Remove sharpness before assembling. Wedge the tenons in the usual way. Check how the bench stands on a level surface. You will almost certainly need to plane the feet to remove wobble, but try moving the bench and turning it around before being satisfied that you have it right.

LIGHT BENCH

If you want a bench seat that is not too heavy for moving about, the wood will need to be thinner than in the slab bench. That means you will have to use additional bracing because joints between the top and legs alone cannot be trusted. This bench is intended to be made of ¾- or ⅞-inch prepared wood. If well made

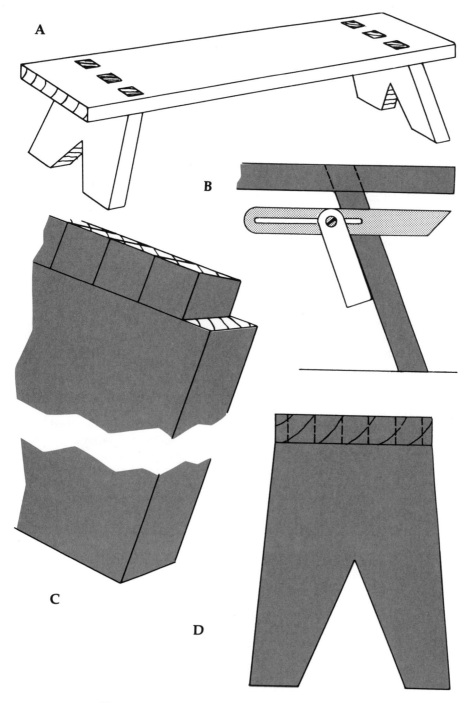

Fig. 4-5. Sloping and cut legs provide stability.

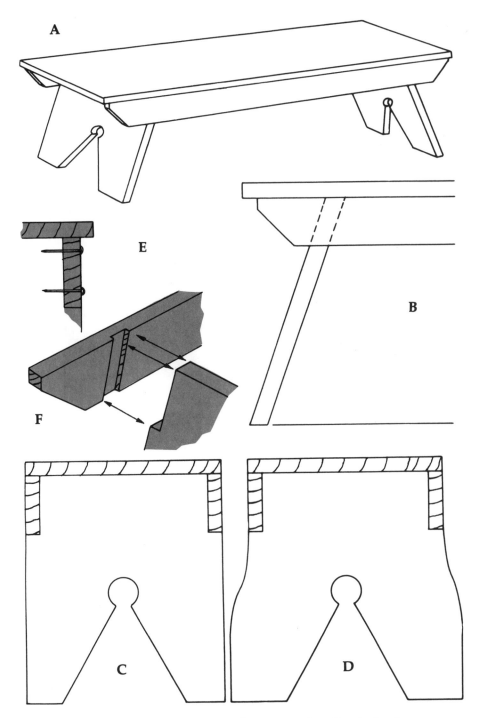

Fig. 4-6. This Light Bench has sides to strengthen the sloping legs.

and given a varnished or painted finish, it will have uses indoors as well as outdoors.

Length and width should be according to your needs (FIG. 4-6A), but 9 inches is about the minimum satisfactory width. The bench can be as short as 18 inches for a one-person stool or up to 84 inches or even longer with thicker wood. Height should be between 15 and 18 inches.

Draw an end to show the angle (FIG. 4-6B). You can make the legs parallel (FIG. 4-6C) or broaden them to increase stability (FIG. 4-6D), particularly if the top is narrow.

Notch the rails under the top into the legs. In the simplest construction, the joints there are directly nailed (FIG. 4-6E), but it would be better to notch the rails slightly (FIG. 4-6F) and use glue and screws. Do not cut more than ¼ inch out of the rail and trim the leg edge accordingly.

The legs have holes drilled for the saw to cut into. Do all the work you need to on the legs, including removing sharp edges, before assembly. Prepare the rails similarly, including well-rounding the lower edges where the hands will grip to move the bench. Assemble the rails to the legs with glue and screws. Bevel strips to go between the rails inside the leg tops (FIG. 4-7A). Glue and screw them in place.

Prepare the seat by rounding its top and bottom edges all around. The simplest way to fit it is with nails driven downward all around. For the simplest construction of a bench that is not regarded as very important, that method would be satisfactory.

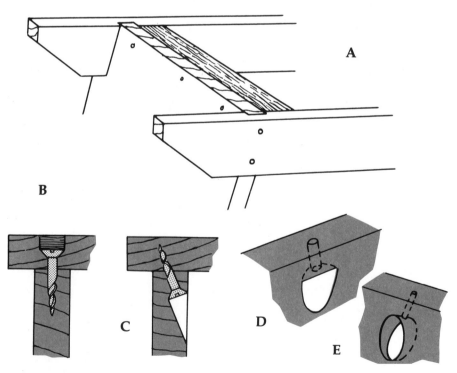

Fig. 4-7. Constructional details of the Light Bench.

A better way to fit the seat to the legs is to screw downward. The screw heads could finish level with the surface, but it would be better to counterbore the screws and fill the holes with wood plugs (FIG. 4-7B). If you do not want screws or plugs to be visible on top, it is possible to do all screwing from below. At the legs, you can place several screws up through the crosswise strips. Along the rails, you can use pocket screws driven from inside the rails (FIG. 4-7C).

Chop the recesses with a chisel and drill so that the holes come about on the center of the top edge (FIG. 4-7D). Another way of making a recess is to drill diagonally with a large bit (FIG. 4-7E). Be careful that its point does not go through. In addition to screwing, by whatever method, use waterproof glue in all joints.

NAILED BENCH WITH BACK

If a plain bench is to have a back, the simplest way to arrange it is to have the bench ends and top level so that the back support can go directly on the end without any need for notching or other shaping.

The bench shown in FIG. 4-8 is intended to be made from wood that finishes about 1¼ inches thick. Some of it could be waney edged. The top or both edges of the back could retain their natural shape, as could the edges of the ends and the underside of the seat rail. The front edge of the seat should be straight and rounded in section.

The sizes listed in TABLE 4-1 suit a seat for two or three. The ends could be attached to the ground (as described for earlier benches). As shown in FIG. 4-8, the seat is intended to be freestanding with a broad enough base to keep it steady in normal use. It would be possible to make the bench with cut and glued joints, but it is shown nailed. Nailing seems more appropriate to a seat that is to have a natural look without a high finish.

Nails 3 inches long should suit most parts made in hard wood, but you will need longer nails if you are using soft wood or driving into end grain. Drill holes in the top piece of wood almost as large as the nail diameter to reduce the risk of splitting. In most places, the nail can force its way into the bottom piece. Near an edge it is wise to drill an undersize hole at least part of the distance the nail will go.

Prepare the seat and its rail (FIG. 4-9A). Nail them together with the seat overhanging the rail enough to fit on the ends. Cut the ends squarely and nail on the seat (FIG. 4-9B). This assembly gives the basic form to which other parts are added.

You can add the feet (FIG. 4-9C) before or after you join the ends to the seat. Make one long piece and use it as a pattern for marking the other feet parts. Taper the projecting parts to half depth. Place matching filing pieces (FIG. 4-9D) between to make up the thickness. The basic bench is shown with the bottom flat, but if it is to stand on uneven ground it would be better to cut back to the width of the end to form feet (FIG. 4-9E). Use waterproof glue and nails driven from both sides in the assembly of the feet. Trim the ends and bottom edges after the glue has set.

The slope of the back is probably best found by experiment. You then can find what angle of the back board seems most comfortable on the particular seat. As shown in FIG. 4-8, the bottom of a back support is about central over the foot, and it slopes to come almost completely on the end of the seat. A support does not need to go right down an end, but it looks neater if it is cut to go against its foot.

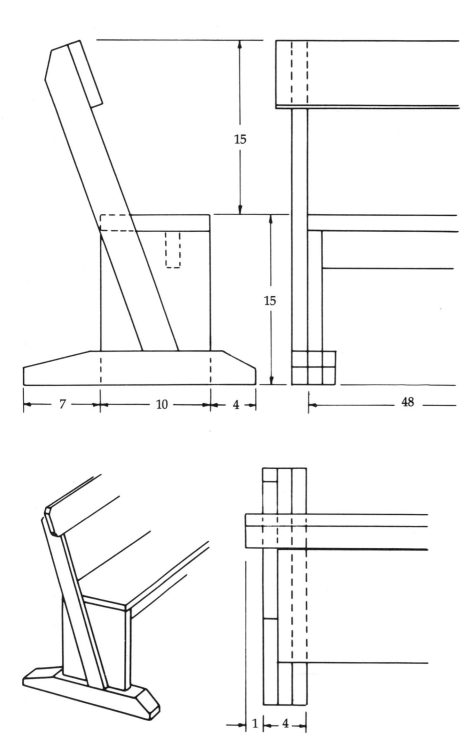

Fig. 4-8. A bench of nailed construction has a back supported at the ends and feet extended behind.

Table 4-1. Materials List for Nailed Bench with Back.

1 seat	10	× 48 ×	1¼
1 seat rail	3	× 48 ×	1¼
2 ends	10	× 15 ×	1¼
4 feet	3	× 22 ×	1¼
4 feet fillers	3	× 8 ×	1¼
1 back	6	× 54 ×	1¼
2 back supports	3	× 30 ×	1¼

Attach the back supports to the ends (FIG. 4-9E), then nail on the back to overhang each end equally (FIG. 4-9F). Check squareness during assembly. The precision required for indoor furniture is unnecessary, but great variations from squareness will spoil appearance. Your final chance of pulling the seat square comes when you attach the back.

There is usually no need to sink nails and cover them with stopping in this sort of construction, however, you must be careful that there are no projecting heads on which clothing could be snagged. If you are using wood that has not been fully seasoned, allow for it to shrink in thickness as it dries out. Punch the nailheads slightly below the surface so that they will not be left above the surface if the wood gets thinner. If it is possible to visit the bench in 6 months, go over it with a hammer and punch to tighten all nails. Unseasoned wood is best left untreated. Paint or varnish on it would tend to peel and come away. Store the wood up to 1 year if you eventually want to paint it.

SLAB BENCH WITH BACK

In a rural setting, a bench made from slabs cut across the log to leave waney edges often will look better than one made from parallel plain boards. It must have straight edges in some places, but elsewhere the natural curving edge helps the bench to match its surroundings.

Comfort comes from sloping the seat backward with the back angled to match. The slope also makes the seat shed rainwater easily. The suggested design is shown in FIG. 4-10. The sizes shown in TABLE 4-2 are for a bench 48 inches long (FIG. 4-11), but other lengths are possible. In any case, you might need to adapt the construction to suit available wood.

For strength, make the seat supports with the grain across and the back supports with their grain crossing them so they provide mutual support and resistance to splitting. Notch the seat around the back supports and keep them straight by two rails underneath.

It will help if you draw an end view full size (FIG. 4-12), taking into account the available materials. Get the slope of the seat on a pattern of 2-inch squares and draw in the other parts to match it.

Make the seat supports (FIG. 4-13A) with their grain across and nail on strips to the front edges after notching them to take the front rail (FIG. 4-13B). The front rail will have a waney edge downward so that the notches at each end will not be the same. At this stage, you can cut the notches only partway down the front. Trim them during assembly when you are putting in the rail.

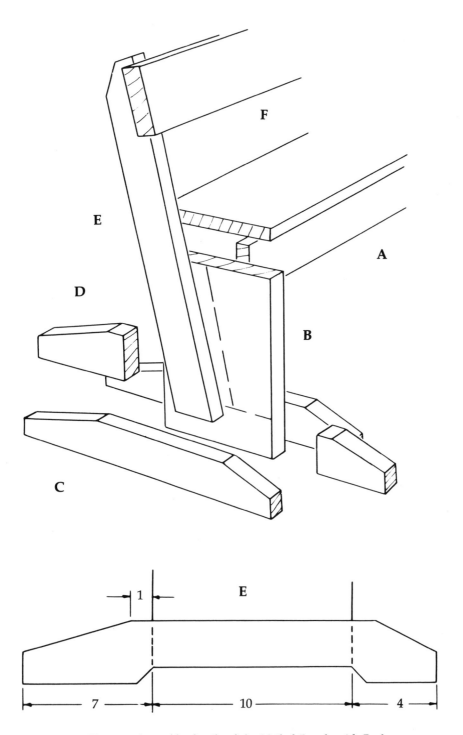

Fig. 4-9. Assembly details of the Nailed Bench with Back.

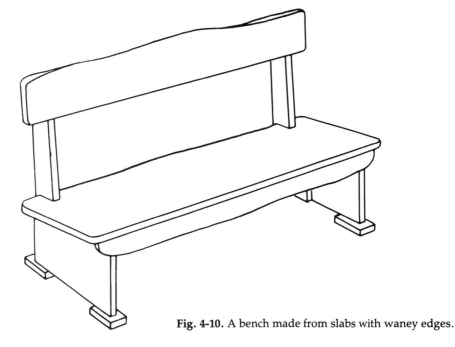

Fig. 4-10. A bench made from slabs with waney edges.

Cut the back supports (FIG. 4-13C) to match the seat slope and overlap the seat supports. Rear edges finish about 1 inch behind the bottoms of the seat supports. At the top, notch the edges to take the back (FIG. 4-13D). Although the back can have an upward waney edge, its lower edge should be straight so the notches can be cut completely. Variations in back width will be upward.

Assemble the ends with the back supports inside the seat supports. Be careful to make a pair of them. You could screw through from opposite sides or use large nails driven through and clenched. The strongest joints will be bolted; four ¼-inch bolts through each overlap should be enough. Have washers under the nuts. If the wood shrinks as it dries out, you will be able to tighten the nuts. Coach bolts are a good choice. If you use ordinary bolts, put washers under the heads

Table 4-2. Materials List for Slab Bench with Back.

2 ends	14 × 15 × 1¼
2 end fronts	1 × 15 × 1¼
2 back supports	7 × 30 × 1¼
4 feet	2½ × 5 × 1¼
1 rail	4 × 42 × 1¼
1 rail	4 × 49 × 1¼
1 seat	16 × 49 × 1¼
1 back	6 × 49 × 1¼

(No allowance for waney edges)

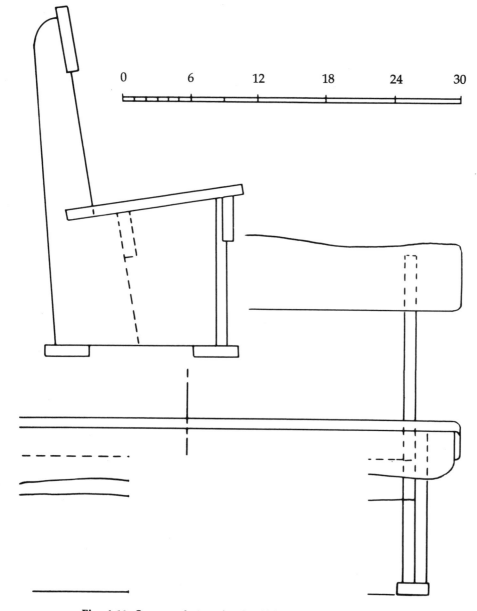

Fig. 4-11. Suggested sizes for the Slab Bench with Back.

as well. It helps to have oversize washers to reduce the tendency to pull into the wood.

The feet (FIG. 4-13E) are simple blocks nailed or screwed underneath. Let them extend about 1 inch back and front. If the bench is likely to be dragged about, take the sharpness off edges and corners to prevent splintering on stony ground.

The inner seat rail (FIG. 4-13F) needs a straight top edge and square ends. It is this rail that decides the bench length and settles its squareness. Its lower edge can be waney or straight. Nail or screw it to the inner edges of the back supports.

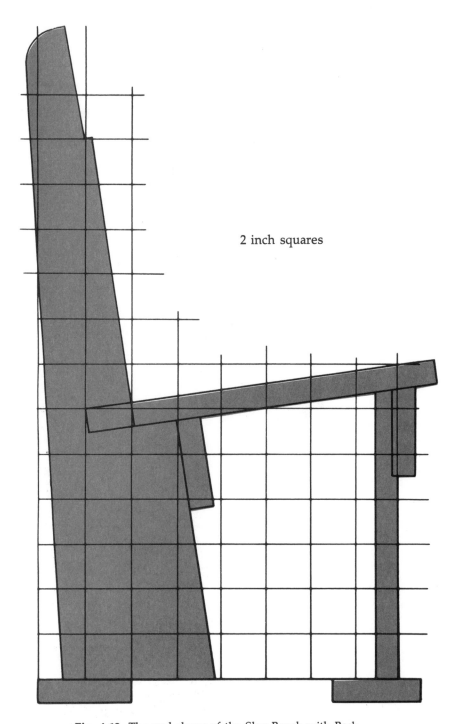

2 inch squares

Fig. 4-12. The end shape of the Slap Bench with Back

At the same time, check that the two ends stand upright when on a level floor.

Make the front rail so that it projects about 3 inches past each end (FIG. 4-13G). Its top edge needs to be straight, but it must be beveled to suit the seat angle. Round the extending ends and take off any sharpness of the waney edge so that a hand put under the bench will not get scratched. Trim the notches to suit and nail or screw on the rail.

The seat (FIG. 4-13H) should have a straight front edge, but the rear edge can be straight or waney. Mark its length to be slightly more than the front rail. Hold the seat against the assembly to mark the positions of the notches around the back supports. Cut them to make a close fit. When you assemble the piece, put small strips (FIG. 4-13J) inside the angles to give support to the overlaps. Round the front edge and outer corners of the seat before the final fitting.

You could nail or screw the seat on, with the heads level, but it is better to counterbore screws and glue plugs over them to give a neat top finish. Hold the seat down with screws at about 2-inch intervals across the ends, and about 6-inch spacing along the rails.

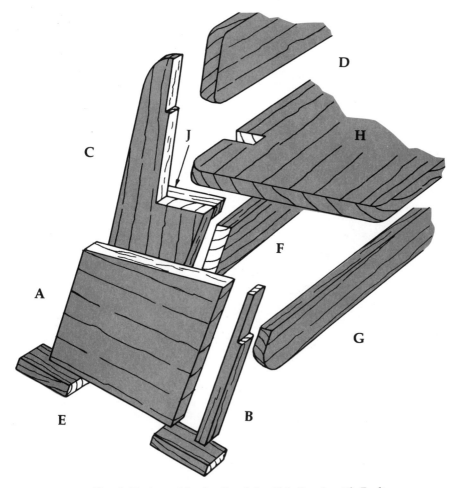

Fig. 4-13. Assembly details of the Slab Bench with Back.

The back can be the width you like, but it looks best if the waney top edge is higher near the center. Make it the same length as the seat. Round the ends and exposed edges. Attach it to its supports the same way as the seat.

You can make this type of bench more attractive by having something carved at the center of the back. It might just be the date cut in with a knife, or a motif formed from your initials. It might be the badge of an organization. Whatever is done should be simple and bold. Natural wood, probably not fully seasoned at the time of carving, does not accept fine detail carving without the risk of breaking out.

SAWBUCK BENCH

The cross-legged arrangement, like a sawhorse (*sawbuck*), allows for providing back support with the extension of a leg at each end. This assembly is not quite as simple as might be expected because the usual symmetrical arrangement of the crossed legs would bring the back support some way behind the seat, and legs would not go far enough to the rear to prevent the risk of tipping.

Instead there must be an asymmetrical arrangement so that the back is more upright and the rear leg extends far enough (FIGS. 4-14 and 4-15). The important parts are the pair of end structures. The lengthwise parts can be any reasonable length; 60 inches would make a seat for two or three. (See TABLE 4-3.)

Fig. 4-14. The Sawbuck Bench.

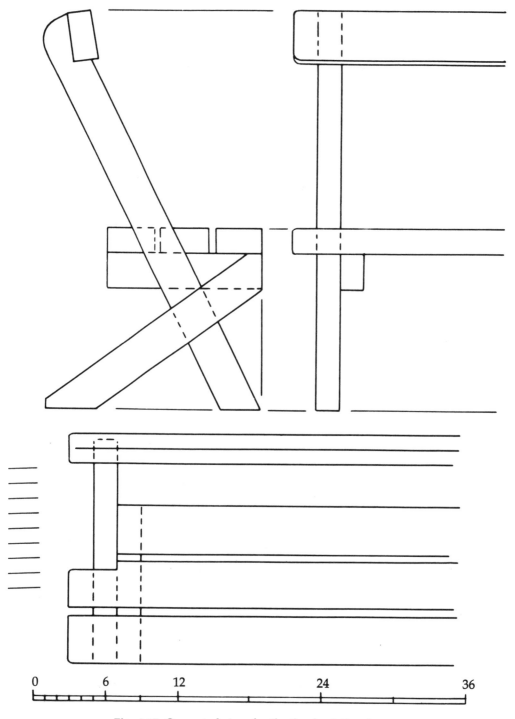

0   6   12   24   36

Fig. 4-15. Suggested sizes for the Sawbuck Bench.

Table 4-3. Materials List for Sawbuck Bench.

2 legs	$3 \times 36 \times 2$
2 legs	$3 \times 24 \times 2$
2 leg stiffeners	$3 \times 22 \times 2$
2 seat supports	$3 \times 14 \times 2$
3 seats	$4 \times 60 \times 2$ (or as required)
1 back	$4 \times 60 \times 2$ (or as required)

The first step is a full-size setting out of an end (FIG. 4-16). Draw a floor line and the seat with its support (FIG. 4-16A). The lower edge of the rear leg slopes from the bottom of the seat support to 14 inches back from the front (FIG. 4-16B). The other leg starts vertically under the front of the seat (FIG. 4-16C) and slopes to 6 inches behind it (FIG. 4-16D). The back rail notches into it to come nearer upright (FIG. 4-16E).

Lay out the legs and make half-lap joints where they cross (FIG. 4-17A). Do this in pairs so that the long part comes inside. Cut the notches at the tops and around the backs. You might prefer to wait to cut the lower ends of the legs until after assembly. Then you can check to see that the cuts come level across the two legs.

Attach the seat supports to the ends with glue and nails or screws from inside. Straighten and stiffen the half-lap joint with another strip on its inside (FIG. 4-17B). Cut it to come close to the seat support.

Make the seat of three pieces of 2-×-4-inch wood, which should be of good quality because later warping or twisting would affect the comfort of the seat. The front two pieces overlap the ends by 2 inches, but the other piece stops between them. Choose the best piece of wood for the front and well-round its exposed edges and ends. Make the next piece the same length, but cut it away to fit around the leg extension (FIG. 4-17C). Cut the third piece to the notched length of the second one.

Fit the seat parts to their supports. Nailing can be sufficient, but for the best quality finish counterbore for screws that can be covered with glued plugs. For a length up to about 60 inches, the seat boards will have enough stiffness in themselves. If the seat is to be longer, you can add a strip under the front board, notched into the supports (FIG. 4-17D) and screwed at intervals to the seat.

Make the back the same length as the seat, but well-round its edges and ends so there is no roughness whatever way it is handled. Screw it to its supports. Check squareness during assembly, using diagonals across the rear of the bench. The seat might need to stand on uneven ground, but check it first on a level surface and trim the bottoms of the legs where necessary. Bevel around the bottoms of the legs to reduce the risk of splintering if the bench is dragged along rough ground. When painting or varnishing, make sure you apply plenty of finish to the end grain of the bottoms to prevent water absorption.

PARK BENCH

A strong bench similar to the types often used in public parks is equally suitable for a garden or yard. If made of teak or another wood that withstands any weather, it can be untreated and left in place all during the year. If made of other wood, it should be treated with preservative and paint. It is not too heavy for two people

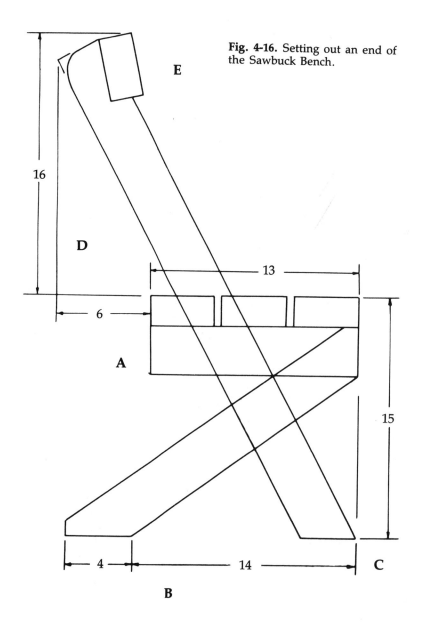

Fig. 4-16. Setting out an end of the Sawbuck Bench.

to carry, so it can be moved under cover in bad weather. The shape is intended to provide reasonable comfort without cushions or other padding. Padding can be added for longer use.

Sizes are for a 60-inch bench designed to seat three people (see TABLE 4-4 and FIG. 4-18). The seat is made of slats arranged on a curve, and the back is inclined to give a restful position.

The front legs are 1¾ inches square (FIG. 4-19A), and the back legs are cut to that bent section from a wider piece (FIG. 4-19B), to provide the slope of the upper

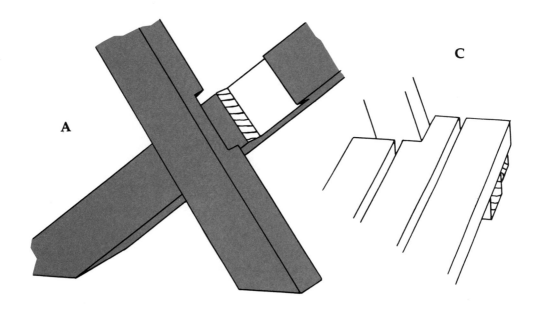

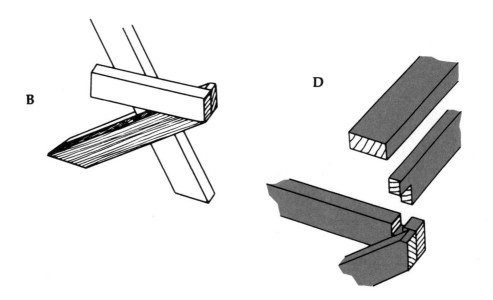

Fig. 4-17. Constructional details of the Sawbuck Bench.

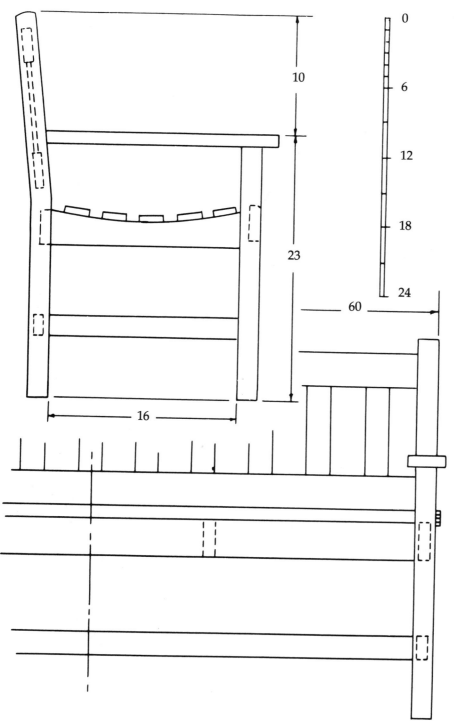

Fig. 4-18. Suggested sizes for the Park Bench.

Table 4-4. Materials List for Park Bench.

2 front legs	$1\frac{3}{4} \times 23 \times 1\frac{3}{4}$
2 rear legs	$3\frac{1}{2} \times 34 \times 1\frac{3}{4}$
2 bottom rails	$1\frac{3}{4} \times 20 \times \frac{5}{8}$
4 rear rails	$3 \times 20 \times \frac{7}{8}$
2 arms	$3\frac{1}{2} \times 20 \times \frac{7}{8}$
2 seat rails	$3 \times 60 \times 1\frac{1}{8}$
2 bottom rails	$1\frac{3}{4} \times 60 \times \frac{7}{8}$
2 back rails	$3 \times 60 \times \frac{7}{8}$
11 back slats	$2 \times 13 \times \frac{1}{2}$
5 seat slats	$2 \times 61 \times \frac{5}{8}$

part. Note that the bend comes just above seat level. The change of direction should be curved—not an abrupt angle.

Mark the legs together to get the seat and bottom rail joints level. Mark the two rear legs together to get the back rail positions the same. Note that they must be in the same plane to match the back slats.

Nearly all joints are with stub tenons, and they should go about $1\frac{1}{4}$ inches into the $1\frac{3}{4}$-inch legs (FIG. 4-19C). For most parts, the tenons can be $\frac{1}{2}$ inch thick.

Mark the seat and lower rails together (FIG. 4-19D). The top of the seat rails dip to 2 inches thick with a fair curve. The two intermediate seat supports must have the same curves. Mark them at this stage, but do not cut them to length yet. Cut the mortises and tenons for the bottom and seat rails at each end.

Make the arm rests (FIG. 4-19E). They are parallel, except for tapering to the rear legs, where they tenon in. At the front, there is not much depth for tenons. You might prefer to screw downward into the tops of the legs. If you are using tenons, it is best to use twin ones to get enough glue area (FIG. 4-19F).

Prepare the lengths. Get all the distances between shoulders the same (FIG. 4-20A). The seat front rail comes almost level with the front of the legs. You can use a barefaced tenon there to allow for curving the front edges adequately (FIG. 4-20B). The seat back rail also comes near the front of the rear legs, but it does not need rounding. Its purpose is to take the ends of the intermediate seat supports.

Top and bottom back rails are the same, with tenons into the legs and a number of light slats arranged ladderlike along them (FIG. 4-20C). Because they are thin, you could cut mortises to take the full thickness or shoulder them on one side only (FIG. 4-20D). Make up the back assembly, but be careful that it is square. Get diagonal measurements the same. It is the squareness of this assembly that controls the squareness lengthwise of the rest of the seat.

Make up the pair of ends. Check squareness and check that opposite ends match. The arms and seat are parallel with the floor; they should be square to the legs. Let the glue set on the end and back assemblies before going further. So far as possible, pull joints together with clamps. If you prefer, you can use dowels through the main joints; two $\frac{1}{4}$-inch dowels set diagonally would be right (FIG. 4-20E).

Join the ends with the lengthwise parts while the ends are standing on a level surface. Check squareness as viewed from above, as well as in other directions, before the glue sets.

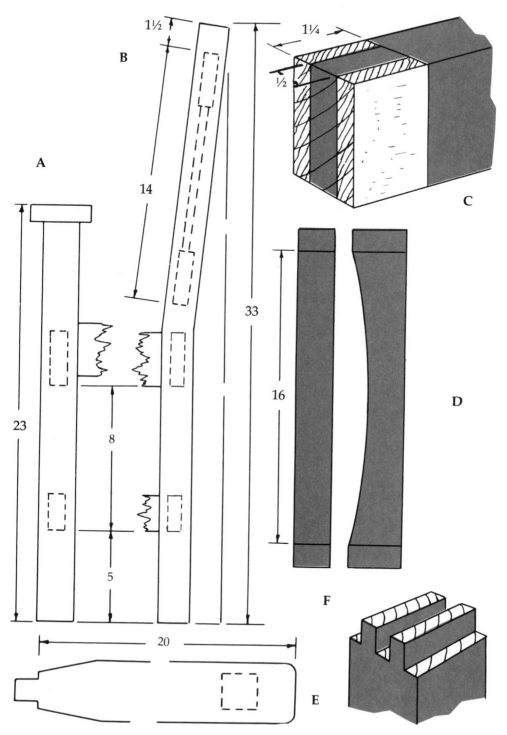

Fig. 4-19. Sizes of parts for the Park Bench.

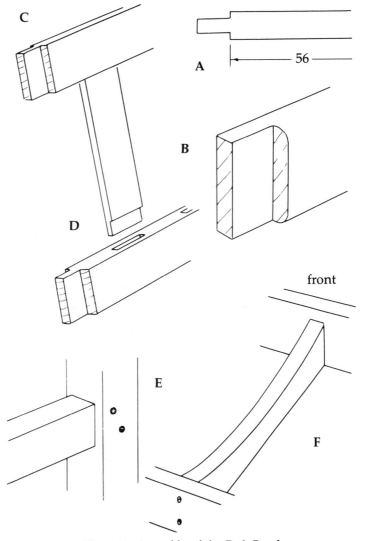

Fig. 4-20. Assembly of the Park Bench.

The seat slats will go past the ends a short distance and will need intermediate supports. Make the supports to fit between the seat rails, where they can be screwed (FIG. 4-20F). You could tenon or dowel them, but screws should be sufficient. Use a long, straight piece of wood between the end seat rails as a guide when fitting the intermediate supports so that you can get the curved tops in line.

Make the seat slats with rounded tops and ends. Attach them with a central screw at each crossing. Space them evenly. So far as possible, have the gap behind the front seat rail the same as the gaps between the slats (for the sake of a uniform appearance).

Take the sharpness off exposed edges. Except for the tops of the rear legs, there is no need for much rounding. If it is a wood that will suffer from water absorption, treat the bottoms of the legs with waterproof glue.

5

Chairs

A GREAT VARIETY OF CHAIRS can be made for outdoor use. Some simple chairs are described in chapter 4, and seats for more than one person are described in later chapters. The rougher and more rustic seats are usually large enough for two or more people.

Building chairs includes rather more advanced woodworking techniques using cut and glued joints, instead of simple nailed construction. Most chairs for outdoor use in the garden or yard are made from planed and seasoned wood, with mortise-and-tenon joints in many, if not all, meeting places between parts.

Chairs often are made to match tables, using generally similar layouts and construction, so there is a balanced appearance when several chairs are grouped around a table. Some seats for more than one person can be made to match as well. It is worthwhile assessing probable needs and keeping in mind a general pattern even if you are only making one chair at first.

For chairs made from prepared wood, stock sizes of sections can be less than specified because the quoted size is the size before the piece is machine-planed. You will find that 2 × 2 inches quoted is actually not much more than 1¾ inches finished. That does not matter, providing you allow for it when marking out. Where you need to cut joints, it is always advisable to mark from the actual pieces of wood, rather than rely on measurements for widths of cuts.

In better quality chairs, you should galvanize or otherwise protect nail from corrosion. You also should protect screws, and you can counterbore them where the wood is thick enough, and glue plugs over their heads. Modern waterproof glue, particularly the type intended for boatbuilding, will help to make strong weatherproof chairs.

SIDE CHAIR

The outdoor Side Chair has a normal sitting height (FIGS. 5-1 and 5-2) for use with a table. With cushions it provides a certain amount of relaxation, but not as much as those chairs shaped for lounging. It is more for working at a table or for having outdoor meals.

The seat is made of slats (FIG. 5-2A) and the back is similar (FIG. 5-2B). Firm attachment of the slats gives stiffness to the chair. The other parts have mortise-and-tenon joints (FIG. 5-3A). There is no need to take the tenons right through. They will be strong enough if they go in about two-thirds the thickness and are one-third the thickness in width.

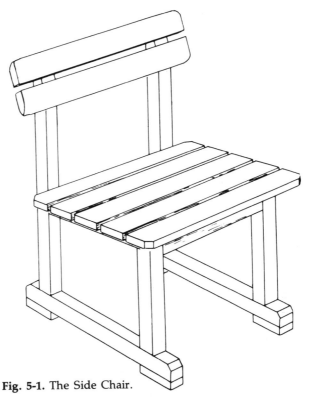

Fig. 5-1. The Side Chair.

Make a full-size drawing of a side view (FIG. 5-3B) to get the sizes of parts. Mark out the pairs of legs together. The bottoms of the legs tenon into the bottom rails. The back of the seat is 1 inch lower than the front. Set an adjustable bevel to this angle and use it for marking out the joints made by the seat rails.

Cut the tops of the rear legs to give the back slats a slope (FIG. 5-3C). Some corners are shown cut off. For neatness they should all be marked the same (FIG. 5-3D).

The chair might stand directly on the bottom rails, but any unevenness in the ground would cause it to wobble. To reduce this risk, you can place feet underneath (FIG. 5-2C). Assemble the two chair sides over the full-size drawing and check that they match each other. Clean off surplus glue and level the surfaces, if necessary, before completing the assembly.

Clamp the front rail tight and check its squareness with the legs. At the same time, nail or screw on the seat slats, checking that the sides are kept parallel. Space the slats evenly and cut off the front corners (FIG. 5-2D).

You can make the back slats more comfortable if you give them a rounded cross section (FIG. 5-3E) above and below. Take off their outer corners at the standard angle. Make sure there is no roughness or raggedness before finishing with paint or varnish. (See TABLE 5-1).

SCREWED ARMCHAIR

Some armchairs are made with mortise-and-tenon joints. They are pieces of furniture to admire and be proud of, and they are the better quality outdoor seats.

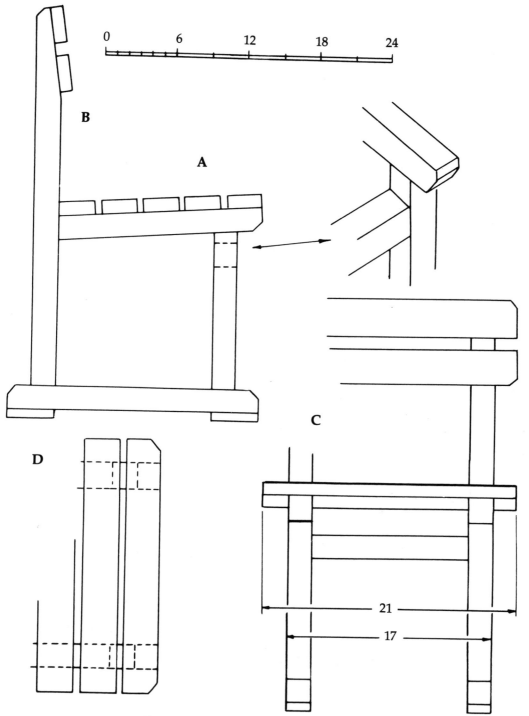

Fig. 5-2. Suggested sizes for the Side Chair.

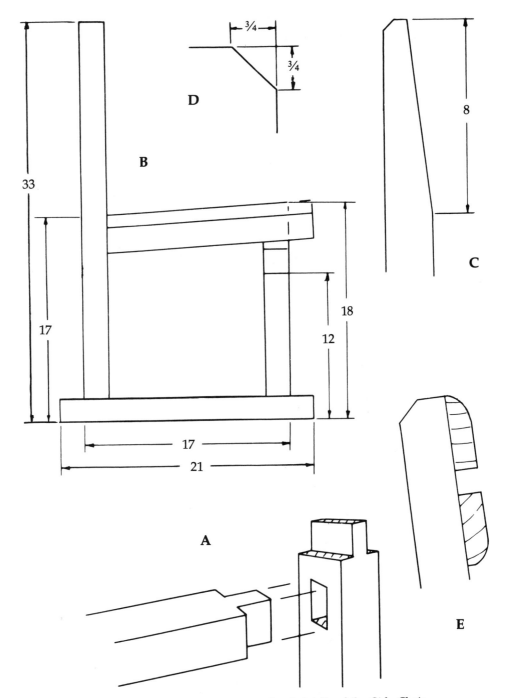

Fig. 5-3. Main sizes and constructional details of the Side Chair.

Table 5-1. Materials List for Side Chair.

2 front legs	2 × 18 × 2
2 rear legs	2 × 33 × 2
2 bottom rails	2 × 22 × 2
4 feet	2 × 5 × ⅞
2 seat rails	2 × 22 × 2
1 front rail	2 × 17 × 2
7 slats	3 × 22 × ⅞

Some situations, however, do not justify high-grade construction. Perhaps the maker has doubts about his skill to make that type of seat. Then there is a case for relying on nails or screws. The armchair shown in FIG. 5-4 is made almost entirely by putting pieces of wood over each other and screwing. Proving the screws are driven correctly and are of adequate length, and that there are enough of them, the chair should have a reasonable life. Nearly all of the wood is 3 inches wide and ¾ inch thick, which will simplify ordering. (See TABLE 5-2.)

Fig. 5-4. The Screwed Armchair.

For most of the joints where ¾-inch wood must be screwed, use 1½-inch or 1¼-inch 8-gauge screws. Where the lower piece is end grain, increase the screw length to 2 inches. You can use glue in the joints as well.

The chair has legs that slope as part of a triangle, in side view, but they are upright when viewed from the front (FIG. 5-5A). The seat and back are made of slats, with gaps between to shed rainwater. The chair often will be used with

Table 5-2. Materials List for Screwed Armchair.

4 legs	$3 \times 30 \times 1\frac{1}{4}$
2 arms	$3 \times 28 \times \frac{3}{4}$
2 arm supports	$3 \times 9 \times \frac{3}{4}$
2 seat sides	$3 \times 26 \times \frac{3}{4}$
1 seat front	$3 \times 24 \times \frac{3}{4}$
1 seat back	$3 \times 24 \times \frac{3}{4}$
5 seat slats	$4 \times 23 \times \frac{3}{4}$
5 seat slats	$3 \times 30 \times \frac{3}{4}$
1 back bar	$3 \times 27 \times \frac{3}{4}$
1 back tie	$3 \times 20 \times \frac{3}{4}$
1 back cover	$1\frac{1}{2} \times 20 \times \frac{3}{4}$

cushions that have securing tapes so the cushions do not move in use, but can be removed and taken indoors when not needed.

Get the shape of the side view by drawing it to full size. The principal lines are the legs and arm (FIG. 5-5B). Then draw the seat square with the front legs (FIG. 5-5C). At this stage, you can decide on the angle of the back. As shown, it slopes back at only slightly more than 90 degrees to the seat. That position provides good support for reading, knitting, or doing some other task. If you expect the chair to be used more for just relaxing, the back could slope more. Some chairs have adjustable backs, but in this simple construction it does not move.

Taper all the legs (FIG. 5-6A) the same. Make the arm supports (FIG. 5-6B). At the front, taper to the extended arms. At the rear, allow enough length to support the back. To take the thrust of a person leaning hard, arrange blocks to come behind the back bar (FIG. 5-6C).

Make the seat up as a boxlike unit. Let the side pieces overlap the back and front. The front is square, but slope the rear to suit the back slats (FIG. 5-6D). Round the seat slats and space them evenly across the framework with the front one on the edge (FIG. 5-6E). Slope the edge of the rear slat.

Screw the arm supports to the legs. Make sure the opposite pairs match. Mark where the seat assembly comes on the front legs and then screw it to the legs. Make sure that the chair will stand level and that the front edge of the seat is parallel with the floor. Put the back bar between the arm supports.

Make the back slats and the back tie that goes across their tops. Space the slats evenly on it and on the rear of the seat (FIG. 5-6F). Screw in place. Make a cover piece to go on top of the back and well-round its edges to improve appearance (FIG. 5-6G).

The arms (FIG. 5-6H) are parallel, but you could taper them slightly to the rear. Well-round them at the front and on the top edges. For the neatest finish, counterbore the screws in the arms so they can be plugged. When sanded level, they would be inconspicuous under varnish.

TENONED ARMCHAIR

The Tenoned Armchair is comparable to the previous one in size and general appearance, but it is more substantial and most of the parts are joined with mortises and tenons. It should have a long life and not suffer much if left outside for most of the year. The suggested wood sections (TABLE 5-3) can be softwood

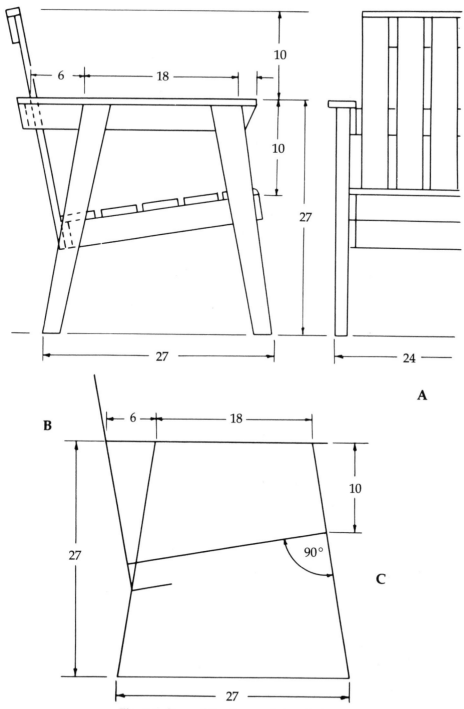

Fig. 5-5. Sizes of the Screwed Armchair.

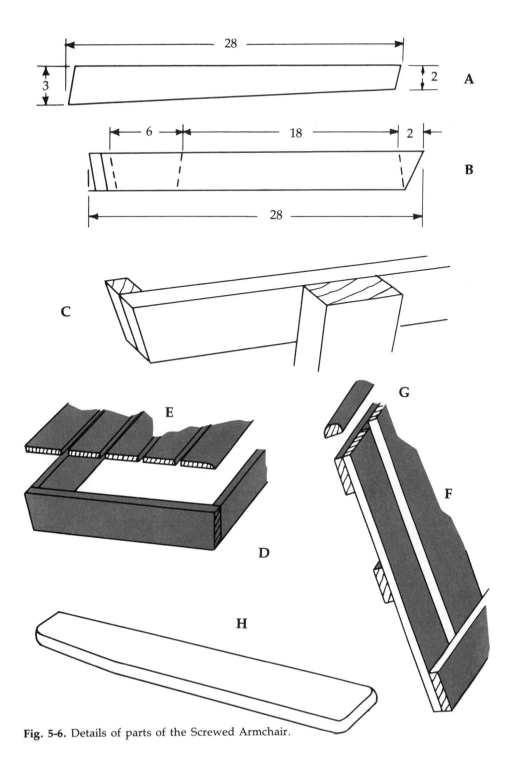

Fig. 5-6. Details of parts of the Screwed Armchair.

Table 5-3. Materials List for Tenoned Armchair.

2 front legs	3 × 23 × 2
2 rear legs	5 × 37 × 2
2 seat rails	3 × 21 × 2
2 arm rails	2 × 18 × 2
2 lower rails	2 × 23 × 2
1 stretcher	2 × 24 × 2
1 front rail	3 × 24 × 2
1 backrail	3 × 25 × 1
5 seat slats	3 × 28 × 1
4 back slats	4 × 28 × 1
2 arms	5 × 24 × 1

providing you protect it well with paint. A rot-resistant hardwood would be better, and you could paint or varnish it, or leave it untreated and allow it to weather to blend in with its surroundings. In that case, you should secure the joints with a boatbuilding-quality waterproof glue and drive dowels across the tenons of the main structure.

The chair shown in FIG. 5-7 is at a size that could be used as it is or with cushions. The ends also could be used to make a longer bench seat. The sections of lengthwise wood suggested should also be satisfactory for a bench up to about 5 feet long to seat two or even three people close together.

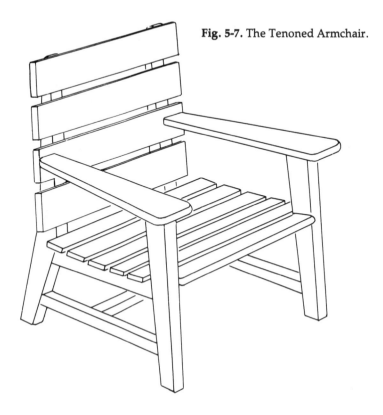

Fig. 5-7. The Tenoned Armchair.

The important shapes are the ends (FIG. 5-8A). In front view, the legs are upright, but from the side both lower parts flare out a little. Cut the slope of the back into the extension of the back legs. The arms slope slightly because they are higher at the front. The seat also slopes at about the same angle. Give it a slight hollow in the top so that the slats across make a little concession to body shape. Make up the ends as identical units and fit the other parts between them, with the bottom rail jointed. Otherwise the parts screw on.

Draw the main lines of the end shape to full size (FIG. 5-8B). The arm is square to the front leg (FIG. 5-8C) and the rake of the back is about the same angle as the front leg. Allow for the slope of the seat, but the bottom rail (FIG. 5-8D) comes parallel with the floor.

Taper the widths of the front legs (FIG. 5-9A). The front edge of the rear leg is in straight lines, but the change of shape at the back can follow a curve (FIG. 5-9B). Do not go too thin near the center of each leg. It is worthwhile examining the grain formation of the wood. Grain is not usually straight along the wood. If you can mark out the wood so that a curve in the grain follows the shape of a leg, it would be stronger than if your cuts go across grain lines.

Mark where the other parts come on the legs. Prepare the pieces that will come under the arms and the lower rails (FIG. 5-9C). Cut the pieces for the seat rails (FIG. 5-9D). The ends for the tenons will be straight, but hollow the top edges so the pairs match. Do not weaken the wood by going too thin at the center.

All of the parts are the same thickness. Mark with the face sides outward and make the tenons ⅝ or ¾ inch wide. They should go about 1½ inches into into the legs (FIG. 5-9E). The exploded view of an end shows the joint arrangement (FIG. 5-10). The top front joints will be covered by the arms. It will be simplest to use open, through, mortise-and-tenon joints there (FIG. 5-9F). At this stage, the two ends are the same except for the mortises in the lower rails, which must face inward.

Pull the joints tight with clamps, if possible, and then drill and fit dowels across them. See that each end frame remains flat. Check the second frame over the first to see that it matches.

Make the bottom lengthwise rail or stretcher (FIG. 5-11A) and the front rail. They must be pulled tight at the ends so they determine the lengths of other parts. Make the back rail that screws to the back legs (FIG. 5-11B). This and the stretcher and front rail will hold the ends in the correct relative positions for the slats to be added. Check squareness and that the assembly is without twist before you add the slats.

The back slats are wider than the seat slats. Make the seat slats, with rounded top edges and well-rounded ends that overlap the supports by 1½ inches. An exception is that the front slat comes between the front legs and is supported by the front rail(FIG. 5-11C). Space slats evenly around the curved supports and screw them down. For a neat finish, counterbore and plug over the screw heads.

Prepare the back slats in the same way as the seat slats and to the same lengths. The space between the bottom back slat and the rear seat slat should be about the same as the spaces between the back slats. The lower back slat must be notched around the arm rail (FIG. 5-11D).

The arms mount on top of the side frames and are best held with counterbored and plugged screws. Round the forward ends. The arms look best if kept parallel on the inner faces, but tapered outside toward the rear (FIG. 5-11E). Well-round all the upper surfaces. Take the sharpness off all exposed edges of other parts before painting or varnishing.

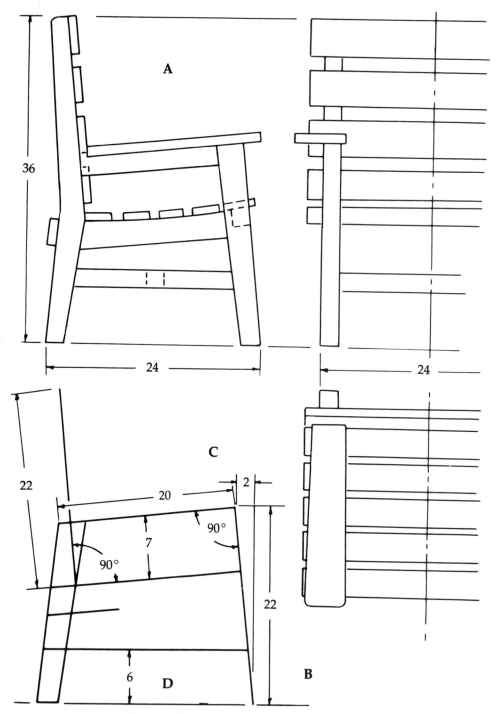

Fig. 5-8. Main sizes of the Tenoned Armchair.

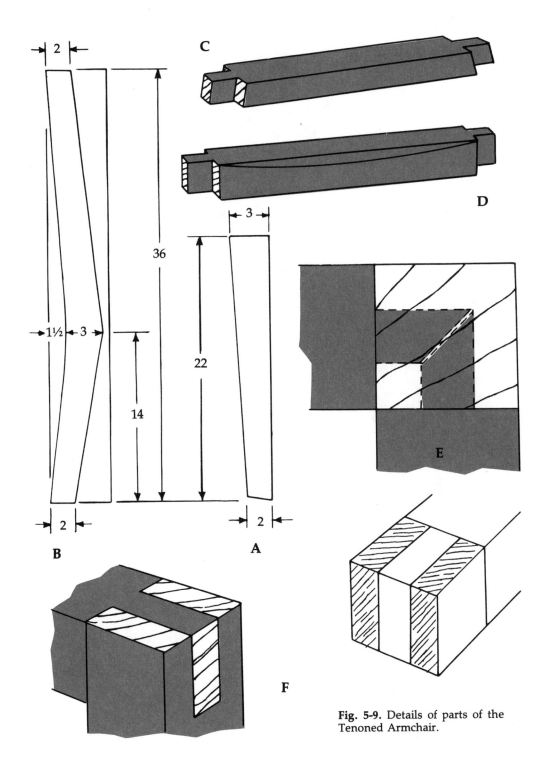

Fig. 5-9. Details of parts of the Tenoned Armchair.

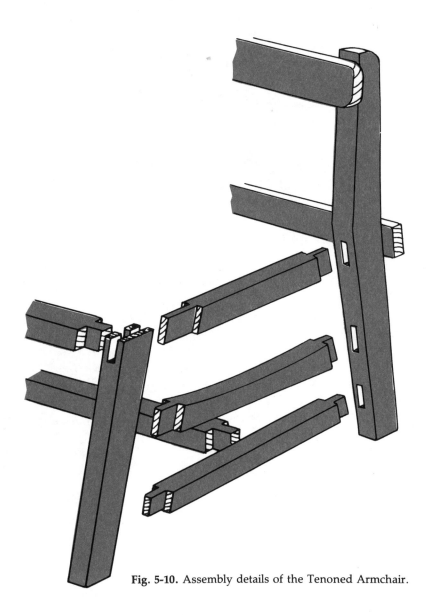

Fig. 5-10. Assembly details of the Tenoned Armchair.

SAWBUCK LOUNGE CHAIR

The chair shown in FIG. 5-12 is intended to fill the need for a light comfortable small chair with a lounging angle. Its shaping allows it to be used without padding, although cushions could be added. It can be carried easily so several of these chairs could be provided for guests to move around as they gather into groups. If made of good-quality wood and given a suitable finish, the chair could also be used indoors.

The main structure consists of two crossing frames, joined with a few crossbars. The seat and back are curved plywood. The wood should be hardwood and the crossing pieces should have reasonably straight grain without knots. You might be able to select pieces with the grain following the curve of each piece.

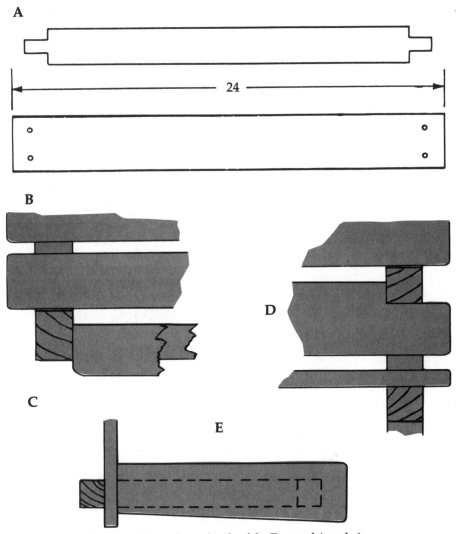

Fig. 5-11. Slat and arm details of the Tenoned Armchair.

The plywood should be exterior or marine grade. If you use veneers, they must be bonded with waterproof glue.

The sizes shown in TABLE 5-4 and FIG. 5-13 are for a chair of relaxing proportions to suit an adult. A slightly smaller version could be made for a child. In particular, the front edge could be lowered to suit shorter legs. In that case, the seat also would need to be reduced back to front.

A full-size drawing is essential, and you can make it on a pattern of squares (FIG. 5-14A). Strength must come where the parts cross; do not reduce sizes there. Mark the locations of the two supporting pieces under the seat and the single one at the back. There is also a rail between the rear legs. The surfaces toward the sitter are straight, but you can curve the other surfaces, except where the parts cross each other.

Fig. 5-12. The Sawbuck Lounge Chair.

Where the pieces cross, notch them into each other, but do not use full half-lap joints to bring the parts to the same level. That method would remove too much wood from each piece. Instead, cut not more than ¼ inch from each piece (FIG. 5-14B) so that the back legs come outside the seat legs.

The seat and back have similar curves. A simple way of forming them is to use two thicknesses of ⅛-inch or 3mm plywood. Cut the plywood with the grain of the outside veneers the straight way of the parts—the short direction—two for each part slightly too large at this stage.

Have two stiff boards that will not deflect when you clamp over them and four strips longer than the width of the pieces being shaped. Take off sharpness of the edges that will come against the plywood. Put the plywood between the strips and boards, then squeeze with clamps (FIG. 5-14C). The exact amount of deflection is not important, but aim to push in about a 1-inch curve. If that dry trial is satisfactory, open up and coat the meeting surfaces with waterproof glue. Then clamp again. If the plywood is rather stubborn dry-clamp and leave the assembly overnight. You should try to curve it a little more than you will eventually want so that the plywood becomes accustomed to curving. Then when you make the glued assembly, the seat or back will hold its shape.

**Table 5-4. Materials List
for Sawbuck Lounge Chair.**

2 inner legs	5 × 34 × 1
2 outer legs	4 × 34 × 1
4 rails	2 × 20 × 1
1 seat	18 × 21 × ¼
1 back	8 × 21 × ¼

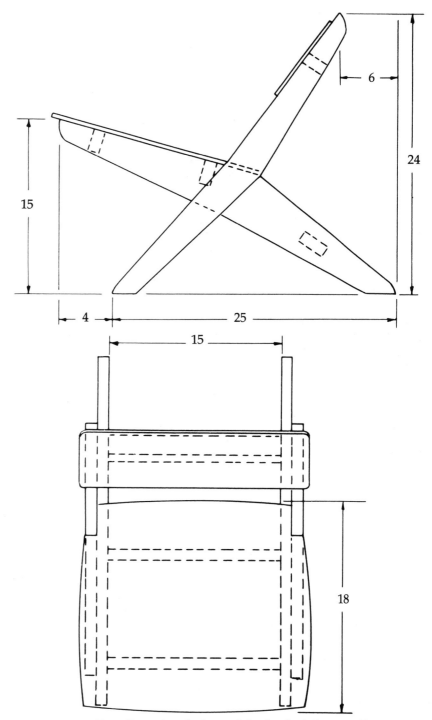

Fig. 5-13. Two dimensioned views of the Sawbuck Lounge Chair.

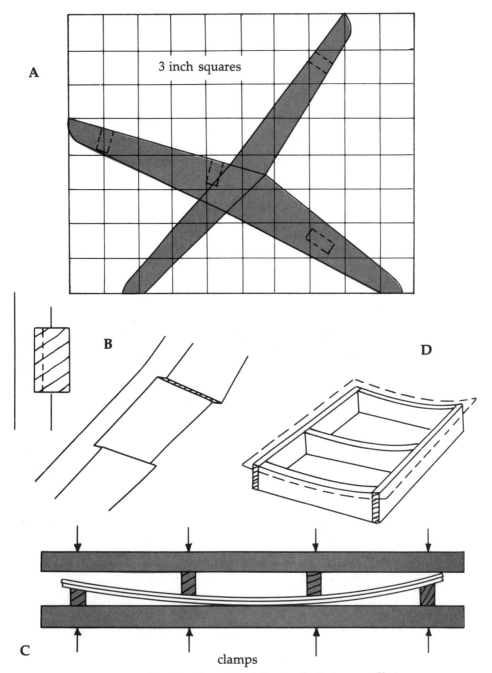

A

3 inch squares

B

D

C

clamps

Fig. 5-14. Shaping the parts of the Sawbuck Lounge Chair.

An alternative is to make your own curved plywood from veneers. If possible, get veneers at least as thick as those used in plywood, which are between 1mm and 2mm, or $\frac{1}{16}$ inch upward. The thinner veneers used in cabinetwork would require too many thicknesses to be glued. To get a smooth, curved shape you must make a jig. It can be a frame with thin plywood sprung to shape on it (FIG. 5-14D). There probably will need to be at least one intermediate crossbar to keep the plywood to a regular curve. Have another piece of flexible plywood ready for applying pressure.

Prepare enough pieces of veneer to make up nearly $\frac{1}{4}$-inch total thickness, but use an odd number of pieces so that both outside veneers have their grain the short way. Put newspaper over the former so the veneers will not become attached with any surplus glue. Apply glue to the veneers and bring them together. Put the loose plywood over the top, with newspaper underneath, and then put on pressure with strips of wood and C-clamps. Leave it until you are certain the glue is hard. Some glues appear to be hard in a few hours, but they need a day or more to build up their full strength.

In whichever method of shaping you use, trim the back piece parallel and to a length that will overhang the supports slightly. Round the outer corners (FIG. 5-15A). The seat also overhangs, but it looks better if the edges are cut to curves. At the rear, you must shape the seat to fit between the outer legs (FIG. 5-15B). Round all edges.

Use the back as a template for marking the hollows in the supporting pieces. All three are the same curve (FIG. 5-15C). They could be tenoned into the legs, but dowels are suggested (FIG. 5-15D). Cut the ends squarely to fit inside the legs. Make the one behind the back longer than those under the seat and between the inner legs.

The curved parts must bear against their supports. The slope of the meeting surfaces is not much and you can screw through without shaping, but it would be better to bevel the edges (FIG. 5-15E).

The lower rail between the rear legs is a simple piece doweled at its ends or tenoned into the legs. Round its edges. If you want to follow on the curved theme of the seat edges, you could give it a hollow in its width (FIG. 5-15F).

Round all ends of the side assemblies and take the sharpness off exposed edges. The tops project above the back so they should be well rounded. Glue the crossed legs with waterproof glue. If you think reinforcement is necessary, drive two screws into each joint from inside—where the heads will not show. Check to make sure that opposite sides match.

Join these parts to the crosswise members, pulling together with clamps. Check squareness at seat level and see that the chair stands upright. The plywood parts will hold the chair in shape. If you think it is necessary, you can glue triangular blocks in the corners of the framing under the seat.

Leave this assembly for the glue to set before adding the plywood parts. Glue them down. If you can get close fits, glue alone might be all that is needed. Then there will be nothing to mar the surfaces. However, glue does not hold well if the joints are less than perfect, and you will probably need to use fine nails with small heads. You can punch the heads below the surface and cover them with stopping. If you prefer to use screws, be careful to get them level with the surface for a neat effect. You might even get their slots all in the same direction across the chair.

For outside use, finish with varnish or paint. If the chair will be taken indoors, you might want to stain it to match existing furniture and finish it with varnish.

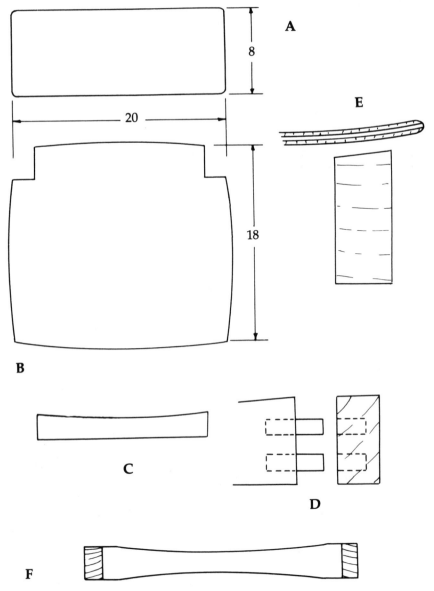

Fig. 5-15. Seat, back, and rails of the Sawbuck Lounge Chair.

STRIP ARMCHAIR

A simple robust armchair can be made of hard or softwood. The softwood must be well protected with preservative and paint or varnish. All of the parts (TABLE 5-5) are made of wood of the same section. In the simplest form, it is possible to make all the joints with screws, using just two 10-gauge, 2½-inch, flat-head screws at most crossings. If you intend to make several chairs, you can prefabricate the parts for all of them to standard sizes—with edges rounded and holes drilled—before you do any assembly work.

Table 5-5. Materials List for Strip Armchair.

2 rear legs	3 × 32 × 1
2 front legs	3 × 23 × 1
4 side rails	3 × 20 × 1
2 arms	3 × 21 × 1
5 cross pieces	3 × 20 × 1
2 cross pieces	3 × 21 × 1

The chair in FIG. 5-16 has a squared shape with some rounding of the arms and a slope to the back. The sizes shown in FIG. 5-17 give a reasonable proportion for most purposes, but you could modify them slightly. Do not extend the design to make a bench for more than one person without introducing additional lengthwise members to give rigidity to the extended shape.

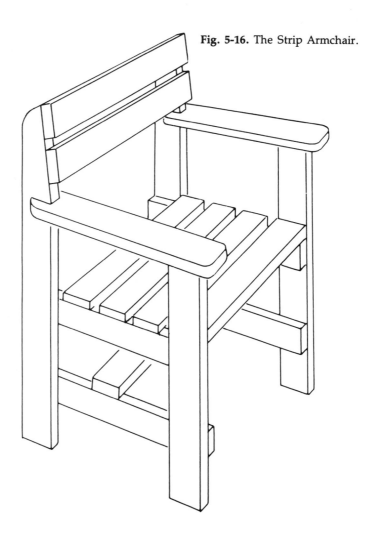

Fig. 5-16. The Strip Armchair.

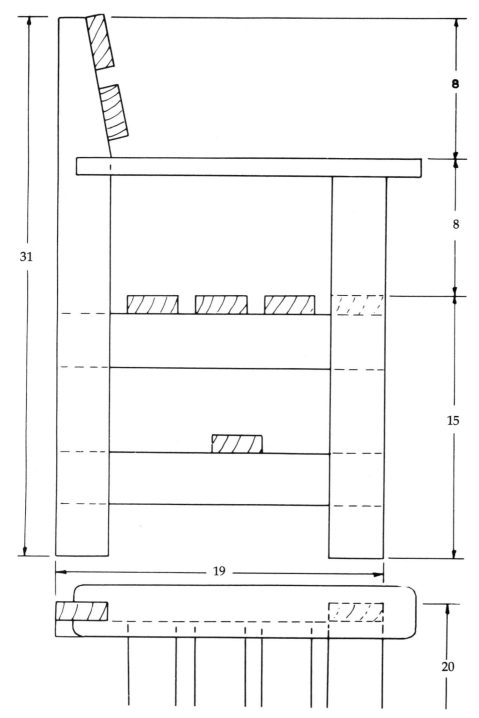

Fig. 5-17. Sizes for the Strip Armchair.

Make all four legs (FIG. 5-18A, B). Make the side rails (FIG. 5-18C) with screw holes arranged diagonally. Make the arms to match (FIG. 5-18D). At the rear, the slot should make a close fit on the leg and be drilled for two screws (entered at opposite sides to miss each other). Round the edges and corners of the arms. Assemble the sides with the crossbars inward. Check that they are square and match each other. If you prefer, use glue as well as screws.

Prepare the five pieces that make the seat and lower rail (FIG. 5-14E). Round the top edges of the seat. Have the front rails level with the legs and space the others evenly. The back rails (FIG. 5-18F) are longer, but check the final length on the chair before cutting and fitting them in place. Screw the lower rail to the side rails.

A simple arrangement of lap and screws at each crossing might be adequate, but if you want a more craftsmanlike construction, you will want to include some fitted joints.

The lower rail would be better arranged upright and tenoned (FIG. 5-19A). Tenons taken through and wedged would be strongest.

If you alter the joint between each arm and its rear leg to include a shallow notch in the leg (FIG. 5-19B), the arm will be positively located and the screws will be relieved of downward strain.

The screws through the arm into the front leg should be counterbored (FIG. 5-19C), but they go into end grain and that might not provide a good grip on the screw threads. One way of making such a screwed joint tighter is to put dowels across so that the screw threads pull into them across their grain (FIG. 5-19D). It would be better to use mortise-and-tenon joints instead of screws between the arms and the front legs. Take the tenons through and wedge them (FIG. 5-19E). You could make stub tenons if you do not want their ends to show.

SLAB ARMCHAIR

Wide boards, cut straight across a log, are often available from a sawmill. This chair is intended to make use of these slabs, which can be 1 ½ inches thick or more. The finished chair is intended to be kept outdoors almost indefinitely. Its sawn surface will weather to blend in with its surroundings. Some woods will benefit from being treated with preservative, but oak and other durable hardwoods do not need to be treated.

The chair is shown freestanding. It can be moved about, but if its position is settled, it could have the legs extended to go into the ground or it might be held down by pegs into the ground or brackets to a concrete base.

Sizes are not crucial and you can adapt them to suit available wood. (See TABLE 5-6). It is possible to make use of waney edges as decorative features. There is certainly no need to plane straight edges that would match surroundings better if left to the natural curve. Only the joints and the bottom edges need accurate cutting. The sizes shown in FIG. 5-20 give a seat of comfortable proportions. If you vary them to suit your wood, keep the seat about the same area and height. Have the back at a moderate slope and a position to come below the shoulder blades.

Examine the wood for flaws. Knots that are obviously well bonded to the surrounding wood will not matter if they come in the body of a part, but they would be weak if they have to be cut to make joints. Look for *shakes*, the natural lengthwise cracks that sometimes occur in a growing tree. If the wood has not yet fully seasoned, the shakes are liable to open as the wood dries further. A

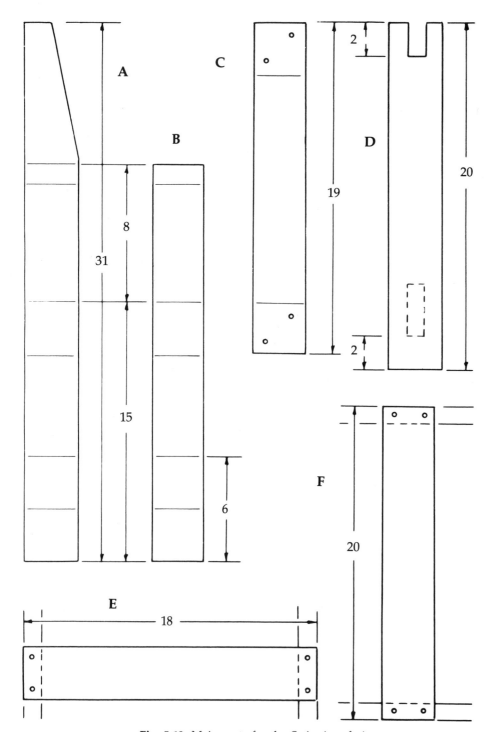

Fig. 5-18. Main parts for the Strip Armchair.

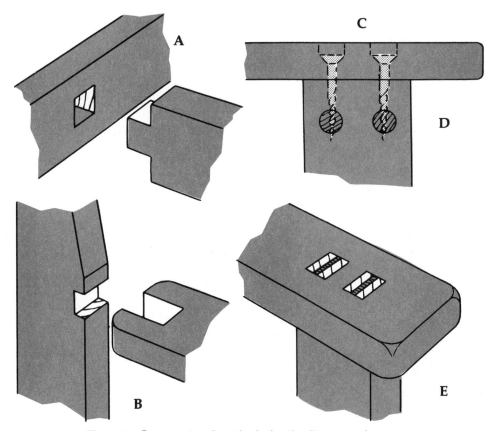

Fig. 5-19. Constructional methods for the Strip Armchair.

Table 5-6. Materials List for Slab Armchair.

2 sides	20 × 38 × 1½
1 seat	15 × 31 × 1½
1 back	12 × 31 × 1½
2 arms	3 × 13 × 1½
4 wedges	2 × 5 × 2

shake that goes through to the end of the wood will not matter, but it would be an unacceptable weakness in a short part, such as the front of the seat or toward the edge of the back piece.

With wood of uneven width, the vital setting out includes the positions and angles of the seat, back, and arms in relation to the floor (FIG. 5-21A). Set out the pieces on a side that has its bottom edge cut straight. Make sure there is enough wood around the marked positions to provide strength. If you must alter sizes to suit the wood, give the seat a slight tilt (5 degrees to horizontal is shown) and slope the back rather more (10 degrees to vertical is shown), but keep the arms horizontal.

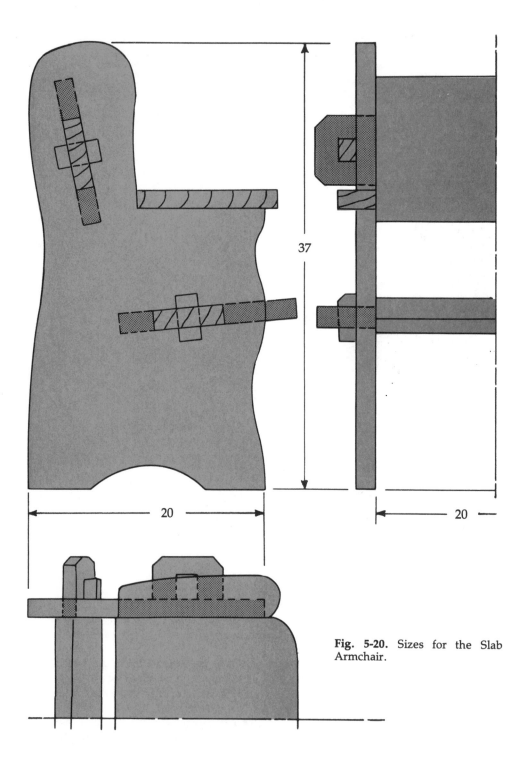

Fig. 5-20. Sizes for the Slab Armchair.

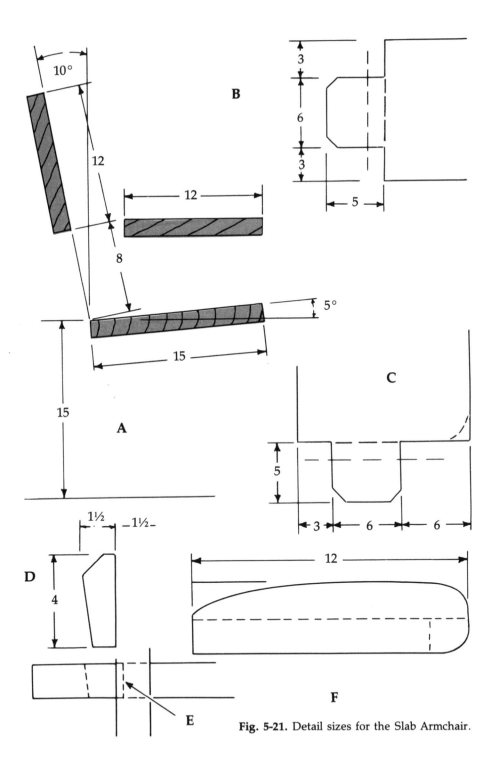

Fig. 5-21. Detail sizes for the Slab Armchair.

Mark the full widths and then the mortises. Both are 6 inches wide, but the ones for the seat are offset in its width. Prepare the seat and back and mark the chair width across both pieces the same so that they fit evenly between the sides. Then mark the tenons—centrally on the back pieces (FIG. 5-21B) and toward the back on the seat (FIG. 5-21C).

Carefully remove the waste from the wide mortise. Drill out as much as possible. Then trim with chisels from both sides toward the center of the thickness so you do not break out the grain fibers. The holes should be a reasonably tight fit on the tenons. Deal with each joint independently and mark so the same parts go together during assembly. This step is particularly important if the wood varies in thickness—as newly sawn wood often does.

Prepare the four wedges (FIG. 5-21D). Give them a slight taper—¼ inches in 4 inches is about right—and bevel the top, which will be hit during assembly. Cut the tapered holes to match the wedges, but have the inner edges slightly inside the thickness of the mortised part (FIG. 5-21E) so the tightening wedge pulls the tenon into the mortise without itself coming against the inner edge of the hole in the tenon.

You can leave some parts of the wood with waney edge, but you should remove the sharpness from those edges that will come into contact with a user. You could use a waney edge at the fronts of the chair sides, but otherwise you can band-saw to a curve (FIG. 5-20). Round the front corners of the seat and remove any sharpness along its front edge.

Nail or screw the arms (FIG. 5-21F) onto the sides with their inner edges level. Make their widths about twice the thickness of the wood. Round the fronts and outer edges and take off any sharpness around the sides. Although a natural and rather rustic appearance is a feature of the other parts of the chair, you should shape and clean up the chair arms so they are comfortable for bare human arms.

CHAIR WITH ADJUSTABLE BACK

The ability to alter the angle of the back of a chair allows you to use it in its more upright position for reading or knitting, while the tilted positions allow for relaxing. The armchair shown in FIG. 5-22 has roomy proportions. You can use it with or without cushions and move its back to three different angles.

The seat is exterior-grade plywood sprung to a curve across. It is supported between two pedestals under the arms. The back is hinged behind the seat, and its angle is controlled by a bar that drops into slots in the arms (FIG. 5-23).

The sections given in TABLE 5-7 are intended to suit softwoods. Nevertheless, the back stop and the arms would be better in hardwood if the chair is to be left outside in all types of weather and given much use. Softwood for these parts might wear excessively at the slots used to adjust the back.

Start by setting out the main lines of a side full size (FIG. 5-24A). Front and rear legs have the same slopes, so lay out each side of a centerline. The seat line drawn is the top edge of the seat sides. Draw the tapers of the legs from 3 inches at the top to 2 inches at the bottom. You can mark out the legs and plane the tapers, but wait to cut the ends until later. This step gives you the angles and sizes of the seat sides. You could screw and glue them to the insides of the legs, but they are better notched in a little. It need not be much and certainly there is no need to make full half-lap joints; ¼-inch notches in both parts will do (FIG. 5-24B). The rear end of each side goes past the edges of the legs so that it can take

Fig. 5-22. Chair with Adjustable Back.

Table 5-7. Materials List for Chair with Adjustable Back.

4 legs	3 × 24 × 1½
2 arms	4 × 28 × 1½
2 arm supports	1½ × 18 × 1½
2 seat sides	2½ × 24 × 1½
4 seat crossbars	2½ × 22 × 1
1 back rail	3 × 24 × 1
1 hinge bar	1 × 24 × 1
1 seat	18 × 22 × ½ plywood
2 back sides	2 × 24 × 1
2 back crossbars	2 × 18 × 1
5 back slats	3 × 24 × ⅝
1 back stop	1 × 24 × 1
1 back retainer	2 × 27 × 1

a crossbar. You can screw on the crossbar, you can allow for cutting a comb joint there (FIG. 5-24C), or you can dovetail the parts.

The curve of the seat across is held by three crossbars (FIG. 5-24D) between the sides. If the 2½-inch pieces curve down to 1½ inches at the center, that will be enough curve (FIG. 5-24E). You can draw a curve around a thin batten sprung to shape through the end corners and mark at the greatest depth. Make sure all three pieces match. You can tenon or screw their ends into the sides.

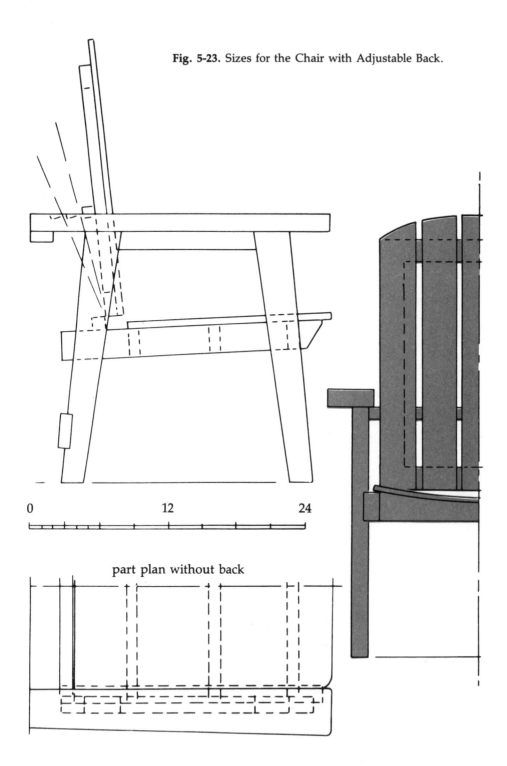

Fig. 5-23. Sizes for the Chair with Adjustable Back.

0   12   24

part plan without back

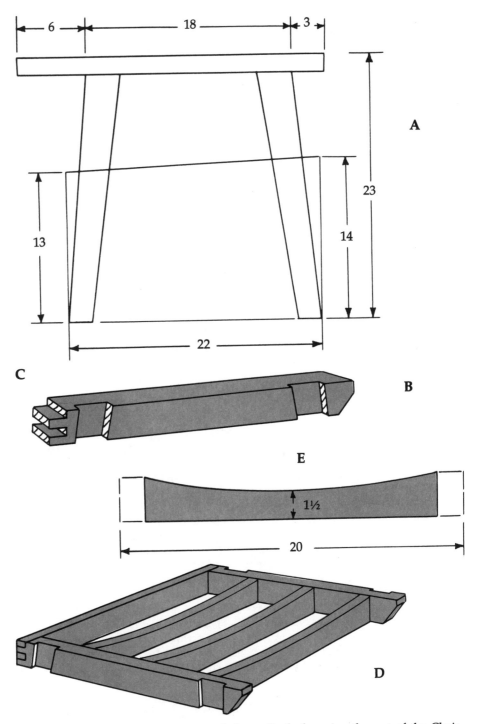

Fig. 5-24. Leg and arm arrangements and the method of curving the seat of the Chair with Adjustable Back.

Join these pieces to the sides and bring in the back rail so that you get a squared assembly (which can be used to mark the plywood seat).

Plywood probably will bend to this moderate curve with its outer grain either way, but it will be easier if you arrange the grain of the outside veneers back to front. The seat plywood comes level with the rear curved crossbar, but at the front it extends a little and has rounded corners. At the sides, cut it to clear the notches at the legs. Fit the plywood with glue and plenty of small nails. It will help to have some stout pieces of wood that you can lay back to front over the plywood and hold down with clamps on their ends while the glue sets. Be careful not to distort the seat. Have the framework resting on a flat surface during assembly.

At the tops of the legs, you can tenon the arm supports into the legs (FIG. 5-25A) or half-lap them to the legs, (FIG. 5-25B) using glue and screws from inside. Join them at the same time as you join the legs to the seat assembly.

Check squareness and see that the assembly stands upright. In addition to the crossbar at the back of the seat, another rail goes across the legs. You could screw it on without letting in, but a shallow notch improves rigidity (FIG. 5-25C). A hinge bar goes across the seat sides between the rear legs.

The arms are shown with a slight taper from back to front on the outer edges (FIG. 5-25D). Keep the insides parallel with each other. At the back, there must be notches for the back stop. The stop is square sectioned and should be a reasonably accurate fit in its notches. The notches must be at different angles in each position. To get these shapes, draw a side view of the parts concerned. Intended sizes are shown in FIG. 5-25E, but check your own chair in case there are slight variations.

The notches do not need to go the full width of an arm (FIG. 5-25F). Cut them carefully. You could leave final paring to size with a chisel until assembly is complete. Then you will have the back swinging and the actual bar to fit.

Well-round the exposed edges and corners of the arms, but leave the edge square where the notches come and below at the back where there will be a crosswise retainer. Fit the arms by screwing downward into the supports and legs (preferably counterboring and plugging). Be certain to get the inner surfaces parallel and square to the chair. Screw the retainer strip under the rear ends of the arms. It is there to prevent the back going right down if the back stop is omitted or improperly fitted. It could act as a fourth position for the back if you need an even more reclined position.

The back is a separate frame made up of 1-x-2 inch strips. You should join the corners with open mortise-and-tenon or bridle joints (FIG. 5-26A). Make the width an easy fit between the chair arms; there can be a ½-inch clearance at each side. The back slats are level with the frame at the bottom, but they are extended at the top so they can be curved. Make them too long and then put them temporarily in position and spring a lath to a curve for the top (FIG. 5-26B). Take off all sharpness on the slats before you nail or screw them to the frame.

You can use almost any available hinges between the back and its bar on the seat. If you must get them specially, two 2-inch hinges should be suitable (FIG. 5-26C).

Fit the back stop. You must keep its ends square, but you can round it elsewhere. Try the back in each position and trim the notches where necessary.

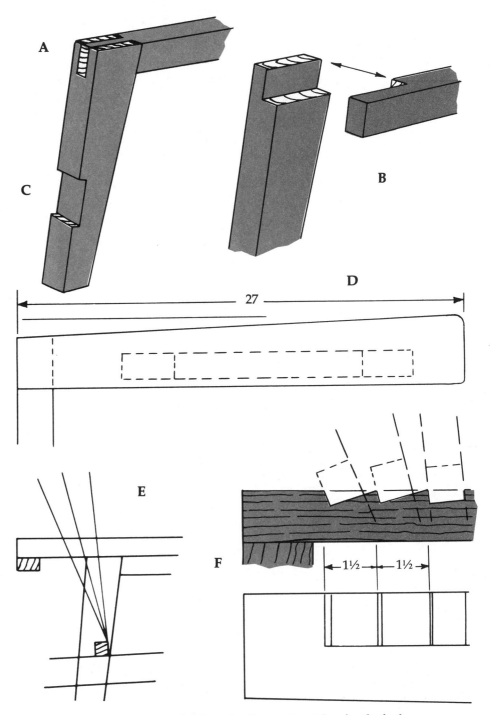

Fig. 5-25. Joint details and adjustment notches for the back.

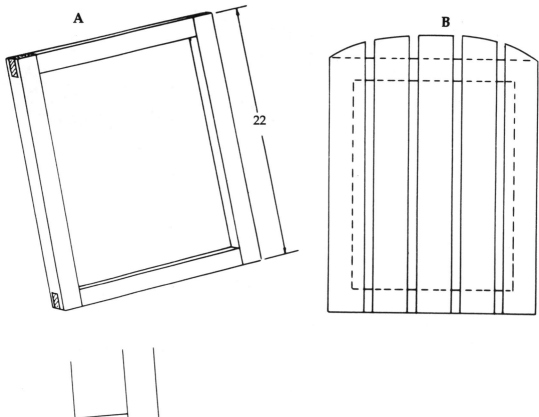

A

22

B

C

Fig. 5-26. Back assembly for the Chair with Adjustable Back.

6

Tables

THE NEED FOR TABLES comes only second to the need for seats in outdoor furniture. Tables will vary from permanent structures attached to the ground and of sufficient size for many people to enjoy meals, to smaller tables that can be moved, to others that can be folded and stowed away. Folding tables are described in chapter 8. Within the other categories are a vast number of designs. The primary need is a flat top at a suitable height from the floor. It is the means of support that designs vary.

Tabletops for use indoors are always without gaps. If boards need to make up a width, they are joined tightly edge to edge. Sometimes such a closed top is needed outdoors, but in many cases the top is made of many boards with gaps between. One advantage of this design is in shedding rainwater more easily. The gaps should not be too wide or there will be difficulty when a cloth is spread over and cutlery and other small items press the cloth into the gaps. For normal use, the gaps should not exceed ½ inch (although there are many tables in use with wider spaces).

A table should stand firmly. The ideal arrangement for stability is three legs that will not wobble no matter how uneven the ground. For most tables, it is preferable to have four legs to give support near each corner. The spread of legs on the floor must be greater than the spread of most chair legs to aid in finding a level stand. If the supports are not individual legs, but there are broad surfaces at the bottom, it is always advisable to thicken at the corners to provide feet (as in the Light Table).

Be careful to brace against diagonal or sideways loads, as well as those pressing directly downward. There must be enough stiffness in the joints. If the top and any shelf are firmly attached, they also serve as stiffeners. Lower rails act as stiffeners, but if people will be sitting on chairs with their legs underneath, the rails must be kept out of their way. In the Light Table, the end rails support a shelf of slats far enough in not to interfere with a sitter's legs at the sides.

LIGHT TABLE

FIGURES 6-1 and 6-2 show a rigid, small table with a shelf below. It is of a height suitable for meals and the use of chairs having seat heights of 16 to 19 inches. The design is intended to match the chair shown in FIG. 5-1. Its construction is basically similar, so you should refer to the instructions for the chair for some

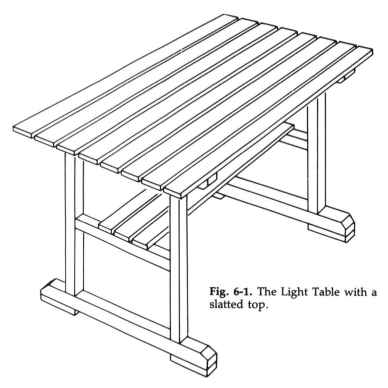

Fig. 6-1. The Light Table with a slatted top.

details. TABLE 6-1 specifies material for a table 36 inches long and 27 inches wide, but these sizes could be modified within reasonable limits. For a much longer table, the supports should be made of thicker wood.

It is not essential to make a full-size drawing. It might help, however, to lay out an end view—either complete or to one side of its centerline—to help in spacing the slats and show the sizes of other parts.

Mark out the legs together (FIG. 6-3A). The mortise-and-tenon joints do not go through and are arranged similarly to those on the chair (FIG. 6-3A). The top and bottom rails (FIG. 6-3C) are the same. Mark them together and cut the mortises. Bevel all the ends. Make and attach feet (FIG. 6-3D) under the bottom rails. Be careful to get the center rails (FIG. 6-3E) the same length between the mortises on the top and bottom rails so that the joints will pull tight. Assemble both end frames. Measure diagonals to see that they are square. Check that they match each other.

It is important that all the top slats are flat and straight. Variations will be very apparent in differences of level or uneven gaps. If you must use slats that are not quite perfect, keep them for the shelf. There they will not be as obvious. Take sharpness of the edges and ends of the slats, but otherwise concentrate on keeping the slats straight and parallel in width and thickness. You can cut off the corners of the outer slats, but otherwise leave the ends square.

Attach the outside slats to the cross rails and measure the top for squareness. Lay the other top slats in place and adjust them to get even spacing (before attaching them). Use a straight piece of wood across an end to get all pieces level.

Check that the legs are square to the top. If there is any difficulty in making the table stand true, nail on temporary diagonal braces while you fit the shelf

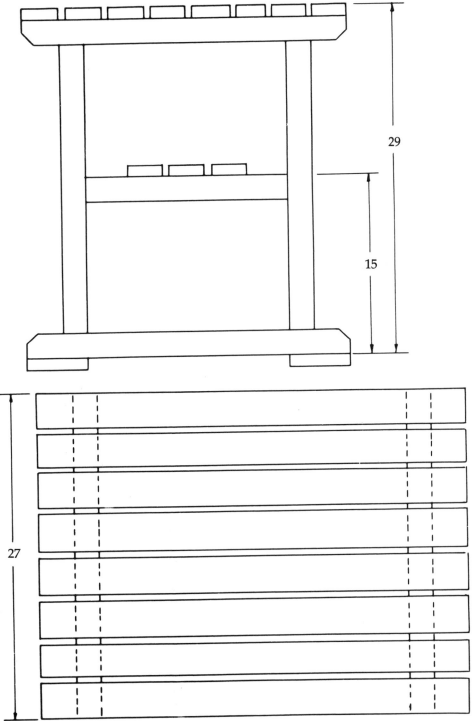

Fig. 6-2. Sizes for the Light Table.

Table 6-1. Materials List for Light Table.

4 legs	2 × 29 × 2	
4 rails	2 × 28 × 2	
2 rails	2 × 22 × 2	
4 feet	2 × 6 × 7/8	
8 slats	3 × 37 × 7/8	
3 slats	3 × 31 × 7/8	

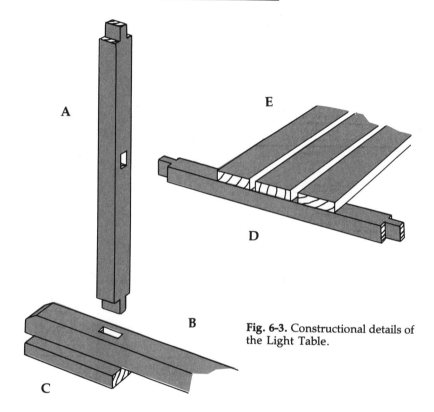

Fig. 6-3. Constructional details of the Light Table.

slats (FIG. 6-3F). Arrange them centrally. They could carry through to the same lengths as the top ones, but they are shown cut off at the rails. You could round the outer edges of the outside slats in case they are knocked by bare legs.

The table should be rigid enough. If you think extra stiffness is needed, you can attach metal angle or shelf brackets between the tops of the legs and the adjoining top slats (where they will be inconspicuous).

SCREWED SLATTED TABLE

A light table will make a suitable companion to some of the armchairs described in chapter 5. It is of simple construction, with all of the joints nailed or screwed, without the need to cut and fit any piece into another. Most of the wood is of the same section. (See TABLE 6-2.)

Table 6-2. Materials List for Screwed Slatted Table.

8 top slats	$3 \times 60 \times \frac{3}{4}$
4 crossbars	$3 \times 32 \times \frac{3}{4}$
2 boarders	$1\frac{1}{2} \times 61 \times \frac{3}{4}$
2 borders	$1\frac{1}{2} \times 33 \times \frac{3}{4}$
4 legs	$3 \times 28 \times 1\frac{1}{2}$
4 leg rails	$3 \times 32 \times \frac{3}{4}$
2 struts	$3 \times 38 \times \frac{3}{4}$

Fig. 6-4. The Screwed Slatted Table with a bordered top.

The slatted top is enclosed (FIG. 6-4) to make a neat surround and give an impression of a more stout construction than would be obvious without the border. The legs are splayed and steadied by struts that also brace the top without getting in the way of a sitter's legs. The sizes give a reasonable table for at least four people to use (FIG. 6-5A).

If the top slats are not a full 3-inch width, it will be advisable to lay them out so as not to have excessive gaps. Then make the overall width of the table to suit the result you get. Spaces should be $\frac{3}{8}$ or $\frac{1}{2}$ inches. Wider gaps might interfere with things put on the table or cause a tablecloth to sag between.

Make up the top by screwing the slats to crossbars at the ends (FIG. 6-5B) and to others that also will take the bracing struts (FIG. 6-5C). For neatness you could screw upward so that the top surface remains smooth. Fit the outside slats and check that the assembly is square by measuring diagonals before adding the other slats. Level the ends and then frame around with strips (FIG. 6-5D and 6-6A).

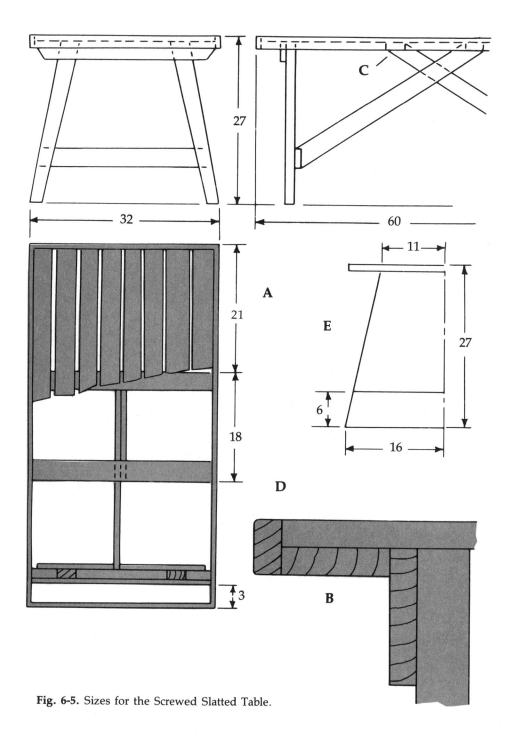

Fig. 6-5. Sizes for the Screwed Slatted Table.

Make the crossbars at the tops of the legs (FIG. 6-6B) to fit into the frame and against the end crossbars. Bevel the ends to the frame, but do not fit the crossbars into the frame yet.

To get the slope of the legs, draw a half section of an end (FIG. 6-5E). The legs taper from 3 inches at the top to 2 inches at the bottom. Make them all the same and cut the ends to the angles obtained from the half-section drawing. Mark where the lower rails will cross.

Assemble the legs to the top crossbars and to the rails. Note that these pieces cross on opposite sides of the legs. Make sure the assemblies are symmetrical by checking diagonals, and see that opposite ends match. Screw the leg assemblies inside the end crossbars (FIG. 6-6C).

The two struts cross and must be notched around the leg rails and crossbars under the top. It is important that they hold the legs upright when viewed from the side. Invert the table. If necessary, nail on temporary pieces of scrap wood at the sides to hold the leg assemblies square to the top. You should get the shapes of the struts on scrap wood and use them as templates for marking the final pieces of wood. Screw the notched ends and the crossing of the struts (FIG. 6-6D).

See that the table stands level. Round the ends and corners of the top before finishing with paint.

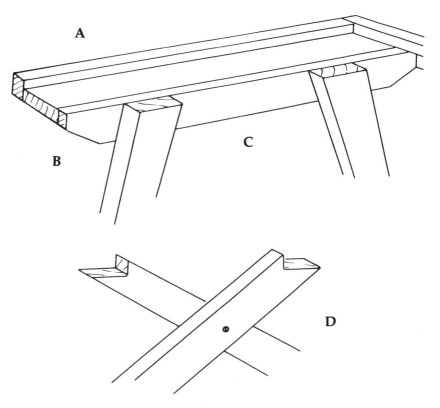

Fig. 6-6. Leg and strut arrangements for the Screwed Slatted Table.

ROUND PATIO TABLE

A round tabletop can be supported with three or four legs. The table shown in FIG. 6-7 has four legs and is intended to stand on a deck or patio where the surface is reasonably flat. It would, of course, be suitable for any level ground. It could be used as a table only, but there is a shelf below with a hole through the center of it as well as through the top to take the upright of an umbrella. The distance between the top and the shelf is enough to support the umbrella without it wobbling.

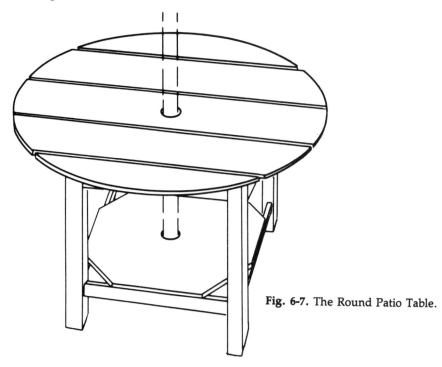

Fig. 6-7. The Round Patio Table.

The top is made of several boards, with gaps between, and held to shape with strips across underneath. These strips also serve as attachments to the underframing (which is made up as a straightforward square table). The sizes shown in FIG. 6-8 and TABLE 6-3 should suit most purposes. If you alter the table, arrange the top to an odd number of boards so that the central hole comes at the center of one and not at a gap.

The framework is best tenoned together, but you could also use dowels. The legs (FIG. 6-9A) are all the same. Top rails (FIG. 6-9B) and bottom rails (FIG. 6-9C) are also in matching sets. The joints are on the same level. Allow for the tenons being mitered in the legs (FIG. 6-9D). The lower rail tenons can be the full depth of the rails, but at the top cut down a little and divide the tenons (FIG. 6-9E).

Make up two opposite sides first by carefully squaring and checking that they match. Pull the joints tight with clamps. If you do not have enough clamps, you can pull a joint tight and drive a nail from the inner surface of the leg through the tenon at each side to hold the parts while the glue sets. Then you can move the clamp to another position. Join the opposite assemblies with the other rails and be certain that the table stands upright and squarely.

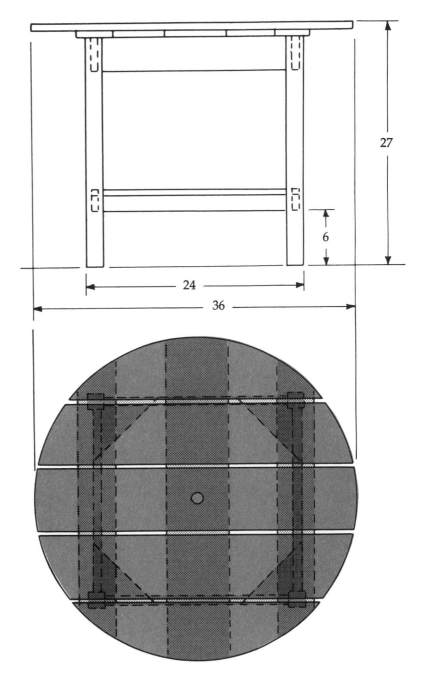

Fig. 6-8. Sizes of the Round Patio Table.

Table 6-3. Materials List for Round Patio Table.

4 legs	$1\frac{3}{4} \times 27 \times 1\frac{3}{4}$
6 tops	$6\frac{3}{4} \times 37 \times \frac{7}{8}$
2 tops	$3\frac{3}{4} \times 33 \times \frac{7}{8}$
4 top rails	$3\frac{3}{4} \times 24 \times \frac{7}{8}$
4 bottom rails	$3\frac{3}{4} \times 24 \times \frac{7}{8}$
1 shelf	$24 \times 24 \times \frac{1}{2}$ plywood

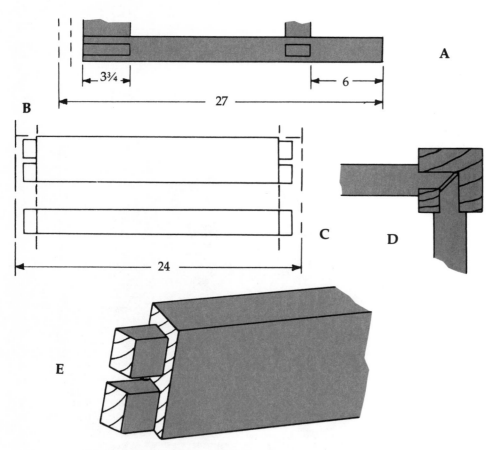

Fig. 6-9. Parts of the supports for the Round Patio Table.

The top is best dealt with in two stages. First cut the boards close to their final sizes. Wait to do the final curving of the edges until after assembly.

Lay out the boards for the top and mark the center of the middle one. Improvise a compass with an 18-inch radius (FIG. 6-10A) so you can draw a circle of the right size. It might help to put temporary spacing pieces between the boards. They need not be full length; they can be short strips positioned near where the circumference of the circle will come. Cut fairly closely to the line, but leave a little for trimming after assembly.

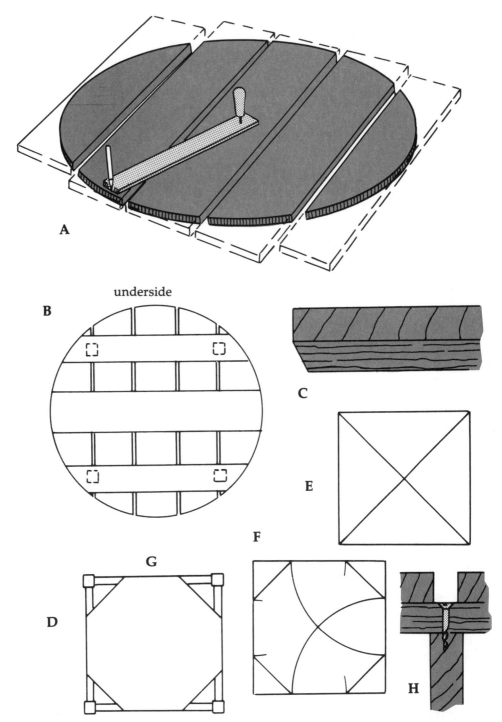

Fig. 6-10. Shaping and constructing the top and shelf of the Round Patio Table.

One stiffening piece goes across centrally, and the other two must be positioned so that they will come over the top rails of the framework (FIG. 6-10B). Make all these pieces too long and then glue and screw them on from below. After assembly, cut the ends to the curve, trim the circle to the final shape, and bevel the cross pieces underneath (FIG. 6-10C).

Make and fit the shelf before attaching the top. The shelf is a regular octagon screwed to the lower rails (FIG. 6-10D). To get a regular shape, mark out the plywood to a square that matches the rails. Draw two diagonals and measure half the length of one (FIG. 6-10E). Use this distance to measure along each edge of the square from each corner in each direction (FIG. 6-10F). Join these marks. If you have laid it out accurately, you will have eight equal sides (FIG. 6-10G).

If the table is to support an umbrella or shade, drill centrally for the upright in the shelf before screwing it to the rails. The hole does not need to be a close fit on the upright because the upright should go in and out easily. As much as $\frac{1}{4}$ inch clearance would be acceptable. Drill a matching hole at the center of the top. Most umbrella uprights are intended to go through to the floor, but if you have one that needs a stop you can put another piece of wood under the hole in the shelf.

Be careful as you position the top on the framing. The two holes must line up to hold the umbrella upright. Where the two crossbars come over the top rails, screw downward, in the gaps between top boards, into the rails and into the tops of the legs (FIG. 6-10H). Those four screws at each position might be enough, but you can put one or two more downward into the other rails where the central crossbar comes. There is plenty of thickness. Counterbore and plug over the screw heads.

As with most outdoor furniture, hardwood would be the best choice for this table, particularly if you expect to leave it outside in wet conditions. It would be lighter and easier to move if made of softwood, but then you would need to store it under cover. If it is well protected with paint, however, an occasional wetting would not matter. In any case, the plywood shelf should be exterior- or marine-grade plywood.

TRIPOD TABLE

A table that wobbles can be quite a nuisance, particularly if drinks are spilled. To get over the difficulty of finding a level base for four legs, you can make the table with three legs. A problem with having three table legs is making a matching top. The usual square or rectangle does not match the configuration of the legs. It is better to either have a round top or one with sides that are a multiple of three. There are tables with triangular tops, but they have long points that are liable to be knocked. There are tops with 12 sides, which are not very different from round. The more common top has 6 sides (FIG. 6-11).

The table shown in FIG. 6-12 has a top and shelf made from plywood (which must be exterior or marine grade). The legs slope outward from strips attached below the plywood at both levels. There are alternative methods of jointing.

Draw a full-size view square to one leg (FIG. 6-13A). This diagram will give you the angle and size of a leg and the same information on the two levels of rails. Set an adjustable bevel to the angle and keep it at this setting when marking out all the parts.

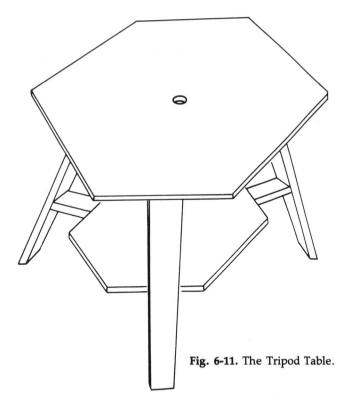

Fig. 6-11. The Tripod Table.

Before marking and cutting any wood, decide on the joints to be used. The legs can be nailed or screwed to the rails at both levels (FIG. 6-13B). At the top, there can be a notched joint (FIG. 6-13C) and a tenon at the shelf level (FIG. 6-13D). A slightly stronger notch at the top is a dovetail (FIG. 6-13E). When cutting the parts, allow for the chosen joints.

Give the legs a taper (FIG. 6-14A). Cut the tops and bottoms to the angle of slope and prepare their joints. Do the same with the rails (FIG. 6-14B, C). The rails come close at the center, but they do not need to meet. There is no need to carefully fit them against each other, and you can cut them slightly short.

Make the top and shelf to the sizes given in FIG. 6-12 and TABLE 6-4. Take care to finish with regular hexagons. Check that all edges are the same length all around. The simplest way to get the shape is to draw a circle and step off the radius around the circumference—it will go six times—and then join the points.

Table 6-4. Materials List for Tripod Table.

1 top	30 × 39 × ½ or ¾ plywood
1 shelf	18 × 22 × ½ plywood
3 legs	3 × 30 × 1
3 top rails	3 × 12 × 1
3 shelf rails	3 × 17 × 1

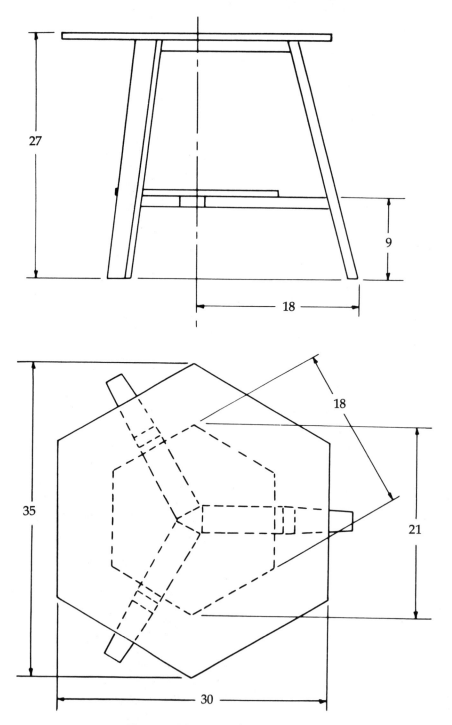

Fig. 6-12. Main sizes for the Tripod Table.

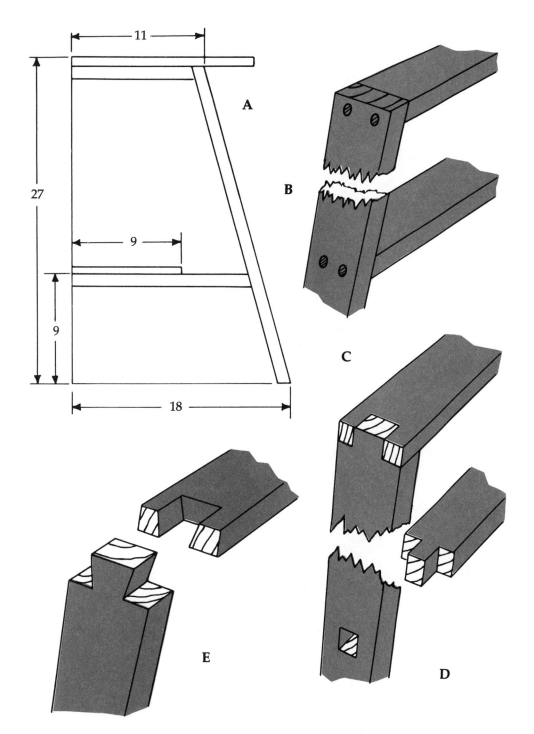

Fig. 6-13. Layout and construction of the Tripod Table.

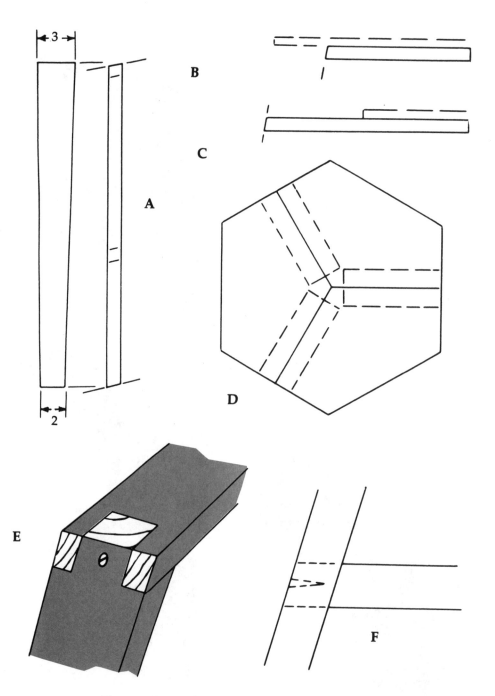

Fig. 6-14. Leg and shelf details of the Tripod Table.

An improvised compass, with a spike through a strip of wood and a pencil at the end, will draw circles. Mark the centers on the undersides of both pieces and draw lines radiating to the centers of alternate sides. Mark the widths of the rails on these lines (FIG. 6-14D).

Attach the rails under the plywood with glue and screws driven upward. If the table is to support an umbrella, drill the centers of the plywood and make sure the rails are clear of the holes. During assembly, put the shelf over the inverted tabletop to check that the radiating rails at each level match their partners. Anything more than a minor error will cause a leg to be out of true and would spoil appearance.

With the table inverted, assemble the legs to the other parts. If you are using screws or nails only, drive them all partway. Then check the symmetry of the assembly by measuring that the shelf is parallel with the top and the legs are at the same slope. Then tighten them. It is difficult to clamp the top joints if they are notched or dovetailed. Drill each for a screw to pull and hold the joint while the glue sets (FIG. 6-14E). If the lower joints are tenoned, let the tenon go through so that it can be tightened by wedging (FIG. 6-14F).

Try the table on a level surface and check by measuring all around that the top is level. If it is not, trim a leg to bring it level. Bevel around the bottoms of the legs to reduce the risk of splitting, particularly if you have used softwood. Even if you do not use preservative all over, it is worthwhile standing each leg in preservative for a day. It will soak into the end grain and reduce the risk of rot from water absorption.

STRIP-WOOD TABLE

A very simple table can be made of strips of wood and with nearly all the joints screwed (FIG. 6-15). It is possible to prefabricate all the parts (TABLE 6-5) for later assembly. This design is suitable for offering as a kit for a customer to assemble or for producing a large quantity.

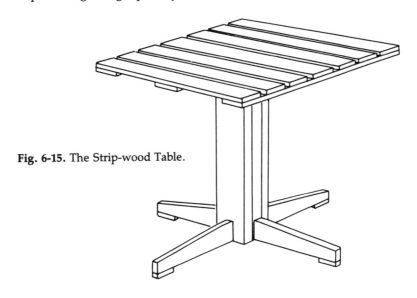

Fig. 6-15. The Strip-wood Table.

Table 6-5. Materials List for Strip-wood Table.

7 tops	$3 \times 31 \times 1$
3 tops	$4 \times 31 \times 1$
2 feet	$3 \times 27 \times 1\frac{1}{4}$
4 feet	$1 \times 4 \times 1\frac{1}{4}$
2 posts	$4 \times 27 \times 1$
2 posts	$1\frac{1}{2} \times 27 \times 1\frac{1}{4}$ or to suit umbrella
2 cleats	$1 \times 5 \times 1$

The top pieces have gaps between and crosspieces below. The central pillar is hollow and the upright of an umbrella can pass through it. The feet are formed by two crossed pieces (FIG. 6-16).

If you have the umbrella or shade that will be used, check the diameter of its shaft and make the thickness of the spacers in the column to suit.

Prepare the feet (FIG. 6-17A); they are halved where they cross. Add the pieces under the ends (FIG. 6-17B) and glue the crossing. Hold it square with weights or other means while the glue sets.

Make the parts for the column (FIG. 6-17C). Notch the 4-inch pieces to suit the feet. In the other direction, notch the filler pieces if they are thick enough (FIG. 6-17D). If you have not needed to thicken them to suit an umbrella, you can cut them short and use packings on each side of the feet, if necessary (FIG. 6-17E). At the top, check that the parts are cut squarely because this will affect the level of the tabletop. Assemble the column parts with glue and screws. Add cleats on the 4-inch pieces (FIG. 6-17F) and make sure the whole top surface is flat, as well as square to the sides.

Assemble the tabletop after cutting or marking all pieces to length. You can drive screws upward so that the exposed surface is not marked by screw heads. At this stage, leave out the center top piece (FIG. 6-18A), but have it ready. Screw and glue the parts together. Then level edges and round the outer edges and corners.

Mark where the column comes under the top on the central crossmember. Drill for screws downward into the column. Use 3-inch screws into the end grain and 2-inch screws into the cleats (FIG. 6-18B). Add the central top strip and then drill downward through the center to suit the umbrella.

Invert the table and check that the pillar is perpendicular to the top. Bring the crossed feet into their slots and check their fit. If the fit is satisfactory, drill for screws each way (FIG. 6-18C) and then glue and screw in the feet. At the same time, measure from the underside of the top to the ends of the feet to see that these parts are parallel and the table will stand level. Try it the right way up and leave for the glue to set. Finish with preservative and varnish or paint.

SIMPLE SLAB TABLE

Boards cut right across a large log suggest a simple table construction. Cut any roughness off the waney edges; otherwise leave the natural shape. End supports can be of similar material. Some lengthwise bracing completes a table. There is a limit to the size that should be made this way. It depends on the widths and thicknesses available; for 2-inch boards a top about 24×48 inches is reasonable.

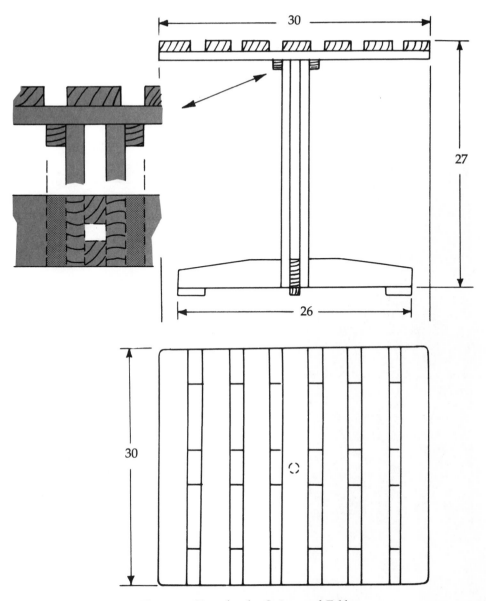

Fig. 6-16. Sizes for the Strip-wood Table.

The table shown in FIG. 6-19 uses the wood as it comes from the sawmill. You might need to do some planing of the top surface to make it acceptable and flat. All of the parts are nailed or screwed. Construction is basic (FIG. 6-20A).

Although the long edges can be far from straight, the ends should be square to a mean line along an edge if the top is to look right. Draw a centerline and mark the ends square to (FIG. 6-20B). At the same time, mark where the supports will come underneath. The sharp corners of waney-edged boards are easily broken, so either bevel or round them.

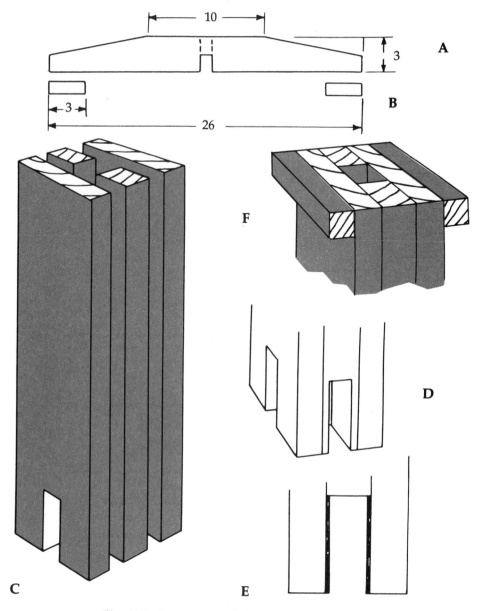

Fig. 6-17. Construction of the pedestal and feet.

Make the leg tops and bottoms parallel in the same way as the tabletop, and cut into the bottoms to make feet for steadier standing than the full width would provide. You will need two lengthwise rails for stiffness. Get their lengths the same. Make a straightedge on the top one (FIG 6-20C). The deeper this rail is, the more stiffness it will provide. The bottom rail can be narrow and can either be parallel or have waney edges.

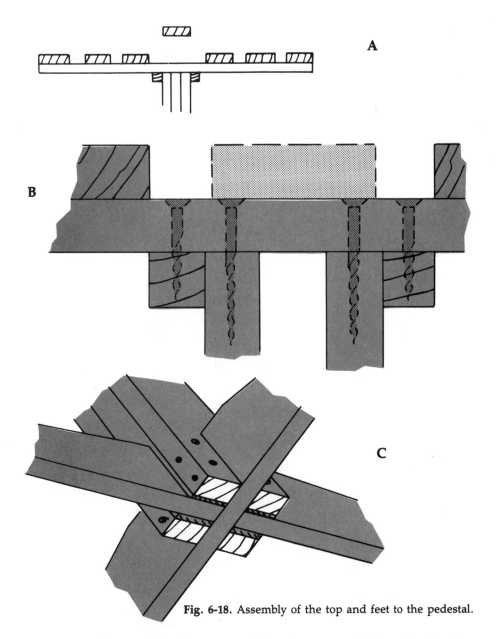

Fig. 6-18. Assembly of the top and feet to the pedestal.

Assembly is with nails or screws. Since they must grip in end grain, they should be fairly long. As a rough guide, with 2-inch wood let the fastening go about 4 inches into the lower part.

In most woods, it is advisable to drill undersize holes for the nails. This practice helps to keep long nails straight and makes driving easier. It also reduces the risk of splitting. For screws, drill clearance holes in the top piece and undersize holes for most of the length of the screw in the lower piece. You can leave the

Fig. 6-19. The Simple Slab Table with screwed construction.

screw and nailheads level on the surface, but it would be better to sink them a little and cover with stopping. Screws are better counterbored and plugged. To strengthen screwed joints, drive dowels across the wood. Then the screw threads will bite into the cross grain of the dowel for increased hold compared with that of end grain (FIG. 6-20D).

TENONED-SLAB TABLE

The Tenoned-Slab Table can be made larger than the Simple Slab Table. The construction is more suited to large sizes. It uses wedged tusk tenons through the ends to make joints that should be stronger than nailed or screwed ones. It also gives a more attractive appearance (FIG. 6-21). The construction is shown with a single top rail (FIG. 6-22), but for a very large top you could use two top rails, spaced about 12 inches apart, for additional stiffening.

The size of the available board for the top will determine the table sizes. Make the height about 30 inches, but relate other sizes to the proportions of the top. You could increase the size of the top by joining two boards, keeping their outer waney edges but straightening their meeting surfaces (FIG. 6-23A). If the wood has been fully seasoned, you could glue this joint, preferably with dowels (FIG. 6-23B). For many tables made from moist wood, you will need to depend on battens underneath.

Battens also will resist the tendency of the top to twist or warp. You can tell if there is much risk of warping by looking at the end grain. A board cut across the center of the tree might shrink in its thickness, but it should remain flat. The farther from the center the board is cut, the greater the risk of warping. If the end shows the center of the annual rings (FIG. 6-23C), it should remain flat. If the annual rings show the board has come farther out (FIG. 6-23D), it can be expected to warp in the direction that tries to straighten the annual rings (FIG. 6-23E).

Battens can be underneath inside where the legs will come and intermediately according to the length. A spacing of 24 inches is reasonable. In addition to the

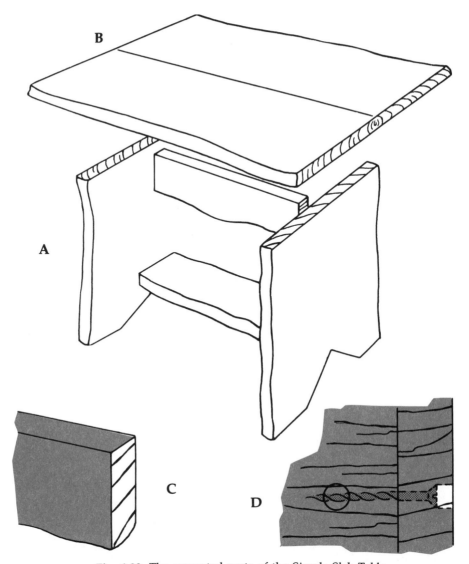

Fig. 6-20. The separated parts of the Simple Slab Table.

tendency to warp, the wood will shrink as it dries and expand if it takes up water. Allow for this movement in the battens. Use a round screw hole at the center, but cut slots for the screws farther out (FIG. 6-23F) so the screws can slide in them if the tabletop gets wider or narrower.

Make the top first, with its ends squared and corners rounded, as for the previous table. The ends can keep their waney edges, or you can cut into the sides as well as the bottom (FIG. 6-24A).

Make sure the two rails are the same length between shoulders. The tusk tenons on the bottom rail will be central, but at the top keep the tenons far enough

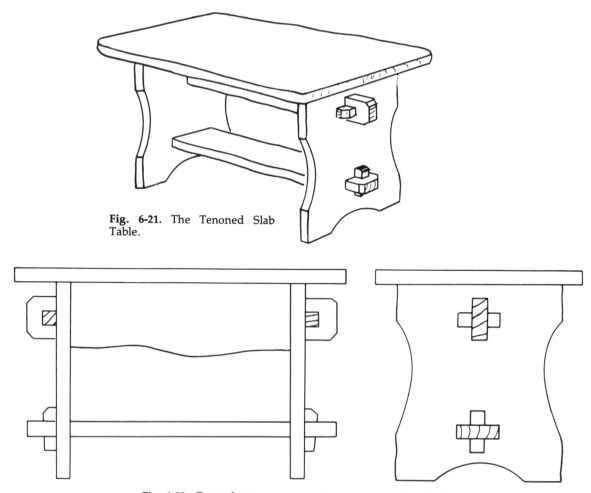

Fig. 6-21. The Tenoned Slab Table.

Fig. 6-22. General arrangements of the Tenoned Slab Table.

down to avoid weakening the short grain in the legs above the mortises (FIG. 6-24B). The widths of tenons will depend on the boards, but if your wedges are made from 2-inch-square wood, the tenons should be at least three times this width (FIG. 6-24C).

Make the tenons extend beyond the wedge hole rather more than the thickness of the wedge so that there is enough end grain there to resist any tendency to break out (FIG. 6-24D). Give the wedges a moderate taper; ¼ inch in 5 inches would do. Taper the holes to match and cut back the hole below the surface of the leg so the tightening wedge does not close against it. The joints almost certainly will slacken after a time. Give the wedges a blow with a mallet periodically until the joints settle down. This will probably be after several months if you start with partially seasoned wood.

With the underframing assembled on a flat surface and battens under the top, center the top over the legs and mark around them underneath as a guide for drilling pilot holes for screws or nails. Fasten the top down by one of the methods suggested for the previous table.

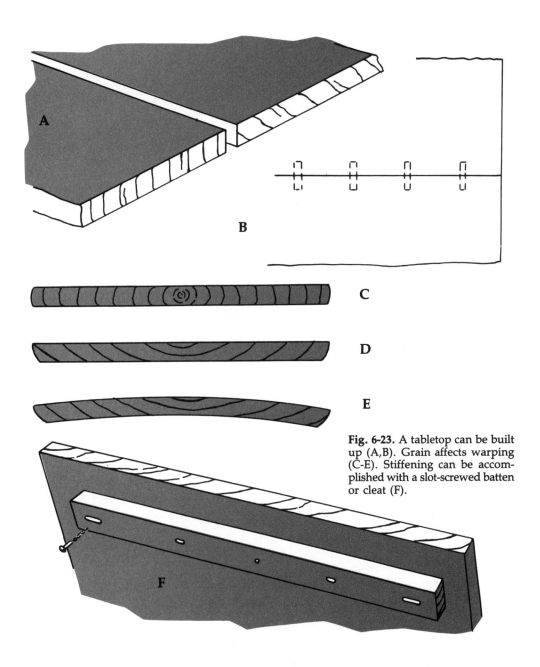

Fig. 6-23. A tabletop can be built up (A,B). Grain affects warping (C-E). Stiffening can be accomplished with a slot-screwed batten or cleat (F).

OVAL TABLETOP

The tabletop that provides the most space within its size is rectangular. If you increase the number of sides or round the corners within the same overall sizes, you must reduce the area. Shaping is often done for the sake of appearance. It also can be done to remove sharp corners. An attractive shape is an ellipse. This is often called an *oval*, but that term really means egg shaped, with one end larger than the other.

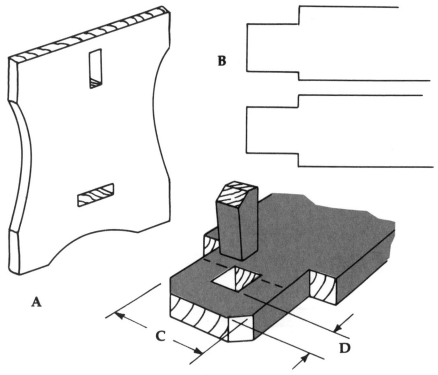

Fig. 6-24. The design of a tusk tenon and its wedge.

You could substitute an elliptical top for one of another shape on the underframings already described. The example has shaped slab ends and a tenoned rail. You can make an elliptical top from one wide board or several joined together. If boards are of different widths, avoid having narrow ones at the sides because not much would be left when the curves are cut.

The special problem is drawing the ellipse. There is no easy way as there is in drawing a circle with a compass. There are, however, geometric ways of finding a large number of points on the circumference that need to be joined. You can use compass curves with two smaller radii at the ends joining two larger ones at the sides. This method gives an approximation, but to the practiced eye it is not as good as a true ellipse.

One practical way, particularly applicable to the large ellipse needed for a tabletop, uses a pencil, a loop of string, and two awls or nails. You must arrive at the arrangement by trial and error, but to start draw a lengthwise centerline, with another the other way (FIG. 6-25A). Measure half of the minor axis along half the major axis and divide the difference by two (FIG. 6-25B). The answer gives you the probable positions for the awls, called the *foci*.

Push the awls or nails into these points and tie a loop of string around them long enough to reach the end of the long line (FIG. 6-25C). Put a pencil in the loop and pull it around; keep the string taut all the time (FIG. 6-25D). That will draw an ellipse. If you find the ellipse is finishing too narrow, bring the awls slightly closer together and adjust the size of the loop to reach the end again. If the ellipse

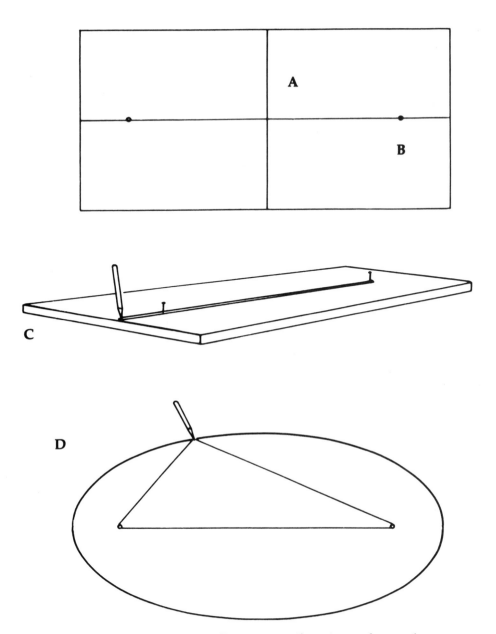

Fig. 6-25. Drawing an ellipse using nails, string, and a pencil.

is too wide, move the awls a little farther apart. You can do this step directly on the tabletop.

If you prefer to work from a template, you can use a scrap piece of plywood or hardboard that is half the width of the top and experiment to get the curve you want. Then cut it and mark around it on the tabletop. If you turn the template over on a marked line, you can check the accuracy of the setting out. You might need to make slight adjustments.

USING EXISTING SUPPORTS

You might not need to make a table completely if you can find some other support of the right height. A sawn-off tree stump can be given a tabletop even if there needs to be some packing to get it level. It might be possible to use a rocky outcrop that will hold one end of the table while you provide legs only for the other end.

There are some interesting bygones that are no longer required for their original uses. Some farm equipment had cast-iron supports. Old mangles or wringers had cast-iron stands. Much older equipment was operated at table height, so it is often possible to take off the upper parts and bolt on your tabletop.

If you use old ironwork, first check it for rust. The protective treatment for some old machines was surprisingly weatherproof. Do not remove it if it is still sound. If there is rust, wire-brush it and treat it with rust-inhibiting fluid. Leave it for the time specified by the manufacturer and then paint over it. Dark paintwork under a wood top finished with varnish or oil in its natural color can be very effective.

7

Combination Furniture

THERE ARE SOME SITUATIONS where it might be better to have one piece of furniture performing two or more functions than to have separate items. Usually the combined piece is more compact, but the parts cannot be moved in relation to each other. There is also the value of mutual support. It is possible to design a combined item with fewer and lighter parts than two separate items, yet with adequate stability and strength. Each part will support the other. If, for instance, you combine a table and a seat, you need have little fear of the table being inadvertently pushed over or a seat being tipped.

It is advisable not to devise some pieces of furniture with multiple functions. You could arrive at something that is inconvenient to use and is not fully functional. There are some ingenious folding combination items that will soon break or fail to function. Always consider fitness for its purpose. The combination item should do all that the separate items would do and, if possible, do them better.

The picnic table is probably the best-known example of a very functional combination piece of outdoor furniture. It is better for its purpose in most situations than separate benches and a table. It stands up to exposure and neglect well, it is very steady, and its construction is simple and sturdy.

PICNIC TABLE

The basic picnic table with attached benches is found all over the world on campgrounds, rest areas, and anywhere that people want to eat outdoors. You can use it in your yard or on a patio or deck, but then you probably will want to give it a rather better finish than if it is to go into more rural surroundings.

The tabletop must be level and of sufficient area, and the seats must come in a convenient relation to it. Several methods have been used in the structure to hold these parts correctly, but a common and successful way uses splayed legs under the tabletop. Crossbars are used to support the seats. The construction described here follows the most common form. As shown in FIG. 7-1, all of the assembly is made of 2-×-4-inch wood. If it is machine-planed, the sizes might be about ¼ inch less, which you must allow for when laying out the work. (See TABLE 7-1.)

The sizes shown in FIG. 7-2 are for a table that will seat up to eight people. The seats are longer than the tabletop so the best use can be made of its ends.

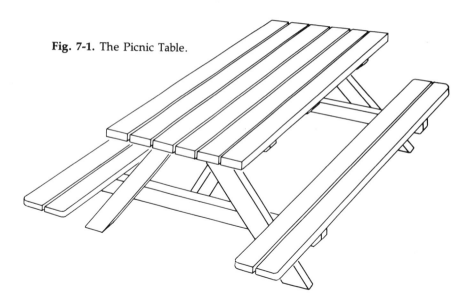

Fig. 7-1. The Picnic Table.

Table 7-1. Materials List for Picnic Table.

6 tops	4 × 61 × 2
4 seats	4 × 73 × 2
2 seat rails	4 × 49 × 2
3 top rails	4 × 26 × 2
4 legs	4 × 60 × 2
2 struts	4 × 33 × 2

If you intend to make the table much larger, you should increase the wood sections. In any case, you could make the top of fewer wider boards, and the seats could be single wide pieces (if they are available). You would need to alter the materials list accordingly.

The important setting out is the splay of the ends. Draw a half view of the main lines of an end (FIG. 7-3A), preferably full size, this drawing will give you the angles of crossing parts. Nearly all of the construction can be nailed, screwed, or bolted with the pieces merely resting against each other. The joints that get the most load are where the seat supports cross the legs. It would be better to notch these parts together. There is no need to go very deeply into each piece; ½ inch should be enough (FIG. 7-3B).

Although the tips of the legs go out to a 48-inch spread in setting out, cut back squarely about 1 inch to remove the risk of the fine angle splitting (FIG. 7-2A). Nail or bolt the cross rails to the tops of the legs (FIG. 7-3C) and check one assembly over the other.

Prepare the boards for the tabletop. They should be level and parallel so that they go together with straight and equal gaps. Bevel or round the outer corners. Mark the positions of the legs on the top pieces and then assemble squarely with equal spaces. Watch that the parts go together squarely both across and between the top and the upright directions of the legs. For the best finish, counterbore screws so that you can plug them to give a smooth surface without metal showing.

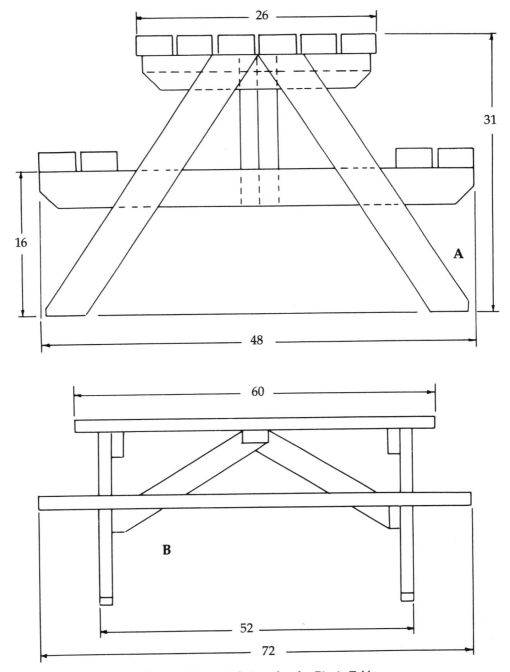

Fig. 7-2. Suggested sizes for the Picnic Table.

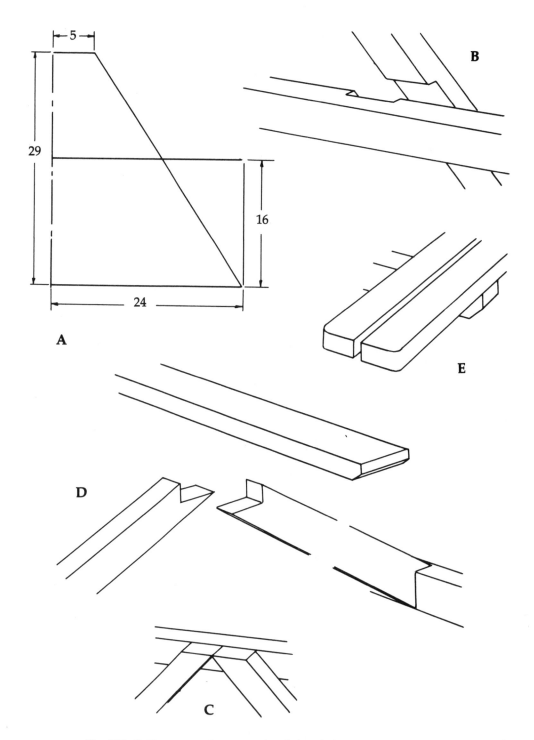

Fig. 7-3. Setting out and constructional details for the Picnic Table.

Invert the table and nail or screw on the central crosspiece under the top. Make the diagonal struts (FIG. 7-2B and 7-3D). Notch them at both ends over the crossmembers and cut them so they finish holding the legs perpendicular to the top. You probably should first cut a piece of scrap wood. Then note any errors on it to be put right when you cut the actual struts. When you assemble, the struts come against each other on the table rail so that their meeting surfaces will be central. Fit the struts with nails or screws.

Bring the table the right way up and check how it stands on a level surface. The top and the seat rails should be parallel with the floor, and the legs should stand without wobbling. If you must trim one or more leg ends, do so at this stage.

Attach the seats (FIG. 7-3E). Allow the same projection on each end and round the exposed corners.

Some woods can be left untreated, but this is the sort of furniture that will be left outdoors almost permanently, so most woods should be treated with preservative. Then you can paint them.

LIGHT PICNIC TABLE

The picnic table just described is the strong and heavy type that is not going to be moved at all, or very rarely. If the table will need to be moved more often, if only to allow the grass to be cut, a lighter version is worth making. Obviously, it will not be as able to stand up to neglect and rough use, but it can be plenty strong enough.

This table (FIGS. 7-4 and 7-5) is made entirely of 1-×-3-inch wood. (See TABLE 7-2). For the minimum weight, it could be a straight-grained softwood. Preferably, it should be one of the resinous types that has a good resistance to water penetration and rot. Because the sections are thin, the wood should be seasoned before use so that there is little risk of warping later. Wood planed all around is advisable, but at least have the top surfaces planed.

Some of the laying out and constructional work is very similar to that of the first table. Refer to those instructions, as well as those following. The tabletop

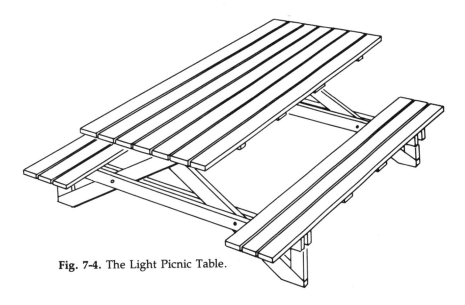

Fig. 7-4. The Light Picnic Table.

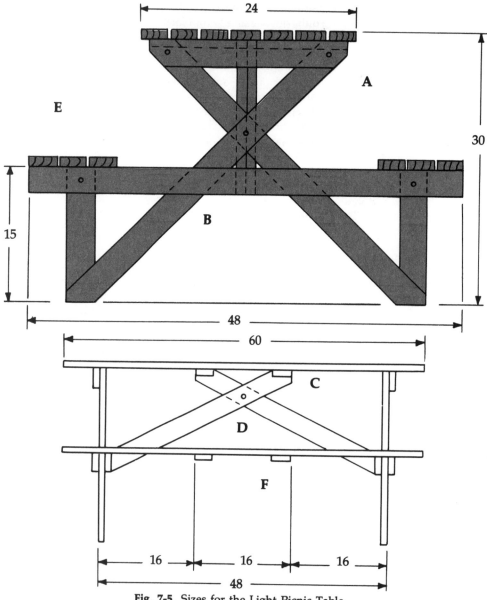

Fig. 7-5. Sizes for the Light Picnic Table.

Table 7-2. Materials List for Light Picnic Table.

7 tops	3 × 61 × 1
6 seats	3 × 61 × 1
4 seat rails	3 × 49 × 1
4 seat posts	3 × 15 × 1
4 top rails	3 × 24 × 1
4 seat rails	3 × 10 × 1
2 braces	3 × 36 × 1

and seats are at about similar spacings to the first table. Top and seats are shown the same length. It would be unwise to incase the overhang of the seat ends in this thinner wood unless you provide more stiffening.

The legs slope at 45 degrees, but it is advisable to set out a full-size end view to get the relative sizes and cuts. The legs must cross at the same level so that they can be enclosed by the seat rails. There should be full half-lap joints between them (FIG. 7-6A). You can use waterproof glue in the joints, but there can also be a bolt through centrally. At the top, the rails are 22 inches long and cut to match the legs (FIG. 7-5A). The joints each have a central bolt. All the bolts in this table can be ⅜ inch in diameter, preferably galvanized or otherwise protected against corrosion.

Mark the seat-rail positions on the legs and attach them with glue and bolts (FIG. 7-5B). Near their extremities also enclose the posts (FIG. 7-6B), which are necessary in this light construction to take the weights of the seat in use.

Simply bolt those joints through. At the bottoms of the posts, the leg and post are in the same plane so you must use a different joint (of which there are several possibilities). The most craftsmanlike joint is a special type of mortise and tenon (FIGS. 7-6C, D). The post comes 1 inch in from the leg end, but do not cut off the leg until after you have glued in the post. A tenon tapering to 1 inch should be sufficient, but you can go deeper if you prefer.

An alternative is to cut the post to bear against the leg and put two ½-inch dowels through (FIG. 7-6E). One can go right through the tapered end of the post, but the other must be shorter. The simplest joint is with long nails into holes drilled slightly undersize—with one each way (FIG. 7-6F). Be careful positioning the posts so they finish upright or they will look unsatisfactory.

Prepare all the tabletop strips. Round the outer edges and corners, but you do not need to do anything to the inner angles. Space the strips evenly across the top rails. The outer strips can come 1 inch outside the ends of the rails. Check squareness as you put on the top. Attach the outer pieces first and measure diagonals before you add the other strips. Counterbored and plugged screws are the best attachments, but you could nail the parts together or use screws with their heads on the surface.

Invert the table and put on the intermediate rails (FIG. 7-5C), screwing from below. They are needed to give stiffness to the thin top. The two braces are similar to those of the first table, but they cross to opposite rails. There is a similar problem in getting their lengths and angles of cuts, so cut a scrap piece to make a template. At the top end, the notch fits up to the tabletop and surplus is cut level with the rail (FIG. 7-6G). At the lower end, the strut goes over the rail (FIG. 7-6H). Nail or screw the end joints and put a bolt through the overlap (FIG. 7-5D). During this assembly, check that the legs are perpendicular to the top.

Turn the table the right way up. Prepare the seat strips in a similar way to those for the top (with the outer edges and corners rounded). Screw them to the rails with similar spaces to those of the top (FIG. 7-5E). Link the strips together intermediately to provide mutual stiffness. Central crosspieces can be sufficient, but two pieces are shown each side (FIG. 7-5F), at the same spacing as the top rails. Screw them from below.

If the table is to be used on concrete, you can add thin strips under the ends of the legs to act as feet and take the wear during dragging. They also will protect the legs from becoming worn and prevent water absorption on damp ground. You can replace the strips when they become worn.

Finish the table by painting.

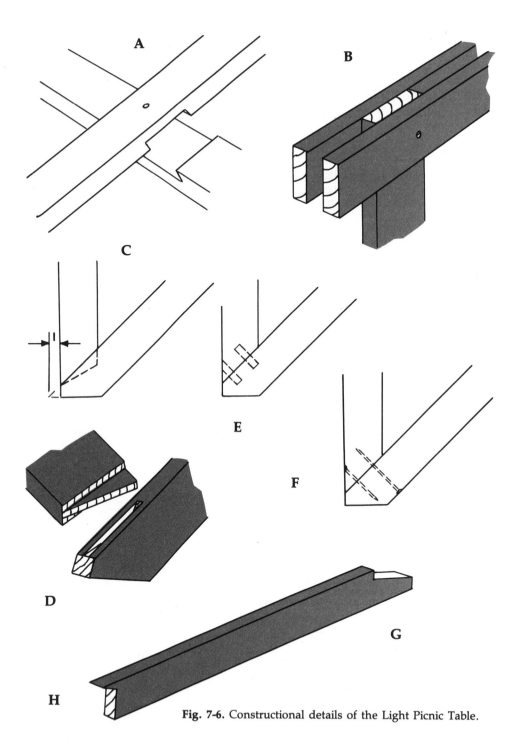

Fig. 7-6. Constructional details of the Light Picnic Table.

DOUBLE GARDEN SEAT

A combination of two chairs and a table and shelf gives two users places beside them for refreshments, things they are using, and storage below. The whole thing is a unit that can have a permanent place or be mounted on wheels or casters for moving about.

The two chairs are very similar to individual seats, but each has only two legs on the ground. If all eight legs reached the ground, there might be difficulty in leveling them all. To give rigidity to the structure, the seat rail at the back and the lower rail at the front are deep and go through from end to end. The seats are shown flat with slats, but you could hollow them. The table and shelf are shown as made of exterior-grade plywood, but they could also be slats.

Much of the construction can be doweled, but the design is shown with mortise-and-tenon joints where appropriate, and simple notches or screwed joints elsewhere. (See TABLE 7-3.) The general appearance (FIG. 7-7) shows that it is easiest to understand if you consider the unit as two chairs with some parts extended to provide the links.

Table 7-3. Materials List for Double Garden Seat.

Legs	
2 rear	$3 \times 32 \times 2$
2 rear	$3 \times 28 \times 2$
2 front	$2 \times 25 \times 2$
2 front	$2 \times 21 \times 2$
Long rails	
1 seat	$3 \times 72 \times 2$
1 front	$3 \times 72 \times 2$
1 rear	$2 \times 72 \times 2$
Chair parts	
6 rails	$2\frac{1}{2} \times 24 \times 2$
4 rails	$2 \times 22 \times 2$
4 back rails	$2 \times 24 \times 1$
8 back slats	$3 \times 15 \times \frac{1}{2}$
4 arms	$4 \times 25 \times 1$
8 seat slats	$4 \times 25 \times 1$
Table and shelf	
6 rails	$2 \times 24 \times 2$
2 trays	$23 \times 26 \times \frac{1}{2}$ plywood

In front view (FIG. 7-8A), the bottom rail goes across. The seat rails and the table rails fit between the legs. The shelf rests on the long bottom rail. The important view for sizes is one end (FIG. 7-8B). To help in your marking out, make a full-size copy of this end. There is no shaping; you can work from measurements only. The back view (FIG. 7-9) shows the seat rail going across in one piece, but there is another rail to support the tabletop and a lighter lower rail going across to take the shelf and inner legs. In both views, the chair backs are shown as vertical slats between horizontal pieces. The chair arms are level with the insides of the legs and extend outside the seats.

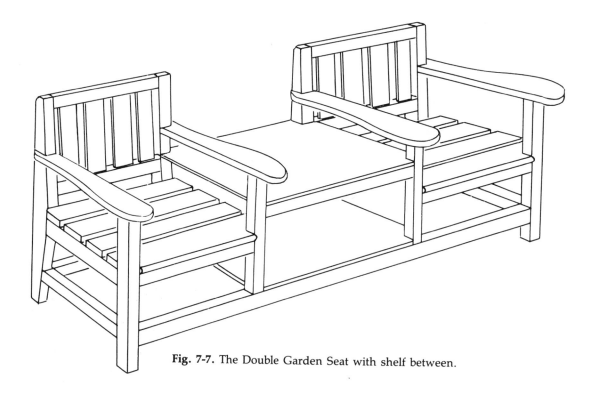

Fig. 7-7. The Double Garden Seat with shelf between.

Mark out the back legs (FIG. 7-10A). The inner ones are similar, but stop at the bottom rail with stub tenons (FIG. 7-10B). The front outer legs reach the floor (FIG. 7-10C), but the inner ones join the long rail with stub tenons (FIG. 7-10D). The tapers on the back legs start above and below the seat slats and rails. The long seat rail notches into the legs, but you should cut more from the legs than the rail so you do not weaken the rail (FIG. 7-10E). Tenon the ends of the rail into the outer legs (FIG. 7-10F).

You can also tenon the long front rail into the outer legs, but at the inner legs make the stub mortises and tenons no more than 1 inch deep. During assembly, you can put a dowel through each joint (FIG. 7-10G).

Other rails that come within the individual seat construction are mortised and tenoned into the legs in the usual way (FIG. 7-11A). All surfaces finish flush, but at the seat level add small cleats to support the ends of the front seat slats (FIG. 7-11B). You must cut the lower side rails at an angle where they join the tapered rear legs.

Join the horizontal chair back rails to the legs with bareface tenons (FIG. 7-11C) or dowels. The slats also can have barefaced tenons into the rails. Space them so the gaps between them are the same as the gaps next to the legs for a uniform appearance. Round the edges of the rails and slats before assembly.

The arms are 4 inches maximum width, but you can taper or curve them, as you prefer (FIG. 7-11D). The best joint at the front is a stub tenon or a pair of them (FIG. 7-11E). Use foxtail wedging if you think that is necessary. At the rear legs, the arms can notch to the legs to take the load, and then be screwed from outside (FIG. 7-11F).

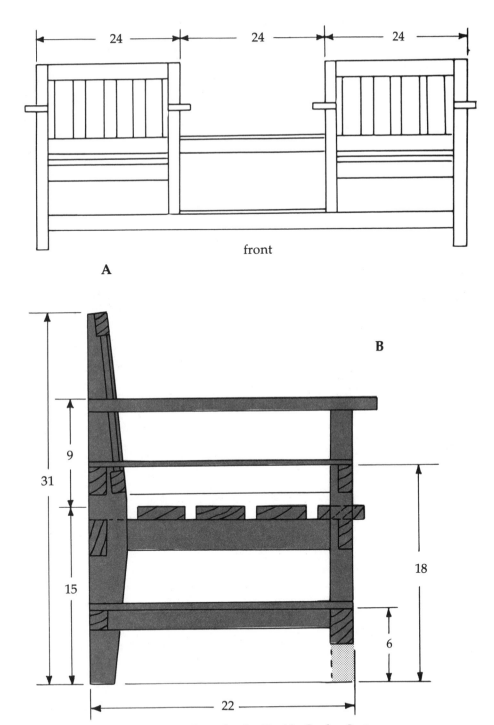

front

A

B

Fig. 7-8. Sizes for the Double Garden Seat.

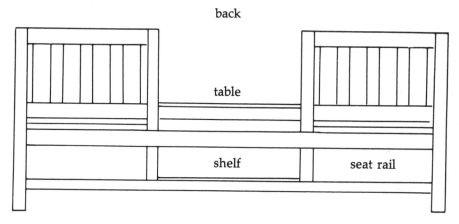

back

table

shelf   seat rail

Fig. 7-9. Back view of the Double Garden Seat.

To support the shelf, there are two long rails running through. You can tenon rails back to front into the long rails a short distance from the legs (FIG. 7-12A). That method will be stronger than cutting the joint into the leg where there is already a joint between a leg and a long rail. You need not cut the shelf until you assemble the framework. Then you can make a close fit of it. Glue and screw it downward into the rails. It is probably satisfactory as a plain surface that is easily wiped off. You can put strips around with gaps for removing dirt (FIG. 7-12B).

The tabletop has rails tenoned into the chair legs (FIG. 7-12C). You could tenon rails the other way into the legs as well, but it is convenient to arrange them similarly to those under the shelf into the front and back rails (FIG. 7-12D). Make the tabletop of plywood and fit it like the shelf. Strips at the sides prevent things falling into the chairs (FIG. 7-12E). A similar strip at the back will stop things falling there, but you can leave the front open or use partial strips—leaving a gap for cleaning.

Unlike for most chairs, do not make the end assemblies first. Instead get the front and back assemblies together as far as they will go. Use the lengthwise pieces to unite the uprights, check for squareness, and try one assembly over the other. Pull the joints tight and put dowels through tenons for extra strength. The back assemblies of rails and slats should hold the parts squarely.

Next join in the rails that go back to front. Start with the lower rails and work up through the seat and table rails. When they are tight, bring in the arms. If you need to make any adjustment, that is most easily done at the arms. Assemble on a level surface and check squareness of the assembly without table, shelf, and seat slats. The plywood table and shelf should go in squarely and lock the assembly to shape. Make the seat slats in the usual way, with rounded top edges and screws downward into their supports. Let the front slats project slightly and well-round its outer edges.

If you want to use wheels, choose casters with wheels about 3 inches in diameter on the stem fittings intended to push into holes in the legs. Be careful of making the seats too high. You will need to shorten the lower parts of the legs, if you are using wheels, to keep the seats about 15 inches from the ground. If you are using cushions, allow for their thickness. It is the compressed thickness that counts and that is not usually very much.

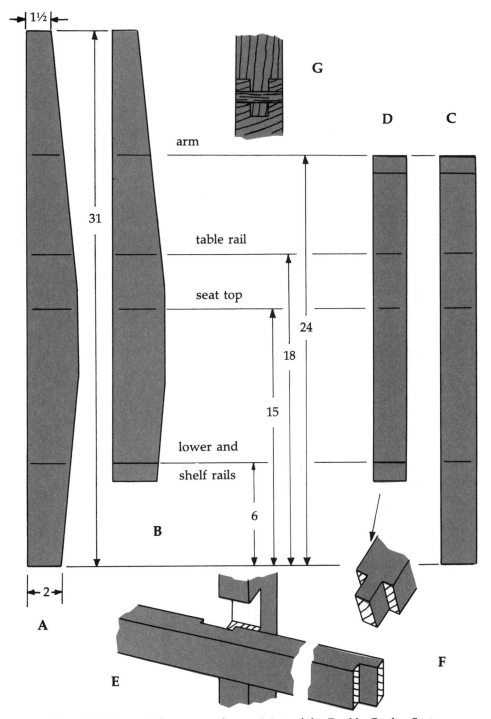

Fig. 7-10. The upright parts and some joints of the Double Garden Seat.

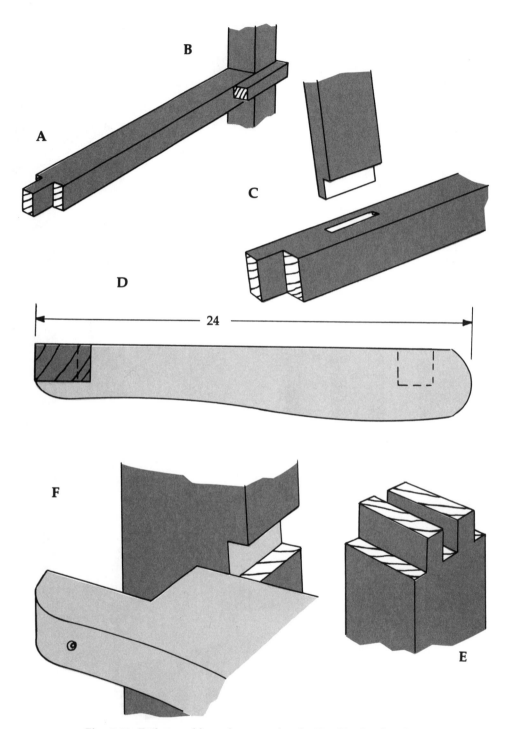

Fig. 7-11. Rail assembly and an arm for the Double Garden Seat.

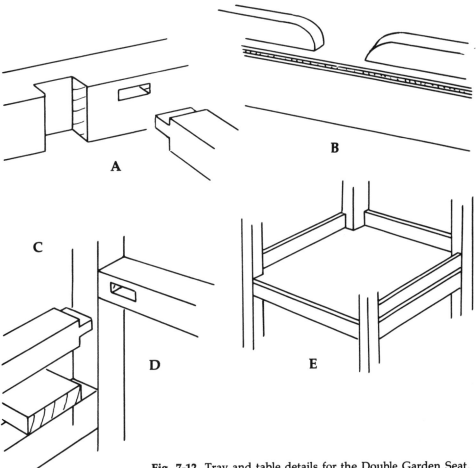

Fig. 7-12. Tray and table details for the Double Garden Seat.

If you paint the seat, you should probably give it the same color all over. You could make it distinctive by painting seat slats, the tabletop, and the shelf a different color than the rest of the woodwork.

Some modifications are possible. You could have shelves at table level extending outside the chairs. Build in supporting rails between the back and front legs and make wooden brackets to come under the plywood shelves (which will serve as additional table space).

You can enclose the space between the tabletop and the shelf to make a compartment for game materials or for anything that needs protection from animals. You can make the sides and back of plywood and make a pair of doors to meet at the center. You could hinge doors at the bottom to drop as a flap.

SEAT/BED/LOUNGER

Something that can be used as a seat, adapted to be a lounger, and then assembled flat as a bed has obvious attractions, particularly when it can be reduced

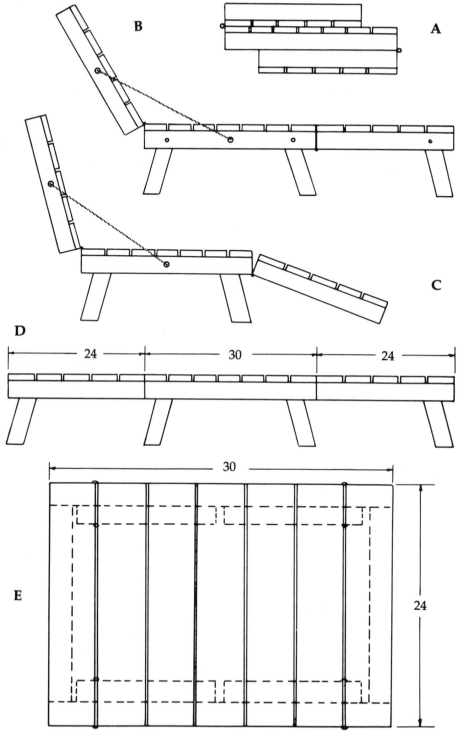

Fig. 7-13. Several layouts are possible with the Seat/Bed/Lounger.

in size for storage. FIGURE 7-13 shows a three-part piece of furniture of very simple construction. It can be used without padding, but could become very comfortable with cushions linked together (as described for use with a lounger). The size is sufficient for use as a bed, indoors as well as outside, if fitted with the linked cushions or a separate mattress. (See TABLE 7-4.) Construction is substantial and the assembly should not suffer if left outdoors for long periods.

Table 7-4. Materials List for Seat/Bed/Lounger.

Center section
2 sides	3 × 31 × 2
2 ends	3 × 21 × 2
7 slats	4 × 25 × 1
4 legs	3 × 13 × 2

Two end sections
4 sides	3 × 25 × 2
2 ends	3 × 21 × 2
10 slats	4 × 25 × 1
4 legs	3 × 13 × 2
2 struts (optional)	2 × 30 × 1
4 leg rails (optional)	4 × 21 × 1

There is a main central part 30 inches long, and two similar end pieces 24 inches long. All of these parts are 24 inches wide. If you want a total length greater than 78 inches, you can make the end parts longer. The height is controlled by the capability of the legs in the central part to fold into it. If you want a greater height you must increase the 30-inch length. You can gain another inch of height for every extra 2 inches of length.

The parts are hinged together. The head end will fold onto the center section with their slats coming together. The foot end is hinged underneath, so that it folds under, with slats outward (FIG. 7-13A). The central part has two pairs of legs. The end parts have single sets at their ends. In all cases, the legs fold inside the framing when not needed. When lowered, the legs rest against the ends of the framing.

As a lounger, the foot end is kept level and the head end raised (FIG. 7-13B). As a seat, the foot end lowers (FIG. 7-13C). As a bed, all the legs are lowered to bring the assembly level (FIG. 7-13D).

Construction could all be by screws or nails. You can tenon the corner joints of the framing. Make the central part first (FIG. 7-13E).

Get the frame square and nail on the slats so that they are spaced evenly. Two or three nails at each end should be sufficient. Plane the slat ends level with the framing. Make the two frames in the same way (except they are 24 inches long).

The legs are all the same and you will need eight of them. They must fold into the framework without projecting so make sure that they are the same width as the frame sides or plane them slightly narrower. Bolt holes come centrally and 4 inches from the corners of the frames (FIG. 7-14A). It is the size of the central frame that controls the lengths of the legs because they must fold to almost touch

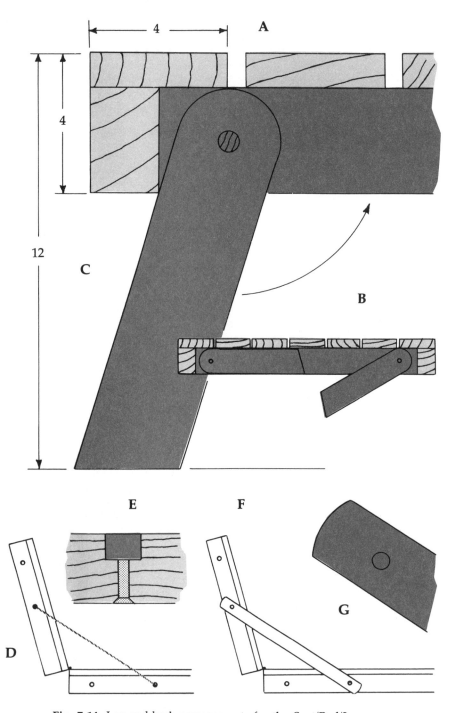

Fig. 7-14. Leg and back arrangements for the Seat/Bed/Lounger.

(FIG. 7-14B). Drill for ⅜-inch or ½-inch bolts and round the tops of the legs so that they will turn on their bolts without fouling the undersides of the slats. Leave some surplus wood at the bottom until you can try a set of legs in place. Open the legs on the center section and use a straightedge parallel with the top to mark across the leg ends. If you are working to the sizes given, the longest legs you can allow for will lift the section 12 inches above the ground (FIG. 7-14C).

The best hinges to use are the strap type with arms extending about 6 inches each way. Mount them near the edges of the sections so that screws go into the sides of the frames. At the head end they come on top; at the other end they are underneath. If you want to use ordinary butt hinges, three 4-inch ones arranged across the joints should be satisfactory.

The head end must be held up in some way for a seat or lounger. You could use ropes—⅜-inch-diameter synthetic rope would do. Drill holes to take the rope at the center of each part on both sides (FIG. 7-14D). On the center section, the knot must not project inside because it would interfere with the legs folding. Counterbore with a larger drill to sink the knot into the wood (FIG. 7-14E). It might be advisable to do the same on the head section, but if you locate the hole where it misses the folded leg the knot will come inside. That will be a help if you want to adjust the angle of the two parts.

The rope can stay in place when the parts are folded and need not be disturbed unless you want to alter the angle of the head or make a bed.

If you prefer a more rigid support, you can use wooden struts. A strut can go from the centers of the parts. Arrange its length to suit the most upright position you want the head to be (FIG. 7-14F). Use bolts with countersunk heads inside and extending enough outside to take washers and butterfly nuts. Do not cut the ends of the struts too short outside the holes because the short grain might break under load. Leaving about 2 inches is better (FIG. 7-14G); that setting holds the head end in position for upright seating.

If you drill more holes in its sides lower, the head will slope back more when the bolts are moved at each side. Small differences are enough. Try coming down in two 1½-inch steps. They should give enough alternative angles.

For temporary folding, you can leave the struts attached at one end, but they will project past the end of the package. For compact out-of-season storage, you should remove them.

The legs are shown as individuals. At the lengths suggested, they should hold without wobbling. If they seem loose or you are making a larger and taller piece of furniture, there should be a rail between each pair of legs. You cannot put it on the surface because that would interfere with folding. You must notch it into the edges or tenon it centrally to the legs. A section of 1 × 4 inches should be satisfactory for the rail.

PICNIC TABLE WITH CANOPY

The common picnic table is a utilitarian piece of outdoor furniture, but it is more of a bench that does its job than a piece of decorative or personalized furniture for your yard or garden. It serves a valuable purpose in many public places. If you want something different on your own property, one way of enhancing its appearance and usefulness is to build it with a canopy and possibly with backs to the seats (See FIG. 7-15 and TABLE 7-5.)

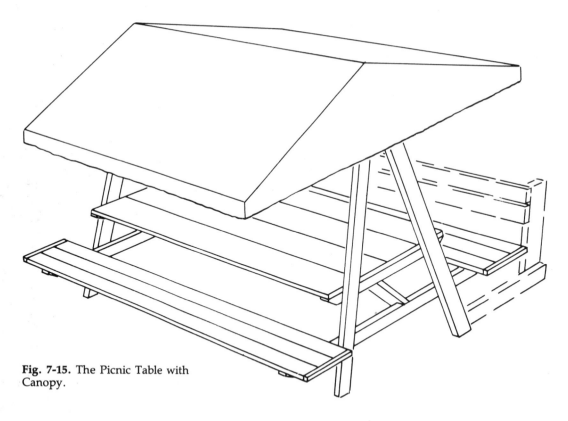

Fig. 7-15. The Picnic Table with Canopy.

Table 7-5. Materials List for Picnic Table with Canopy.

4 legs	4 × 84 × 2
2 seat rails	3 × 68 × 2
2 table rails	3 × 38 × 2
2 canopy rails	3 × 80 × 2
4 gussets	6 × 10 × 1
8 canopy rafters	2 × 98 × 2
1 ridge	4 × 102 × 2
2 canopy rails	2 × 98 × 2
4 table tops	9 × 96 × 2
1 table rail	4 × 38 × 2
2 table struts	3 × 54 × 2
6 seat tops	4 × 102 × 2
8 seat cleats	2 × 13 × 2
1 ridge	4 × 102 × 2
4 seat ends	4 × 13 × 1
with seat backs:	
Increase seat rails to	3 × 88 × 2
4 back supports	3 × 34 × 2
4 bottom rails	3 × 28 × 2
4 back rails	4 × 102 × 2

This combination table/seats/canopy is first described without backs to the seats, but seat backs are described later. Sizes suit an overall length of 96 inches, but the ends can be used with tables and seats of other lengths. The wood sections are intended for softwood; you could reduce them slightly for hardwood.

The sizes (FIG. 7-16) allow for eating at a convenient height. The canopy gives ample clearance as you stoop to sit. The canopy overhang is not much, but there must be a limit. You can increase its width.

If possible, set out an end, or half of it, full size on the floor to get the angles and sizes of the legs. It is also possible to lay down a pair of legs, move them into the correct relative positions, and mark angles and the positions of other parts on them. The ridge goes between the tops of the legs so notch them to suit, but cut them back enough to clear the slope of the canvas canopy (FIGS. 7-16A and 7-17A). Join the legs under the ridge with gussets both sides (FIG. 7-17B). Bevel the ends of the table rail (FIG. 7-17C) and the seat rail (FIG. 7-17D) underneath. They go across the legs symmetrically and parallel with the floor. Measure carefully. Errors might not be obvious until assembly is complete. Then it will be too late for correction.

For strength, it will be best to bolt through these joints; two ⅜-inch bolts at each position are suitable (FIG. 7-18A). If you prefer to use screws, you should cut shallow notches for the rails in the legs to resist any tendency for the rails to slide down (FIG. 7-18B). You could bolt through the gussets at the top, but screws should be strong enough there.

The seat and table rails are on the inside of the legs, but the canopy rail goes on the outside, bolted to the legs. Make sure it is parallel with the other rails (FIG. 7-17E). A pair of rafters go from the ridge to its ends. They do not need to provide much strength, so you can nail them in place. Cut them to fit against the ridge (FIG. 7-17F). At the other end, bevel them and the ends of the rail down to 2 inches deep (FIG. 7-17G) so there is a smooth slope on the roof angle.

The table and its struts brace the whole assembly. It is suggested that you use four pieces, 9 inches wide to make up the top. However, you could use other widths available; they need not all be the same. Allowing for planing to width, there will be gaps of ¼ inch or so between the boards. Nail the top boards to their rails on the ends. Under their centers, put a rail across. You can cut it a little short and bevel its lower edge so that it is inconspicuous and does not interfere with users.

The two struts go from the seat rails to the rail (FIGS. 7-16B and 7-18C). Notch them over the seat rails and cut the center notches so that each strut goes across the full width of the rail and its full depth is against the top boards (FIG. 7-18D). Let the struts overlap each other on this rail so you can nail them to the rail and to each other. Check that the table and legs are square to each other. Measure diagonals from them top and bottom corners of opposite legs. It will help to have the ridge piece in position, but not finally nailed until you are satisfied that the parts are square. Because getting the strut ends correct is important, it will help to cut a thin piece of scrap wood to size first. Allow for corrections to it as you use it as a template for the actual struts.

The seats are shown made of three pieces, but you could use other widths. As for the tabletop, assemble them with narrow gaps. The ends could be open, but they look neater closed (FIG. 7-18E). Put cleats across the ends and two others spaced evenly between to brace the boards to each other. Make strips, well-rounding their outer edges and corners. Use them to close the ends. Nail the seats to their rails.

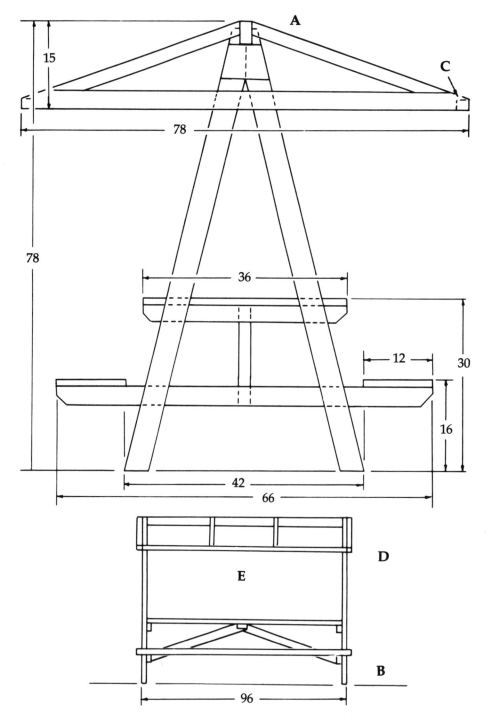

Fig. 7-16. Suggested sizes for the Picnic Table with Canopy.

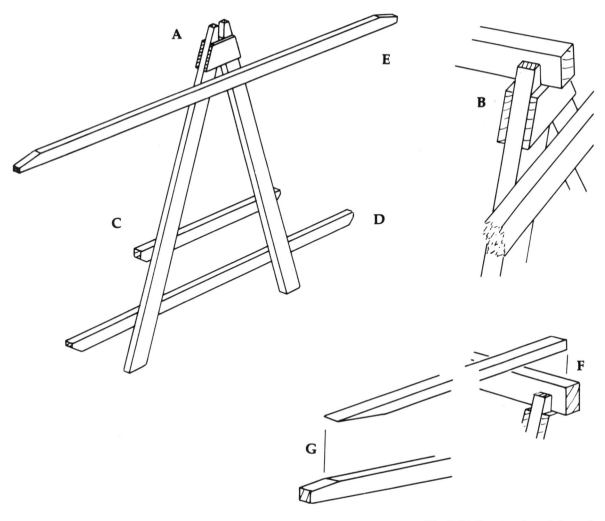

Fig. 7-17. Construction of the end frames of the Picnic Table with Canopy.

Check the rigidity of the assembly at this stage. It should not flex lengthwise. If necessary, put metal brackets between the ridge piece and the inner gussets to the legs.

To give shape and support to the canvas canopy, put lengthwise rails between the end rails (FIGS. 7-6C, D). Join them to the ridge with intermediate rafters (FIG. 7-16E) to keep the shape and prevent the canvas from sagging. Sight along from the ends as you fit these rafters to check that the slopes are the same.

You could get a canvas cover made from paper templates or sew a cover of light canvas on a domestic sewing machine. The latter choice gives you an opportunity to get an exact fit. Assemble panels of material inside out over the framework and pin them together on the lines that must be sewn. Allow for the edges to hang down about 6 inches. You can turn those edges under in a straight

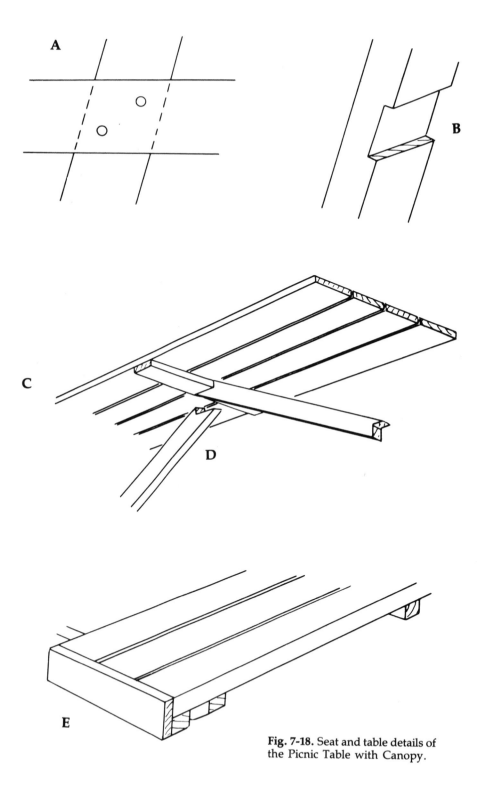

A

B

C

D

Fig. 7-18. Seat and table details of the Picnic Table with Canopy.

E

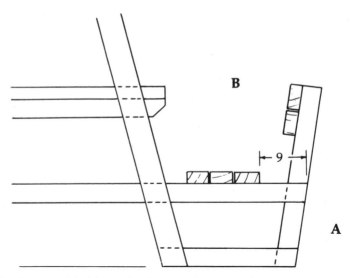

Fig. 7-19. Modifying the framework to provide a back to each seat.

line or scallop them. While sewing the seams, include pieces of tape at intervals long enough to tie around the framework at about 24-inch spacing.

Comfort is increased if the seats are given backs (FIG. 7-19). Construction is the same as already described, except the seat rails should be made about 20 inches longer. The back angle will be about 10 degrees from vertical, or a little more, but make sure all four supports are the same. During the assembly of the ends, put the short bottom rails across the insides of the legs and arrange the supports inside them and the seat rails (FIG. 7-19A).

If you want to fasten the table to the ground, it would be better to take these bottom pieces across in single lengths. Then attach brackets or pegs to the ground.

The backs are shown at the same height as the table, but you could make them a few inches higher or lower, if you prefer. Two rails similar to those of the seat are shown in FIG. 7-19B. They should be stiff enough without intermediate supports. You could brace them to each other by putting short packings between them at one or two places. If the seat needs stiffening, you can add struts similar to those under the table. Place them from the bottom rails to other rails put across under the seat.

8

Folding Furniture

MOST OUTDOOR FURNITURE is used only occasionally. In some cases it will be convenient for the furniture to be rigid and permanently in shape, but for many things it is better if its size can be reduced. If furniture can be folded or disassembled, parts will occupy much less storage space. Care is needed with disassembled parts so that none are lost, particularly nuts, bolts, and washers. Most folding furniture does not require loose parts, so there is nothing to lose, but the folded item will not reduce to quite as small a package as some disassembled tables, chairs, or other items.

In addition to the convenience of reducing bulk for storage of furniture used in the vicinity of the home, folding furniture is useful for camping and other trips where you need to stow everything as compactly as possible if you are to get it all into the vehicle.

It is important that a folding piece of furniture be strong enough during use and when folded. Some things are satisfactory when assembled, but a comparatively fragile part will be exposed to damage when folded. Of course, it is important to guard against inadvertent folding when the item is in use. There must be a definite lock in some way. There must be no risk, for instance, of a chair collapsing under a normal load.

Some folding furniture is designed most ingeniously and usually with rather complicated mechanisms. This type is more suitable for factory production because there are special parts that most individual craftsman cannot make. In any case, a simple action is preferable to a complicated one because it is easier to make and it is less likely to go wrong.

Folding furniture manufactured in quantity is mostly metal formed by machine. This technique is unsuitable for the home shop. Wood is the preferred material, but some simple metalwork is needed, including sawing, filing, drilling, and some simple bending. All of these tasks can be done with hand tools, if necessary.

For the sake of lightness, wooden folding outdoor furniture is normally made with sections no thicker than necessary. Therefore, it is advisable to select straight-grained hardwood that is free from knots. Softwood would not normally be used. If you do choose to use softwood, you should increase sections, and you must reinforce joints in many places with metal brackets or plywood gussets.

You should paint or varnish folding furniture to prevent the wood from absorbing moisture, as well as to improve appearance. A boat varnish gives good protection and allows the grain to show through, resulting in a lighter appearance than a painted surface. Pay particular attention to any end grain that will rest on the ground because it is particularly prone to soak up moisture.

FOLDING STOOL

The Folding Stool is a basic type of seat that uses canvas and is comfortable to use. It packs to under 3 inches thick. It is suitable for camping and fishing trips, as well as for use in your yard. The parts are made as two frames pivoted near their centers (FIG. 8-1) with canvas across the top bars. The frames are the same except, that one is narrow enough to fit inside the other. (See TABLE 8-1.)

Mark out the two top bars (FIG. 8-2A), but do not round the edges until after you cut the joints. Mark out all four legs (FIG. 8-2B). Leave the cutting of the bottom angled ends until after assembly. The joints are simple mortise-and-tenon joints (FIG. 8-2C). They should be strong enough, but if you have any doubts you can add strip metal brackets inside each (FIG. 8-2D). Check that the legs of the narrower assembly fit inside the other ones.

The braces on the outer pair of legs should come below the pivot points (FIG. 8-1A); otherwise they will interfere with the action by hitting the inner legs when the stool is opened. This problem would not occur with the inner legs if the braces were higher, but it is standard to put both sets at the same height. As shown in FIG. 8-2E, put the braces on through the marked positions on the legs and hold them at each place with one screw, then cut the braces level. Where the braces cross, spring them over each other. It would weaken them too much to cut half-lap joints there. Fit the legs into each other when you put on the braces so you see that they will be able to move.

The pivots can be coach bolts. Let the square neck pull into the outer leg, include a thin rivet between the legs, and then have a washer and nut inside (FIG. 8-2F). Cut off the bolt end fairly close to the nut and hammer over its edges all around while you support the head on an iron block (FIG. 8-2G) so the nut cannot work loose. Instead of a bolt, you could use a rivet if you prefer.

The seat can be a plastic-coated material or plain—proofed canvas—about 15 ounce per square yard grade. The width needed is 15 inches. If you are able to get this stock width, it will have a *selvage* where the thread turned back during weaving (this will not fray). If you must cut wider canvas, allow enough for turning under. This method is advisable in any case because a *tabled* edge will provide strength where it is needed.

If you cut the canvas with pinking shears, you can machine-sew a single line of stitches without turning the canvas in (FIG. 8-3A) because the edge will not fray. If you cut straight, it will be better to fold the edge in and stitch through it (FIG. 8-3B). Rub down the folds with the handle of a knife, or something similar, before stitching.

Where the canvas is attached to the top pieces, allow folding under so that you can drive tacks there (FIG. 8-1B). Bringing the canvas around three edges of the wood relieves the tacks of strain. Fold the canvas around the tops of the legs and arrange tacks or large-headed nails closely; 1 inch apart will probably be close enough.

As you fit the canvas, check the amount of opening and the height of the stool (FIG. 8-1C). Allow for the canvas stretching a little. When you have finished attaching the canvas, open the stool fully so that you can mark and cut the bottoms of the legs parallel with the top.

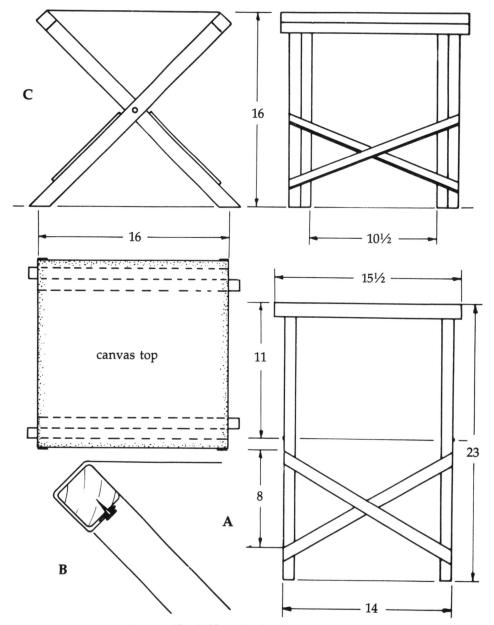

C

16

10½

16

canvas top

11

8

15½

23

14

A

B

Fig. 8-1. The Folding Stool with a canvas top.

Table 8-1. Materials List for Folding Stool.

2 tops	$1\frac{1}{8} \times 16 \times 1\frac{1}{8}$
4 legs	$1\frac{1}{8} \times 24 \times \frac{7}{8}$
4 braces	$\frac{7}{8} \times 18 \times \frac{1}{4}$

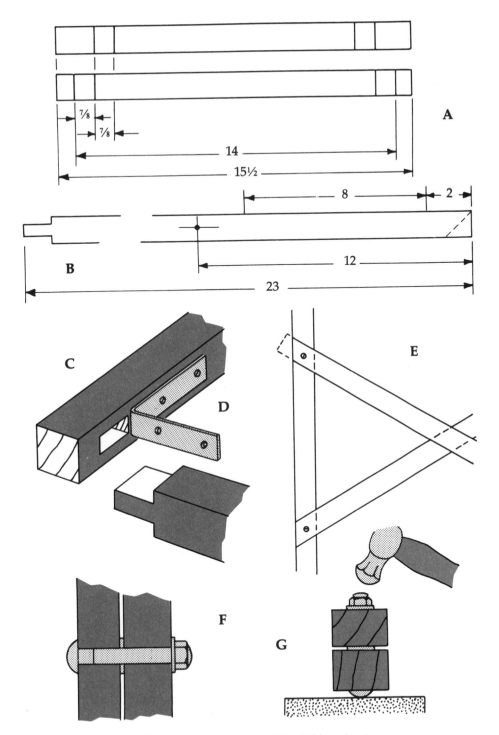

Fig. 8-2. Construction of the Folding Stool.

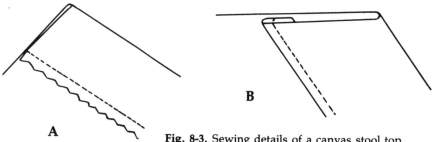

Fig. 8-3. Sewing details of a canvas stool top.

FOLDING ARMCHAIR

The Folding Stool has many uses, but if you want more comfort there must be a back; attaching arms would be even better. A type of folding chair that is built around a folding stool is a well-tried design for wood construction. As shown in FIG. 8-4, the chair has ample size for comfort when opened, and it stands rigidly. It packs to only a few inches thick. Its side view is the same size whether opened or closed. (See TABLE 8-2.)

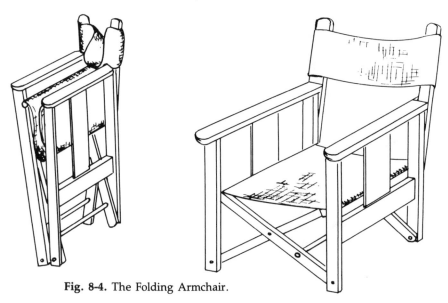

Fig. 8-4. The Folding Armchair.

Table 8-2. Materials List for Folding Armchair.

4 stool legs	$1\frac{1}{4} \times 26 \times \frac{5}{8}$
2 stool crossbars	$1\frac{1}{4} \times 18 \times 1\frac{1}{4}$
2 stool rods	$\frac{5}{8} \times 18$ round rods
4 side legs	$1\frac{3}{4} \times 28 \times \frac{7}{8}$
2 side rails	$3 \times 18 \times \frac{7}{8}$
2 side slats	$4 \times 15 \times \frac{1}{2}$
2 arms	$3 \times 22 \times \frac{7}{8}$
2 backs	$1\frac{3}{4} \times 26 \times \frac{7}{8}$

The framework, including the arms, is made of wood, but the seat and back are canvas, which will conform to body shape and provide comfort. There are some simple metal links and spacers to be made. The most attractive finish would be boat varnish, with the metal parts painted. You can paint the wood as well, if you prefer. It would be unwise to leave the wood bare because it would absorb moisture.

The general drawing (FIG. 8-5) shows that the seat is a stool. A pair of sides is linked to the stool and joined with canvas to form the back. You can make the stool first and fit the sides to it, but it is probably easier to get an accurate assembly if you start with the pair of sides then adjust the spacings of the stool sides and legs to suit.

Set out the chair side full size (FIG. 8-5A). Make the parts with square edges. After cutting the joints and doing general shaping, you should round all edges that will be exposed (FIG. 8-6A). Most joints can be doweled, but you could use mortise-and-tenon joints, if you prefer.

Mark out the four upright legs together (FIG. 8-6B). Drill ¼-inch holes for bolts 1 inch up from the bottom to form stool pivots. Dowel the side rails into the marked positions on the legs (FIG. 8-6C). The tops of the legs have dowels into the arms (FIG. 8-6D).

The arms are parallel except for rounding at the front and a taper at the back. The side slats are too thin for dowels and it will be better to slot them into the arm and rail (FIG. 8-6E).

Mark and cut the back piece and the arm that attaches to it to match. Cut the bottom of the back (FIG. 8-5B) to an angle against the leg; it would weaken it to go to a feather edge. Well-round the top. The joint between the end of the arm and the back must resist the thrust of a person sitting and leaning back. A joint that cuts too much out of the back can cause it to break there under pressure. So there is enough wood left in the back, join the arm with a single ⅝-inch dowel. Drive a wedge from behind (FIG. 8-6F). There should never be much load on the joint at the bottom of the back because thrust at the top tends to push that joint together. Use glue and one or two screws there. After you have prepared all parts, rounding where advisable, assemble to make a matching pair.

The stool is made up of two crossbars to take the canvas, with four crossed sides held below the pivot with lengths of dowel rod (FIG. 8-7A). The sizes of the sides shown (FIG. 8-5C) will give a satisfactory spread when opened.

As you set out the stool, the crossbars should be as long as the widths of the sides, but the joints between them and their legs must be spaced to suit the spacing of the chair side legs. The pair of stool legs that come outside the others must fit between the chair side legs with just enough clearance for thin washers. The inside stool legs must fit between them with similar clearance.

You can join the legs to the crossbars with dowels, but it would be better to use tenons, either right through (as in the Folding Stool) or with stub tenons (FIG. 8-7B). Round the top edges of the crossbars (FIG. 8-7C). Drill for ¼-inch pivot bolts, 1 inch from the rounded bottoms of the stool legs and again at the pivot points.

Drill for the dowel rods that brace the lower parts of the stool legs. When you assemble, you can fit the rods right through and hold them with glue and nails driven across.

The central pivot of the stool is a ¼-inch bolt or rivet taken through washers. The pivot of the outside stool legs to the bottom of the side rigid legs is the same

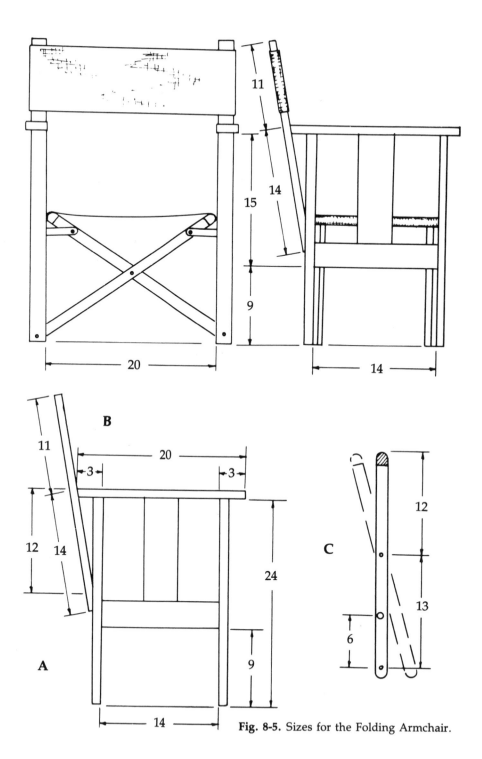

Fig. 8-5. Sizes for the Folding Armchair.

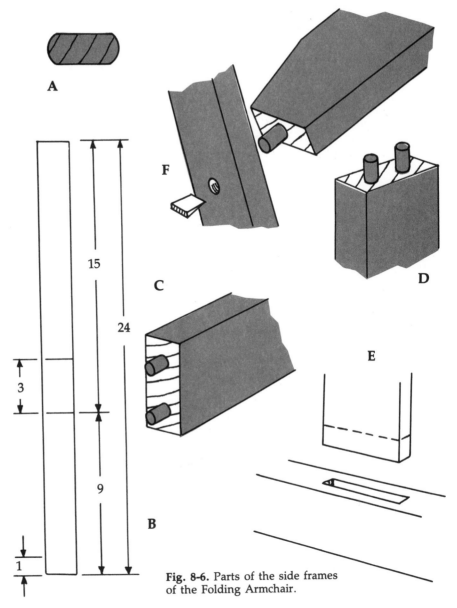

Fig. 8-6. Parts of the side frames of the Folding Armchair.

(FIG. 8-7D). You could use coach bolts, as described for the first stool, but rivets are shown. When you do the final assembly, have the prepared rivet head outside and hammer over on the washer on the inside.

At the other side, there is a gap to be filled between the stool leg and the side rigid leg. Use short pieces of tube on the rivets. Make the length to take up the thickness of the outer stool leg (FIG. 8-7E). You can make a trial assembly with the rivets or bolts loose, but do not tighten them until you have the canvas on and the metal links ready.

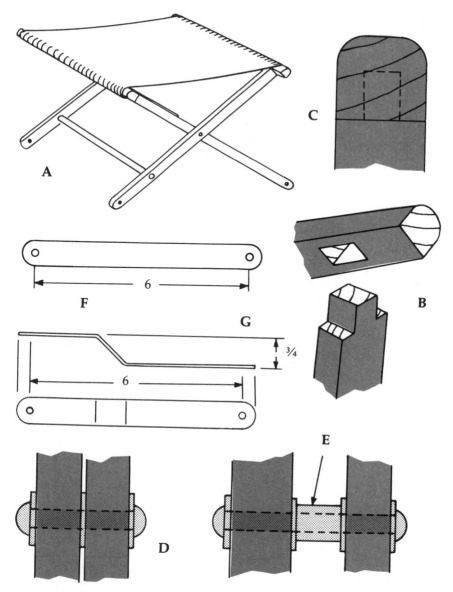

Fig. 8-7. Details of the folding seat of the armchair.

The links that join the stool to the sides and permit folding are pieces of strip metal about ⅝ inch wide and under ⅛ inch thick; ³⁄₃₂ inch would be ideal, but any strip about this section could be used. Iron is the obvious choice, but that is liable to rust. Painting iron before assembly will give ample protection. Brass would resist corrosion. Stainless steel would be a good choice, but some of it is difficult to bend and drill.

The straight links that join the outside stool legs to the rigid side legs (FIG. 8-7F) are simple, straight pieces. Mark the centers of the holes with a centerpunch and use these dots as centers for drawing the end curves before drilling.

At the other side of the chair, the links should have the same distance between the holes, when finished, but you must bend the links to allow for the legs being in a different plane (FIG. 8-7G). You can do this task while the strip projects above the vise jaws. Drill holes to suit the screws used; 10-gauge screws are suitable. Countersink the holes so the heads will not project and interfere with folding.

To find the best positions for the links, make a trial assembly. Put the rivets or bolts in loosely and open the chair to the sitting position. Attach the links temporarily to the rear stool legs only, about 3 inches down from the crossbar. Put screws into the side legs when the links are about horizontal. Try the folding action, altering the screw positions until the action is correct. Mark and drill similar positions for screws at the front. Measure across the top of the stool in the open position to determine the length of canvas to fit.

Do any finishing to the woodwork before you attach the canvas, including the parts that will be covered by canvas for the sake of protection. Attach the seat canvas in the same way as described for the Folding Stool. A width of 15 or 16 inches would be suitable. Roll the canvas over the crossbars and tack closely underneath. In the first fitting of the seat canvas, aim to have it finish taut in the open position to allow for some stretching. When the seat canvas has been fitted, you can assemble the pivot rivets or bolts together with the links. You should then have the seat standing with its sides upright.

The back strip of canvas should be 7 or 8 inches wide. Deal with the edges in the same way as for the edges of the seat. Do not stretch it as tightly as the seat; it can start with a little slackness. Wrap the ends around the wood and tack inside in the same way as for the seat.

CHAIR WITH FOLDING BACK

A seat without a back support does not provide as much comfort as a chair. It is possible to make a chair that is a development of the Folding Stool, yet that packs to almost the same size. It is a folding stool with the crossed legs supporting a canvas top, but on one pair of legs there are pivoted the uprights of a back that will swing down when the legs are folded (FIG. 8-8). When a stool without a back is used, the sitter usually has his legs toward a free canvas side. If there is a back, one of the bars must come to the front.

In FIG. 8-9, you can see that the back pivots on the outer legs and their crossbar is extended for it to press against (FIG. 8-9A and TABLE 8-3). At the top, there is a plywood back support (FIG. 8-9B). The parts must be arranged to give clearance when the back uprights fold down. The inner legs have a crossbar that does not extend to the width of the outer legs, and the canvas comes inside that crossbar (FIG. 8-9C).

The four legs are the same except for the pivot holes for the back in the outer ones (FIG. 8-10A). Leave the cutting of the angled bottoms until after assembly. The joints to the crossbars will be the same as in the Folding Stool (FIG. 8-2C), and you can include metal brackets (FIG. 8-2D) if you prefer.

Make the back uprights (FIG. 8-10B). The simplest back is a flat piece of ¼- or ⅜-inch-thick glued plywood and screwed to the side pieces. A more comfortable back is curved. The amount of curve is not crucial, but about 1½ inches in the width is enough.

You can make a curved back with two pieces of ⅛-inch plywood, cut to width, but with some excess length at this stage. Prepare two stiff boards and three

Fig. 8-8. The Chair with Folding Back.

packings that will go across the plywood. Round their edges. Put glue on the meeting surfaces of the plywood and squeeze it in a vise or with clamps to a suitable curve (FIG. 8-10C). When the glue has set, trim the wood to size. Allow for slightly curved ends (FIG. 8-11A) and round the back edges in section, whether you make it flat or hollowed. For the hollowed back, notch the uprights to suit the slope on each side so they remain parallel when you glue and screw the back on.

You must make the distances between the back uprights and the two sets of legs to match each other. Work to the actual wood; this might be slightly thicker or thinner than drawn. Put the back parts together with the outside edges 17 inches

Table 8-3. Materials List for Chair with Folding Back.

4 legs	$1\frac{1}{8} \times 24 \times 1\frac{1}{8}$
2 backs	$1\frac{1}{8} \times 21 \times 1\frac{1}{8}$
1 crossbar	$1\frac{1}{8} \times 19 \times 1\frac{1}{8}$
1 crossbar	$1\frac{1}{8} \times 16 \times 1\frac{1}{8}$
4 braces	$\frac{7}{8} \times 18 \times \frac{1}{4}$
1 back	$3 \times 18 \times \frac{1}{4}$ plywood
or 2 backs	$3 \times 18 \times \frac{1}{8}$ plywood

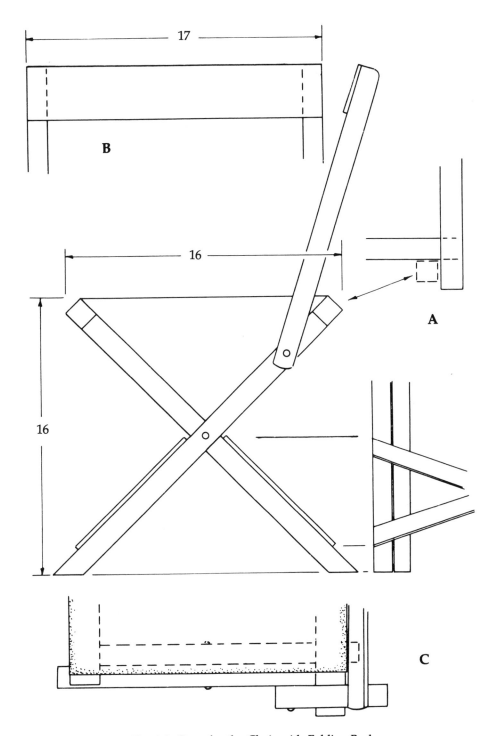

Fig. 8-9. Sizes for the Chair with Folding Back.

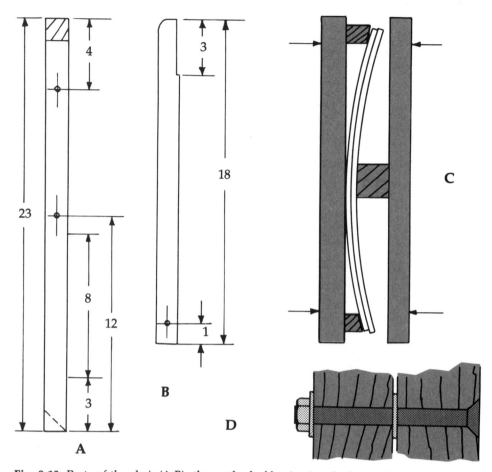

Fig. 8-10. Parts of the chair (A,B), the method of laminating the back (C), and the details of the pivot bolt (D).

apart (FIG. 8-11B). Make the back crossbar long enough to extend ½ inch past the back uprights, and make the joints for the outer pair of legs so they will come inside the back uprights (FIG. 8-11C). Allow for thin washers between them.

Make the length of the front crossbar so that it does not quite reach the outside edges of the outer pair of legs, and position the joints for its legs to come inside the outer legs (FIG. 8-11D). Round the edges and ends of the crossbars and then assemble the legs to them. Also attach the braces (FIG. 8-11E) in a similar way to those for the Folding Stool. Spring them over each other where they cross. Keep them below the pivot position so that they do not obstruct the legs when opening.

Make the central pivots between the legs with bolts or rivets, as described for the first stool or the chair. Make the back pivots in a similar way, but there must not be any projections on the insides of the outer legs—they might interfere with folding (FIG. 8-12). Use bolts or rivets with countersunk heads on the inside (FIG. 8-10D).

Varnish or paint all the woodwork before assembling the parts. Then fit the canvas as described for the first stool. You must keep its width a small amount

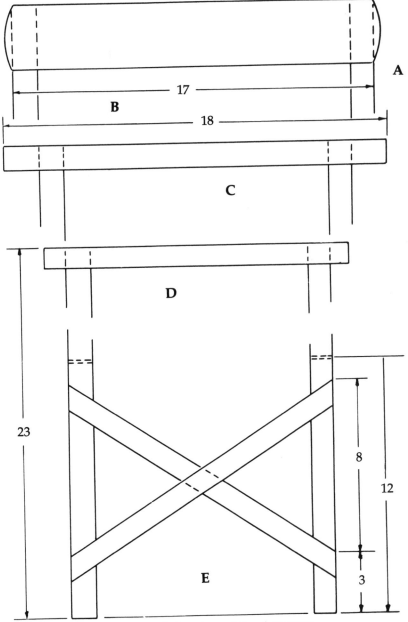

Fig. 8-11. Relative sizes of the chair parts.

in from the ends of the front crossbar so that the chair will fold without obstructing the back.

DECK CHAIR

The fold-flat deck chair is common in many forms in most parts of the world. There are versions with leg rests, canopies, arms, and other additions, but the

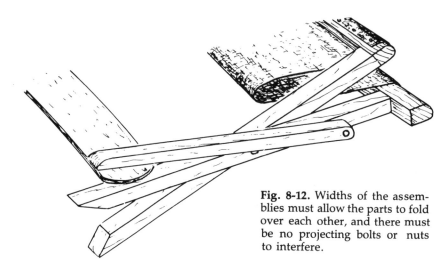

Fig. 8-12. Widths of the assemblies must allow the parts to fold over each other, and there must be no projecting bolts or nuts to interfere.

basic pattern is the most common form. It serves as a simple and comfortable adjustable seat that can be stored in a minimum of space. The example in FIG. 8-13 is of straightforward construction with no extras. The sizes given will make a chair of average size. If you use other sizes, remember that the inner assembly must fold inside the outer one and that the strut part must swing over the top of the outer frame for folding. If the canvas is flat and moderately taut when the chair is folded, it will curve into a comfortable shape when the chair is set up.

Fig. 8-13. The folding Deck Chair.

There are two frames pivoted together. A strut assembly allows the chair to be at any of three angles (FIG. 8-14A). When the frame is folded, the two four-sided parts close into line and the strut part rests on them (FIG. 8-14B). This brings the assembly down to less than 4 inches thick.

Fig. 8-14. The general arrangements of the Deck Chair.

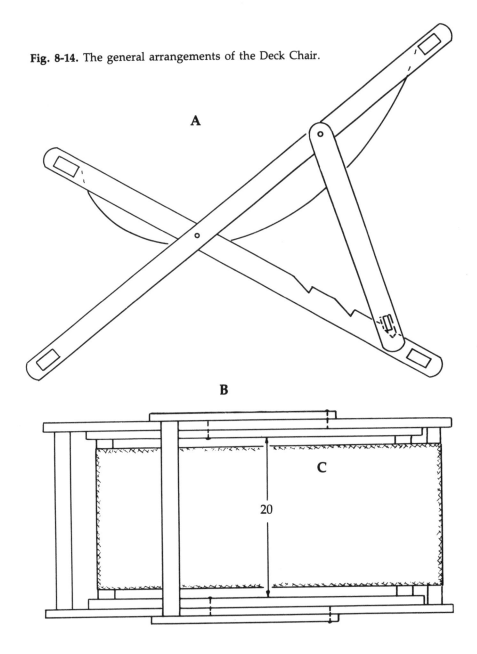

Table 8-4. Materials List for Deck Chair.

2 sides	2 × 52 × 1
2 sides	2 × 43 × 1
2 struts	2 × 24 × 1
5 crossbars	2 × 27 × 1

All of the parts are of 1-×-2-inch section and should be of straight-grained hardwood free from flaws. (A heavy person using the chair puts considerable strain on some parts.) The width shown is intended to take canvas 18 inches wide, but you can adjust that width if only canvas of another width is available. (See TABLE 8-4.)

Mark out the long sides (FIG. 8-15A). Make all of the ends with crossmembers tenoned in the same (FIG. 8-15B). Round the ends using the edge of the crossmember as the center for the compass. Mark out the shorter sides (FIG. 8-15C). Cut the notches for the strut into a ⅜-inch hole (FIG. 8-15D). It is possible to make all the notches the same and have the strut crossmember an average shape. Because the angle the crossmember meets the side is different in each position, you will obtain the best fit by making the furthest notch as shown and match the strut crossmember. Alter the other positions to suit during a trial assembly. You will cut all of the notches into ⅜-inch holes, but the angles into them will be slightly different at the inner two positions.

Make the strut sides (FIG. 8-15E). Make the bottom joint similar to the others but cut the tenon back to allow the bevels on the crossmember (FIG. 8-15F). Cut the top semicircular and drill in it for the bolt (FIG. 8-15G).

The joints are all tenons about ½ inch wide (FIG. 8-16A). Round the edges of the crossmembers of the four-sided frames (FIG. 8-16B). Cut the tenons slightly too long and put saw cuts across them so that you can tighten the joints with wedges (FIG. 8-16C). Plane the tenons level after the glue has set. Make sure assemblies are square. The inner frame should fit inside the other with just enough clearance for a washer on each side.

Pivots can be ¼- or ¹⁄₁₆-inch coach bolts. For the main pivots, have the heads outside. Have them inside for the strut pivots. Include washers between the parts and under the nuts (FIG. 8-16D). After the final assembly, cut off any surplus threaded end of each bolt and rivet the remainder by hammering onto the nut to lock it. If you are fitting the notches for the strut individually, do so during a temporary assembly.

Take off the sharpness from the edges of the main parts. This is particularly important for anyone sitting in the chair. However, do not reduce the cross section much. Varnish the wood before final assembly so that you can get at the parts that would otherwise be difficult to reach.

If you buy the canvas the right width, you can use its selvages as they are because they will not fray. If you must cut wider canvas, turn in the edges, as described for the Folding Chair.

Have the frames folded so that they are in line. The canvas must go from the front rail of the inner frame to the top rail of the outer frame (FIG. 8-14C). Allow enough to wrap around the rails and turn in to be tacked. You can tack to the edges of the rails (FIG. 8-16E), but for the strongest joint the canvas should go around to the flat part (FIG. 8-16F). Tacking in this way is easy enough for the first end, but you can get enough slackness in the canvas to swing a hammer at the other end by folding the frames the wrong way (after you have settled on the canvas length). If fastened in that way, the canvas under load helps to keep the tacks in place.

SLAT-TOP STOOL

A canvas-topped stool can provide more comfort, but it could suffer if left out in all types of weather. An all-wood stool will have better weather resistance.

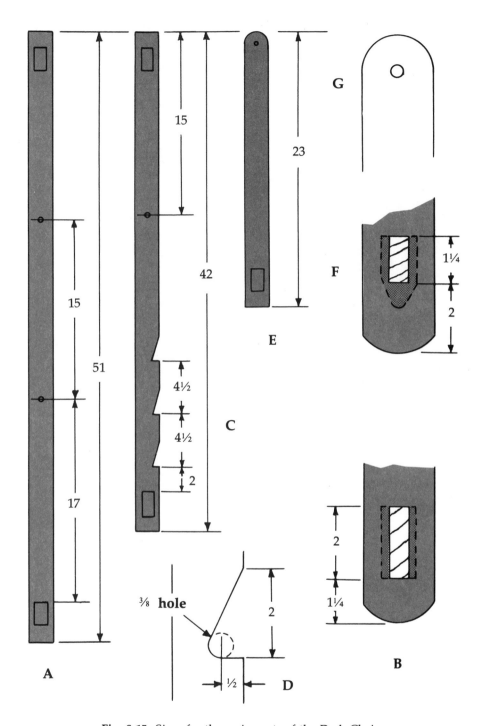

Fig. 8-15. Sizes for the main parts of the Deck Chair.

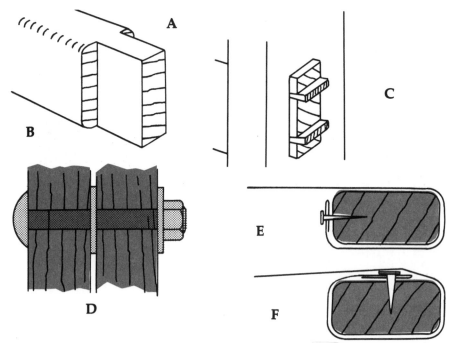

Fig. 8-16. Assembling (A-C) the Deck Chair, adding the pivots (D), and attaching the canvas (E,F).

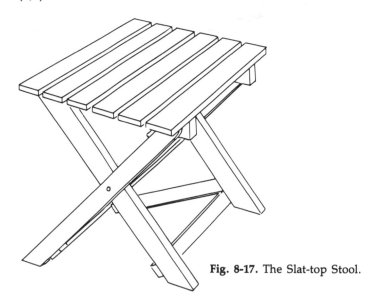

Fig. 8-17. The Slat-top Stool.

The Slat-top Stool (FIG. 8-17) has a top made of narrow strips so that it does not trap water on crossed legs, which fold flat with the top alongside. The sizes shown in FIG. 8-18 and TABLE 8-5 are for a stool of minimum size that can be stowed compactly. It is just big enough to act as a reasonable seat. The top can be softened with a cushion, possibly provided with tapes for lashing on.

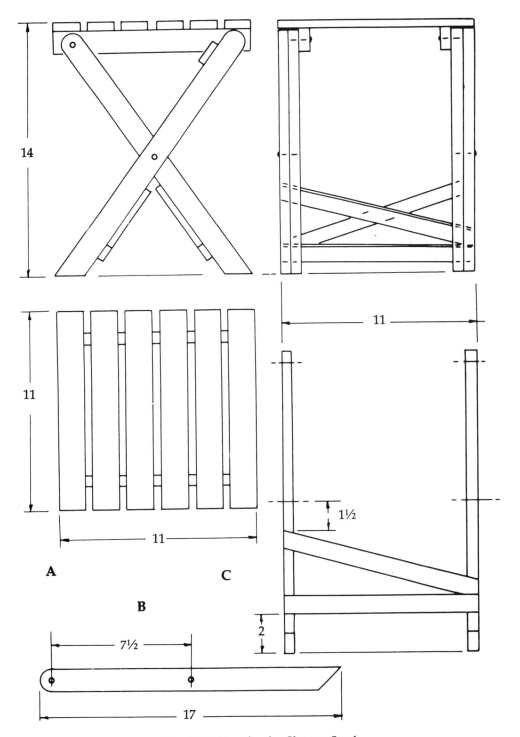

Fig. 8-18. Sizes for the Slat-top Stool.

Table 8-5. Materials List for Slat-top Stool.

6 tops	1½ × 12 × ⅜
6 top supports	1¼ × 12 × ⅝
4 legs	1¼ × 18 × ⅝
2 braces	1 × 12 × ⅜
2 braces	1 × 13 × ⅜
1 ledge	1½ × 12 × ⅜

The wood is all of fairly thin section so the design is unsuitable for most softwoods. The best choice will be one of the lighter straight-grained hardwoods. Sizes quoted are the finished ones. Some parts would not be strong enough if sawn sizes were used and planed thinner.

There is no need to make a full-size drawing unless you want to alter the sizes. As shown, the ledged end of the outer leg assembly swings down to close in line with the other leg, and the top drops between them.

Start with the top. Take the sharpness off the slats. Mark out and cut the supports (FIG. 8-19A), but do not cut the notch yet. Its exact size and angle will be determined later in a temporary assembly with the legs. Attach the slats to the supports (FIG. 8-18A). The distance the supports are in from the ends of the slats must be equal to the thickness of two legs with a washer between. It would not matter if the distance is up to ⅛ inch farther in than that, but do not allow too much.

Make the four legs (FIG. 8-18B). The tops are semicircles about the centers of the holes in the inner legs. Although the tops of the outer legs are the same shape, they do not require holes. It is best to use a straightedge to mark the final angles of the bottoms during a temporary assembly.

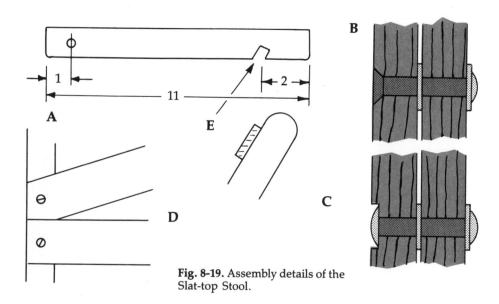

Fig. 8-19. Assembly details of the Slat-top Stool.

The pivots can be rivets or bolts ¼ inch in diameter, but there must be clearance at their heads where parts cross when folded. That only happens at one side in each place. You can use countersunk rivets or bolt heads (FIG. 8-19B). The nut or other rivet head can project at the other side. If you must use a snap head, counterbore enough to get it below the surface (FIG. 8-19C).

The leg assemblies must be square and parallel if folding is to be smooth. You can use the top you have assembled for squaring. Join the legs with their central pivots temporarily, then attach the inner legs with their pivots to the top. Fold the pivots between them to find the distances the legs must be apart.

The braces must come on the undersides of the leg when the stool is in use, and the tops of the diagonals must be kept low enough to clear the opposite legs when the legs are spread. Put the straight braces across (FIG. 8-18C), then arrange the diagonals close to them (FIG. 8-19D). Glue and a single screw at each position should be sufficient.

Adjust the stool to its position for use. See that the top is parallel with the floor. Hold the ledge strip against the legs so you can mark the shape of the slot each side by penciling along the edge of the leg and marking the thickness of the top ledge. Cut the slat to about half the thickness of the top support (FIG. 8-19E). Make it an easy fit on the ledge. Move the ledge up to the position to go into the slots and mark where it goes on the legs. Open the stool and attach the ledge to the legs.

When you are satisfied with the action, separate the parts for varnishing or painting. Then bolt or rivet them together.

SLAT-TOP CHAIR

A stool provides a simple and compact seat. If it is to be used for long, there will be a need for a seat back. The Slat-top Stool would not be satisfactory if it was made into a chair by extending one of its legs. That would give the back too much slope and extend it so that it would be unstable if the user leaned back. The arrangement of legs must be altered to bring the back more upright and extend the rear legs to give support (FIG. 8-20).

General construction is very similar to the stool. The shape and sizes given in FIG. 8-21 and TABLE 8-6 show how the chair form is obtained. A full-size drawing is not essential. You can mark angles during assembly. A full-size side view will help in understanding the layout.

To fold the chair, bring the legs into line while you slide the seat up the back to also finish in line. If you alter sizes, you must allow enough space in the back for the seat to accommodate below the back slats.

Make the long legs (FIG. 8-22A) and the short legs (FIG. 8-22B). Get the angles of the ends from your full-size drawing or wait to mark and cut them until you make a trial assembly. The pivots can be as suggested for the stool, either rivets or bolts (FIG. 8-19B, C), with the same need of clearance where parts come together when folded. Drill for the pivots.

Make the seat supports (FIG. 8-22C) and drill for the pivots. Round the lower front corner. You must arrange the slats to take the seat as far back as possible, but the rear one must have enough clearance on the long legs to allow it to fold (FIG. 8-21A). Extend the crossbar below (FIG. 8-22D) to the outer legs and bevel it to fit against them. Bevel the ledge across the long legs to match (FIG. 8-21B). These parts come together and take much of the chair's load, so you should securely glue and screw them on, and accurately fit them.

Fig. 8-20. The Slat-top Chair.

Stiffening of the leg assemblies is similar to the stool, but the braces come on the outsides of the legs because of the different method of folding. Make up the seat except for the crossbar underneath. Temporarily pivot the legs to it and to each other so you can swing the parts into their folded position and attach the braces (FIG. 8-22E) and the back slats (FIG. 8-22F) to keep the legs at the correct widths.

Try the action of the chair opened and closed. Check that the seat is level. Trim the angles at the bottoms of the legs, if necessary. Separate the parts for sanding and follow with varnish or paint. Close the pivots finally and attach the crossbar below the seat.

SLAT-TOP TABLE

A table with a slat top is an obvious companion to the slat-top stool and chair. This one is lightweight and arranged to fold in a very similar way. Its general appearance is like a larger version of the stool (FIG. 8-17). It does not need to carry as much weight as a stool or chair, so sections of wood do not need to be proportionately greater. However, the increased size means that there is more tendency to push out of shape if it is not adequately braced.

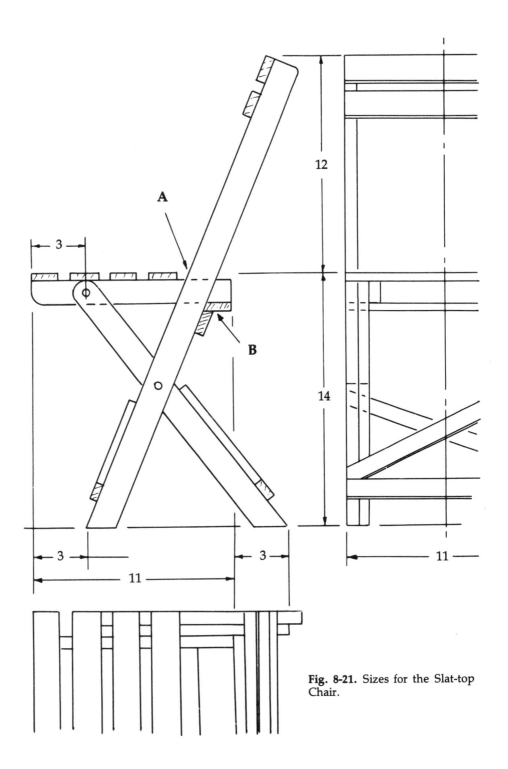

Fig. 8-21. Sizes for the Slat-top Chair.

Table 8-6. Materials List for Slat-top Chair.

4 seats	$1\frac{1}{2} \times 12 \times \frac{3}{8}$
2 seat supports	$1\frac{1}{4} \times 12 \times \frac{5}{8}$
1 seat crossbar	$1\frac{1}{4} \times 12 \times \frac{5}{8}$
2 legs	$1\frac{1}{4} \times 21 \times \frac{5}{8}$
2 legs	$1\frac{1}{4} \times 30 \times \frac{5}{8}$
3 back slats	$1\frac{1}{2} \times 12 \times \frac{3}{8}$
2 braces	$1 \times 12 \times \frac{3}{8}$
2 braces	$1 \times 15 \times \frac{3}{8}$

Construction is the same as for the stool, except for the following differences. (See TABLE 8-7.) The table shown assembles to 22 inches each way. It folds by the legs with the ledge swinging down; then the top closes against them.

Make the top of slats on two supports (FIG. 8-23A). Arrange them to overhang enough to cover the legs (FIG. 8-23B). Because of the size, there is a risk of the top going out of shape. To prevent this, put strips across the inside and level with the outer edges of the third slat in from each end. You could tenon these parts together, but it should be satisfactory to nail them. Inside the pieces, glue and screw triangular blocks on stiffeners (FIG. 8-23C).

Make the legs (FIG. 8-23D) like those for the stool. Make pivot holes where they cross and other pivot holes at the top of one pair of legs only. To give greater rigidity, use two diagonal braces on each pair of legs (FIG. 8-23E). They can spring over each other where they cross. There is no need to cut a joint there; a half-lap joint would weaken the wood too much. Let the braces come as high as they can on the legs (providing they do not foul each other or the opened legs). Set the widths of the leg assemblies with the tabletop as a guide.

As with the stool, make a trial assembly so that you can mark the slot for the ledge and its position on the legs. When that assembly works satisfactorily and the tabletop finishes level, take the assemblies apart for painting or varnishing. Then tighten the rivets or bolts.

LONG TRESTLE TABLE

It is often useful to have one or more fairly light tables that can be folded flat when not needed. It is even more useful to have a folding arrangement that does not involve any special action or loose pieces.

The table shown in FIG. 8-24 has a framed plywood top and legs. The legs are held upright by struts, which are held in place by gravity. When folded upward toward the center, the legs come close to the top and the total thickness is only a few inches. It is the folding of the legs that controls the length of the table. It would not be impossible to let the leg ends overlap, but that method would increase the folded thickness. Otherwise the length must be enough to keep the legs clear of each other.

If the table is to stand 30 inches high, the length of the top cannot be less than about 65 inches. The example shown is 72 inches. The main parts are shown $1\frac{1}{4}$ inches thick for rigidity. They could be increased to $1\frac{1}{2}$ inches, but it would be unwise to reduce them much unless lightness is the most important requirement. Width can be anything you want to make it, but it is shown as 27 inches. The leg assemblies and the top are the same width. (See TABLE 8-8.)

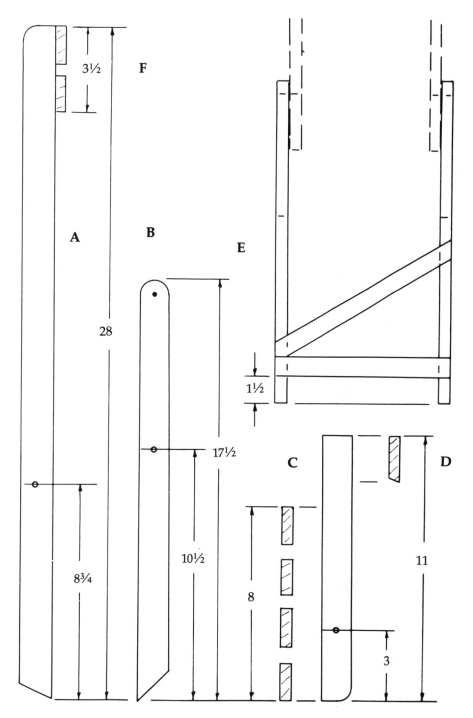

Fig. 8-22. The main parts of the Slat-top Chair.

Table 8-7. Materials List for Slat-top Table.

9 tops	$2 \times 23 \times \frac{1}{2}$
2 top supports	$1\frac{1}{4} \times 23 \times \frac{5}{8}$
2 top supports	$1\frac{1}{4} \times 20 \times \frac{5}{8}$
4 legs	$1\frac{1}{4} \times 30 \times \frac{5}{8}$
4 braces	$1 \times 27 \times \frac{3}{8}$

The plywood supports the top framing, and there is little need for joints between the top parts. You can miter corners or half-lap the flat pieces. Use glue and plenty of nails through the plywood. Make up the top with the strips framing the plywood, but do not attach the other cross pieces yet.

Make up two leg assemblies (FIG. 8-24A). At the top, it is best to tenon the rail into the legs (FIG. 8-25A). For a simpler construction, you could screw the rail into the inner surfaces of the legs. The lower rail comes 6 inches from the ground. Screw and glue it to the outer surfaces of the legs (FIG. 8-25B). Except for seeing that the parts are square and match each other, you will have a simple assembly.

In order to make the table so the legs fold neatly, you must get certain distances correct. The distance from the center of the hinge between the legs and table (FIG. 8-25C) to the center of the hinge at the top of the strut (FIG. 8-25D) must be the same as the distance from the first hinge to the hinge on the lower leg rail (FIG. 8-25E). With a leg in place, measure the distance between the hinges when the leg is square to the top. Then measure the same distance along the top. At that point, put another piece across (FIG. 8-25F). Place another one across the same distance from the other end.

Measure the overall length of a strut when the leg assembly is square to the top. Make each strut in two equal parts (FIG. 8-25G).

All of the parts can be joined with 3-inch hinges. Hinge the tops of the leg assemblies to the ends of the top framing (FIG. 8-24B). Hinge the ends of each pair of struts together so that they meet closely when laid out straight. Any space between the ends will cause the struts to sag in use. Join the struts to the rails with hinges on top. Leave the central hinges underneath. When the table is standing the right way up, the struts should stay in place. To fold, push them toward the top and lay the legs against the top.

This plain table can have a cloth over it for outdoor use. You can frame the edges round with thin wood to cover the plywood edges. You can use a laminated plastic on the top. If you prefer a solid top, you can use several boards with battens across underneath for hinging the legs.

FOOTREST

If you are sitting in a chair and want to put your feet up, you can use a stool. For greater comfort, however, it is better to have a support with a cushion at the same height as the front of the chair seat. The support shown in FIG. 8-26 looks like a stool, but it is not really intended for that purpose, although it could make a temporary seat. It is meant to come against a chair, where it can be adjusted to bring its cushion close to the height of the chair. There is a rail at one end to keep the cushion from being pushed off when the user changes the position of his feet.

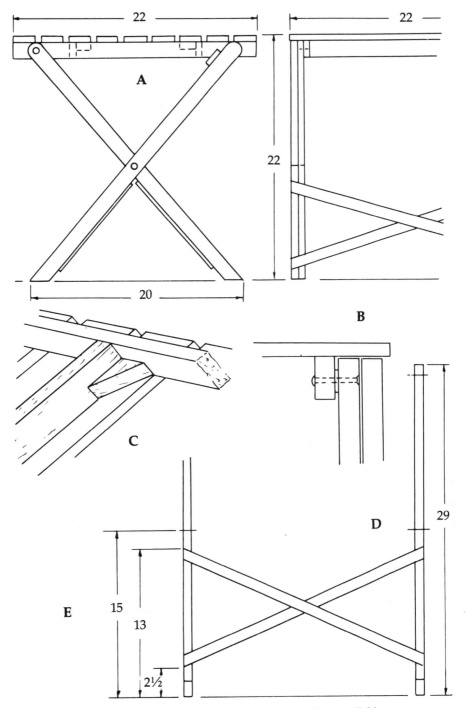

Fig. 8-23. Sizes and assembly of the Slat-top Table.

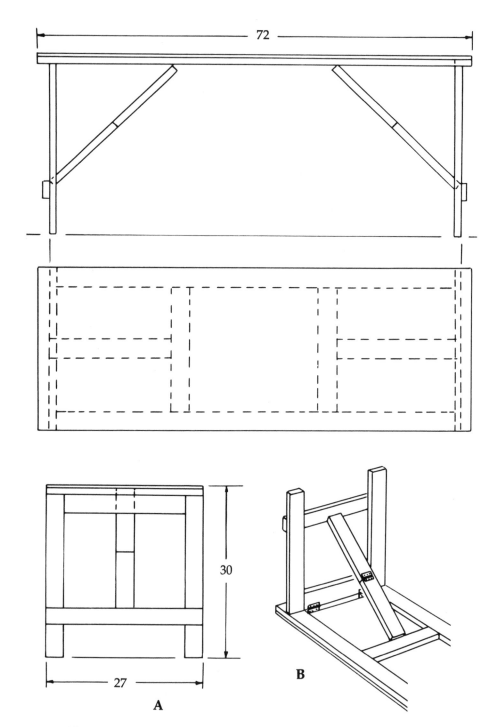

Fig. 8-24. Sizes and folding action of the Long Trestle Table.

A

B

Table 8-8. Materials List for Long Trestle Table.

1 top	27 × 72 × ½ plywood
2 top frames	3 × 74 × 1¼
4 top frames	3 × 28 × 1¼
4 legs	3 × 30 × 1¼
4 leg rails	3 × 27 × 1¼
4 struts	3 × 16 × 1

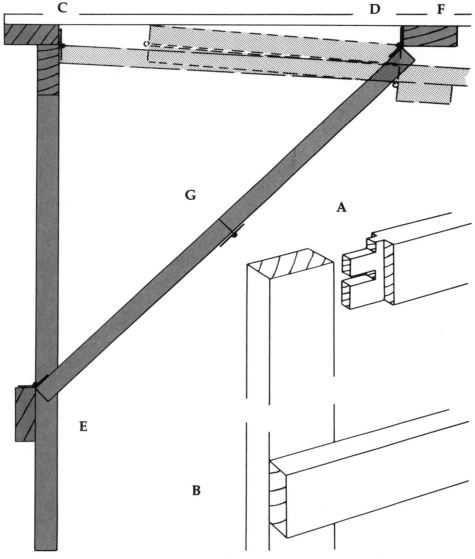

Fig. 8-25. End details of the Long Trestle Table.

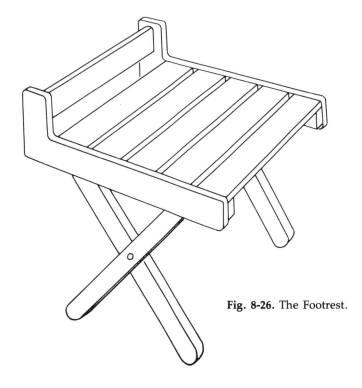

Fig. 8-26. The Footrest.

You can make the footrest with adjustable legs to give three different heights. The average height is 15 inches to the top of the slats (FIG. 8-27). If another height would suit your needs, you can alter the leg length. The sizes of wood suggested suit a close-grained hardwood. For softwood, increase them slightly. (See TABLE 8-9.)

The legs cross as in a folding stool. Two legs have a crossbar (FIG. 8-29A) that engages with slots in the top rails. Changing slots alters the footrest height. The other two legs cross between them and are pivoted to the other end of the top rail. There is a packing (FIG. 8-29B) to allow for the thickness of each outer leg. The footrest can be folded to reduce thickness, but it is not intended to go flat.

The top rail and its slots control other sizes (FIGS. 8-28A and 8-29C). To get the shapes and angles of the slots, set out a side view of the rail with its centerline and the centerlines of the legs, using the middle slot position (FIG. 8-28A). With the pivot point as a center, draw an arc through the leg crossing (FIG. 8-28B). The arc shows the path the crossing takes when the leg swings to other positions. With the same radius and the other slot locations as centers, mark two other center positions on the arc (FIG. 8-28C). Through those points draw new centerlines of the leg and its crossbar. With those lines as guides, you can draw the shapes of the slots (FIG. 8-28D). Drill holes first to suit the thickness of the crossbar and cut the sides of the slots into them. Round the entrances to the slot for easy adjustment.

If you do not want to go to that trouble, mark the shape of the center slot from the layout and draw the approximate shapes of the other two slots by estimation. You can trim them to their final shapes during assembly by trying the fit of the crossbar. You do not want a tight fit.

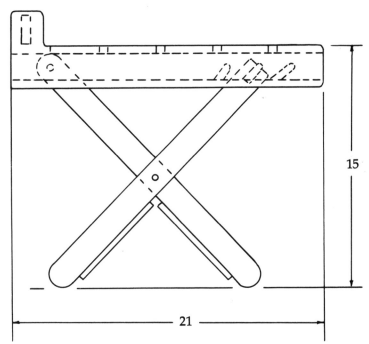

Fig. 8-27. Sizes for the Footrest.

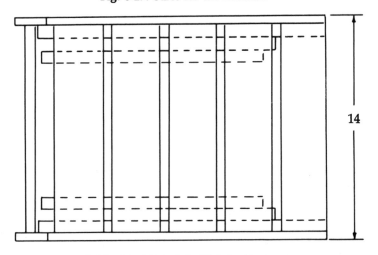

Table 8-9. Materials List for Footrest.

4 legs	$1\frac{1}{2} \times 20 \times \frac{3}{4}$
2 top rails	$1\frac{1}{4} \times 21 \times \frac{3}{4}$
2 top cover rails	$5\frac{1}{2} \times 21 \times \frac{1}{2}$ plywood
5 slats	$3 \times 15 \times \frac{1}{2}$
1 slat	$2 \times 15 \times \frac{1}{2}$
2 leg braces	$1 \times 20 \times \frac{3}{8}$
1 leg crossbar	$1\frac{1}{2} \times 14 \times \frac{1}{2}$

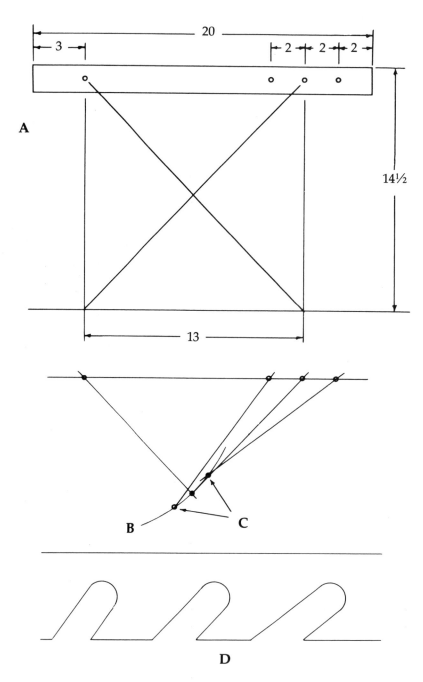

Fig. 8-28. Set-out of the Footrest to allow adjustment.

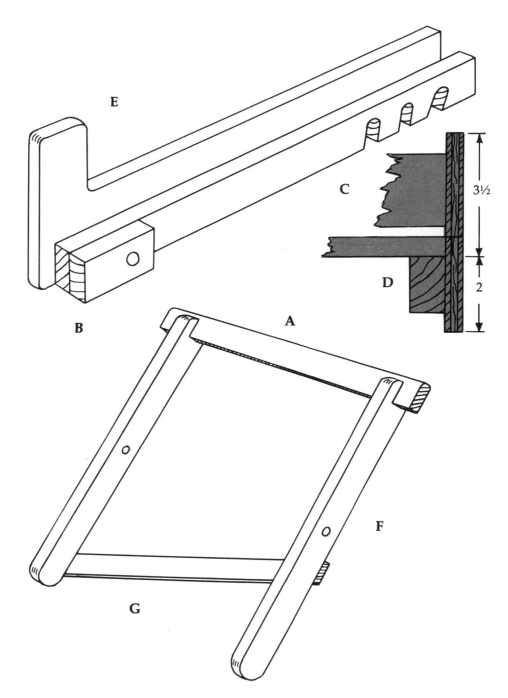

E

C

3½

D

2

B

A

F

G

Fig. 8-29. A side and leg of the Footrest.

Make the pair of top rails (FIG. 8-29C) and join them with the top slats. Space them evenly and with their ends cut level with the outsides of the rails (FIG. 8-29D). Make the outside pieces of plywood that will cover these ends (FIG. 8-29E). They go ½ inch below the rails, come level with the tops of the slats, and have ends projecting upward to take another rail that retains the cushion. Have these pieces ready, but do not fit them yet.

Make the four legs (FIG. 8-29F). One pair has their tops rounded and drilled for pivot bolts. The other pair is cut back with slots to take the crossbar, which projects enough to fit into the slots in the top rails. Allow for ⅜-inch bolts. To brace the legs, put diagonals across. One on each pair of legs should be enough (FIG. 8-29G). Arrange them at opposite angles.

You must let in the heads of the top pivot bolts through the rails flush at the outside so that you can fit the cover pieces. If you use countersunk bolts, this task is easy, but with other heads you will need to counterbore to let them in. Fit these bolts and attach the plywood cover rails. Make the end rail and fit it with screws through the plywood into its ends. If you prefer, you can cut mortises through the plywood and tenon the rail ends. Screws should be strong enough.

Assemble the footrest and test its adjustments. Then disassemble and get ready for painting.

9

Butcher-block Furniture

THE TRADITIONAL BLOCK on which a butcher chops meat is made up of many pieces of wood joined together with their end grain upward. The name *butcher block* is also given to an assembly of pieces laid with their grains parallel to the surface and built up to the area required in much the same way as a wall is built with layers of bricks.

Some furniture for indoor use is made in this way. The method is also suitable for outdoor furniture made of softwood or hardwood. The effect is of a substantial and massive assembly. A complete piece of furniture is usually fairly heavy. Weight can be an advantage in outdoor seats and tables that must be left out and will need to resist knocks or loads which might move them or turn them over. Nevertheless, they are not always as massive as they appear because inner parts are not as thick as outer ones.

For indoor furniture, the parts are glued. Outdoor furniture can be glued, but for many things it will be enough to use nails. For softwoods of fairly large sections, nails alone are satisfactory. Each layer is nailed to the next (FIG. 9-1A). A zigzag arrangement of nails that go well into the lower piece will make a strong joint. For instance, 2-inch planed wood finishes about $1\frac{3}{4}$ inches thick. A 3-inch nail then goes $1\frac{1}{4}$ inches into the lower wood, which is adequate, but a nail much shorter would not be adequate. Of course, nailheads will show on the last piece in a series, but you usually can arrange for it to be at the back or be hidden by another part. Glue in a nailed joint would strengthen it further and prevent water seepage between boards.

If the wood has been completely seasoned, you might rely on glue only, particularly with hardwoods, but unseasoned wood or softwood still containing much moisture will not take glue reliably. You can strengthen a glued joint by using dowels (FIG. 9-1B). The number depends on the joint, but a dowel near each end will resist any tendency for the joint to open.

Joints in the length would be inappropriate in a small assembly, but in a long bench or similar thing you can include an occasional joint to use up shorter pieces. It could even be considered a design feature. The simplest joint is a plain butt (FIG. 9-1C). For this type of joint, make sure the meeting ends are square and forced close together. The meeting angle need not be square so long as both pieces are the same (FIG. 9-1D). If you cut them to a long angle, you can nail through during assembly (FIG. 9-1E). Even with a wider angle, you can drive a nail

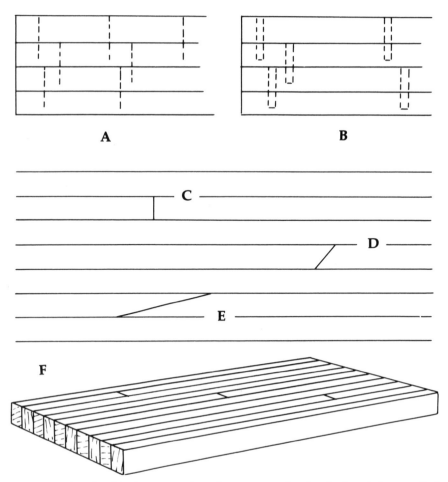

Fig. 9-1. In butcher-block construction, the parts can be glued, doweled, or nailed (A,B), and can be assembled with occasional lengthwise joints (C-F).

diagonally across the joint. For most softwoods, you can nail direct without drilling. Near the ends and in places where accuracy is important, drill undersize almost as far as the nail is to go.

Do not have many joints in the length and always arrange short pieces between others being full length. Even then it looks better and is stronger if you stagger the joints (FIG. 9-1F).

You can use stock sizes of softwood: 2 × 4 inches is the obvious selection. The quality you choose depends on the project, but occasional knots can be regarded as decoration. The method of construction provides mutual support. You can sometimes include a piece with flaws that might not be suitable for an assembly where it must form a part unaided. Straight wood is usually the best choice, but you could cut a curved piece for shorter parts or to butt between other layers that would flatten it.

Hardwoods need not be as massive as softwoods; 2-×-2-inch sizes would suit many things. Much depends on the wood. You could use one wood throughout, but you can get an interesting effect by mixing two or more of different colors.

Alternate strips of dark and light colors or some other arrangement can give an unusual effect.

SOFTWOOD BENCH

A simple bench, sometimes called a *parson's bench*, can be made with the legs included in butcher-block layers (FIG. 9-2A). A short bench is shown, but you can use this method to build up any length bench when you want to provide seating all around the edge of a patio. Intermediate supports would be needed for a length greater than 8 feet.

For a simple bench, have enough pieces ready to make up the width you want and mark across the ends of all of them to get matching lengths. Cut them squarely. You might need to plane the ends after assembly. If you get them fairly accurate first, you will not need to remove much to level them. Alternatively, leave the wood too long and trim all the ends together after nailing. In whichever method you use, you must cut two pieces short by the width of the legs (FIG. 9-2B). Squareness in both directions is important in their ends because it affects the squareness of the legs.

Nail the strips together and include the legs as you progress (FIG. 9-2C). Make up the thickness of the legs with pieces on the outsides (FIG. 9-2D). It is best to leave the tops of the legs very slightly too long so that you can plane them level. Cleanly planed end grain looks good between adjoining long grain.

If the bench is to remain in one place, possibly against something else, legs nailed only should be strong enough. If the bench can be moved about or it might get rough usage, it would be better to provide brackets. They can be simple iron angle or shelf brackets that extend both ways underneath (FIG. 9-3A). If you prefer an all-wood construction, you can nail or screw in wood brackets (FIG. 9-3B).

If the bench is long enough to need intermediate legs, include them during assembly (FIG. 9-3C) at back and front. Thickening pieces should be the same as at the ends.

During the assembly of any bench, watch that it is going together with the top flat and without twist. So far as possible, assemble the top downward on a flat surface, but you will want to tilt the work sideways for convenience in nailing. Bring it back to the inverted position after each series of nails and see that the top still rests close to the flat surface. You also can check by standing the bench on its legs and sighting along. To aid in this check for twist, have long straight strips across the ends to exaggerate any twist (FIG. 9-3D). An old-time carpenter called these *winding strips*, and a twisted assembly was *in winding*.

CORNER SOFTWOOD BENCH

If you want to arrange bench seating around the edge of a patio or if you need to angle the seats for any reason, one way is to merely make separate seats and bring them together. If it would be better to join them, you could use strips of metal or wood underneath (FIG. 9-4A). With that method, you can disassemble them later to rearrange seating. If there is no doubt that the seating will remain where it is made, you can build the seat tops into each other.

It will help to have a frame against which you can assemble the butcher-block strips. You could make the frame from pieces that will be later cut and used in the assembly. Make that frame to match the angle the seat will be. Even if it is apparently 90 degrees, there is no point in carefully getting your bench square

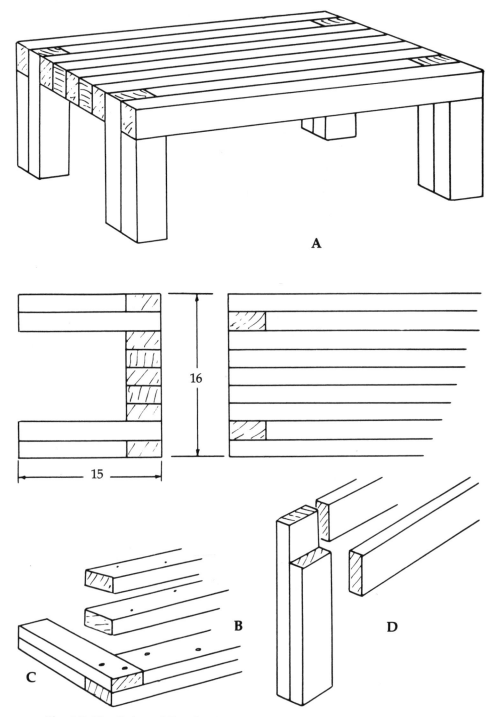

A

B

C

D

Fig. 9-2. The Softwood Bench is built up from standard sections of lumber.

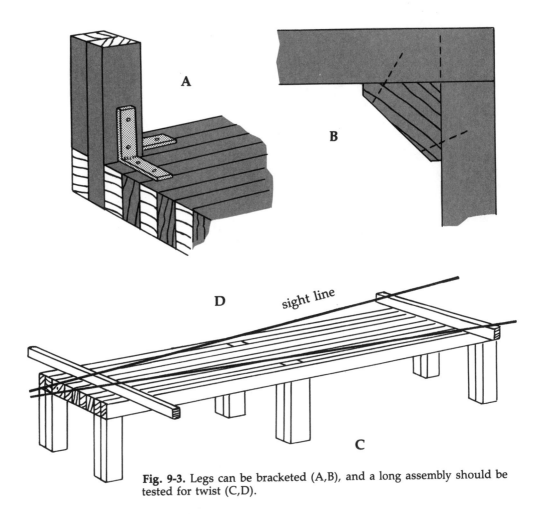

Fig. 9-3. Legs can be bracketed (A,B), and a long assembly should be tested for twist (C,D).

into the corners (FIG. 9-4E). Bring in the legs as you progress. Work upside down, when the deck below or the corner of a house is a degree or so different. Make the frame to the actual shape and brace it with a diagonal strut (FIG. 9-4B).

Decide where you need legs. Their location will vary according to sizes and situations. If the seat fits inside a corner, you can put one leg near the corner at the back and two front legs a short distance each way from the angle (FIG. 9-4C). If the seat goes around an outside angle, a leg can come right at the corner and back legs need not be as close (FIG. 9-4D).

You could make the corners straight and butted, with straps below, but they look better with a herringbone arrangement. Using the frame as a guide, bring the ends together in alternate ways as you nail them in layers. Then add nails as with a straight bench, checking that the assembly is flat and that the legs are upright as you go. Use brackets at the legs. Once the assembly has progressed to many layers, there is little risk of it going out of shape. You can remove the temporary frame and use its parts in further assembly work.

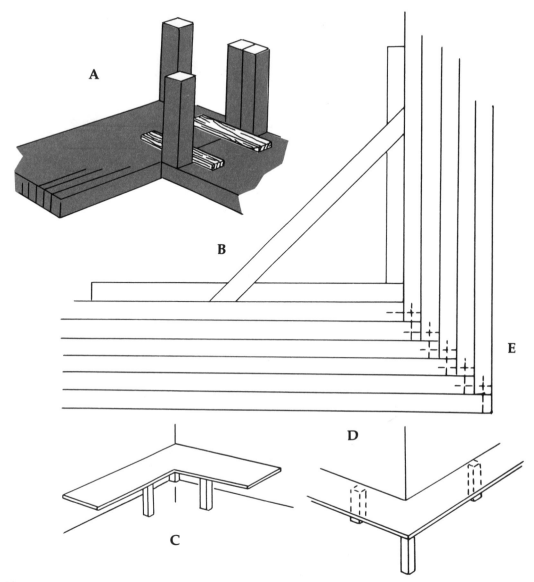

Fig. 9-4. At a corner, parts can be abutted (A), or they can be joined in a herringbone fashion (B-E).

OPEN SOFTWOOD BENCH

The solid benches have smooth, level tops and an attractive massive appearance. They are also heavy and rainwater can settle on top. It might be better in some situations to have gaps between the strips. In a given width, that would be lighter than a solid top and water would be able to run through. In the simplest construction, alternate pieces can be cut short. That method would leave rather wide gaps which would be uncomfortable to sit on, and even cushions would become caught in the spaces. It would be better to have thinner spaces; 1 × 4 inches is a suitable stock section.

The small bench shown in FIG. 9-5A has full-length, 2-inch widths alternating with short sections of 1-inch width. The legs are made up to 5 inches thick. Ends could be left showing the end grain (FIG. 9-5B) or a strip could be put across between the outer sections of the legs (FIG. 9-5C).

Decide on the lengths of filler pieces. They should be shorter than the spaces between them (FIG. 9-5D). Plan the layout to suit the size bench you are making, but fillers between 6 and 12 inches will do. Make enough fillers for the whole bench so that you get them the same length.

For the legs, make the inner and filler pieces the full depth of the bench, but cut back the outer piece (FIG. 9-5E). Nail the parts of the legs together. It will be best to make all the legs so they are ready for fitting to the other parts as you come to them. Set back the tops (FIG. 9-5F) if there is to be a strip across the end of the bench.

Mark on the first outside piece where the legs and spacers will come. Join this piece to the legs and the first set of spacers. As you add more strips, use a try square to mark across so you will fit all the spacers level. Also watch the squareness of the ends if there is to be a strip across them. If the end grain is to be exposed, it would not matter if you left some excess length to be trimmed after complete assembly.

The simplest, closed end has the strip square between the outer pieces (FIG. 9-5G), but you can make a neater corner by mitering (FIG. 9-5H). Although all the parts are shown with sharp angles, you should round the outer edges and corners. You also could round the lengthwise strips and arrange the spacers a short distance below the top level.

For an angled corner of an open bench, there are several ways of arranging a herringbone effect. You could treat each layer, whether a full-length piece or a spacer, separately (FIG. 9-6A) and alternate the laps. Another method is to regard a long piece and its spacer as a unit and alternate these pairs (FIG. 9-6B). Whichever way you do it, the spacers could be all the same length. They should form a diagonal line with the inner ones getting closer to the next spacers (FIG. 9-6C), or you could arrange their lengths so that they come square across (FIG. 9-6D). Keep spaces along the bench the same.

If you want to put a leg at a corner, whether inside or outside the angle, cutting its top away to allow the outer seat pieces to go right through takes rather a lot from the leg. You could allow for this by increasing the wood section to 2 × 6 inches. In any case, there should be wood or metal brackets underneath. Another way would be to cut off the leg below the seat, allowing the top assembly to go right through to the corner, and then secure the leg with angle brackets in both directions to as many top pieces as can be included.

HARDWOOD BENCH

Any of the softwood bench designs could be made in hardwood, but that would result in great weight, increased costs, and a construction far stronger than required. A reasonable section for most benches built solidly is 2 inches square, which finishes after planing to about 1⅞ inches square. The tops can be of that size throughout and legs can be the same or larger section.

In the simple bench shown in FIG. 9-7A, the top is made up in the usual way. It could be of different woods for an unusual appearance. The exposed end grain

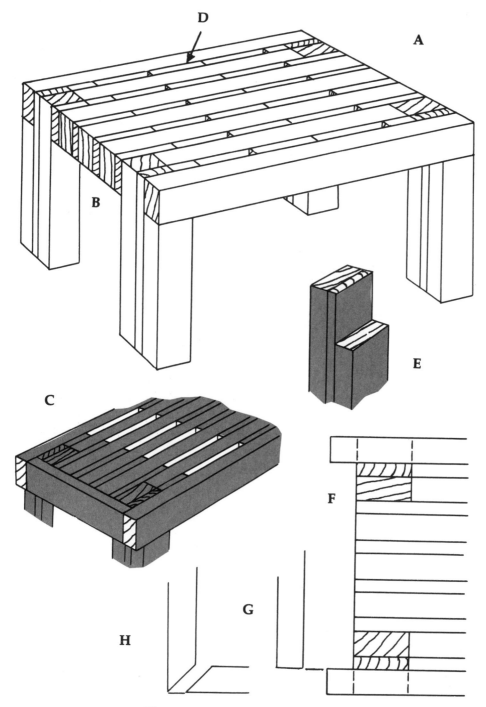

Fig. 9-5. Assembly of the Open Softwood Bench.

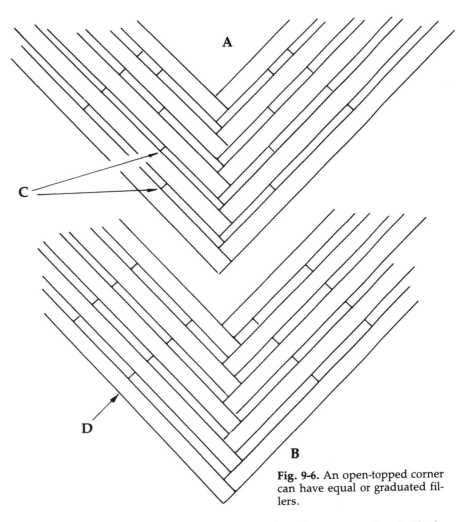

Fig. 9-6. An open-topped corner can have equal or graduated fillers.

adds to the effect (although it would be possible to frame across there). The legs are set in from the ends and are braced with framing. All have their joints to the top hidden. It is possible to do some assembly with nails, but cut joints are more appropriate to good hardwoods. Joints to build up the laminations could be nailed, but elsewhere glued cut joints are better.

Start by making the two assemblies that each consist of a lengthwise piece with legs attached (FIG. 9-7B). Set out the shapes at one leg. For a short bench, the bracing strut can be at 45 degrees. If the bench is long, it is better to take the strut further along (FIG. 9-7C).

Use a mortise-and-tenon joint at the top of a leg (FIG. 9-8A), but do not take it through the top piece. A length of 1 inch or slightly more will be enough for a tenon. Tenon the strut into the leg (FIG. 9-8B). You could use a tenon at the other end of the strut, but it is easier to half-lap it—either straight (FIG. 9-8) or dovetailed (FIG. 9-8D). There will be a rail between each pair of legs. You cannot make the rail yet, but you can cut its mortise in readiness (FIG. 9-8E).

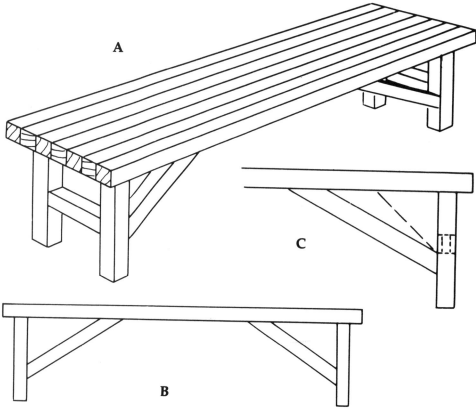

Fig. 9-7. The Hardwood Bench.

With these two assemblies made up, further assembly is just a case of starting at one side with a plain strip outside one legged piece, and adding more layers until you are ready to take in the other legged piece. Glue each joint and then nail it to its neighbor. Doweling is easy. Clamp the glued joint. Then drill through it at about 10-inch intervals so that you can drive in glued dowels (FIG. 9-8F). If you keep the dowels short, they will hold just as well, but you will not have to level their tops after driving. Stagger the dowel positions as you progress.

When you reach the stage of bringing in the second long piece with legs attached, measure the length between shoulders of the lower crosswise rails. Make these rails and glue them in when you build in the legged piece.

If you want to close the ends of the top with strips, make the outer strips long enough to enclose the end pieces (FIG. 9-8G). The end pieces can merely fit between, or you can miter them (FIG. 9-8H). If the size of bench you want to make would be better with thicker legs, there is no difficulty in making them any reasonable section. All that is necessary is to cut a suitable tenon at the top and arrange the rail and strut joints centrally in the leg.

BUTCHER-BLOCK TABLE

A tabletop in the butcher style could be made of thick pieces as described for the benches. The result would be quite heavy, which might be an advantage in

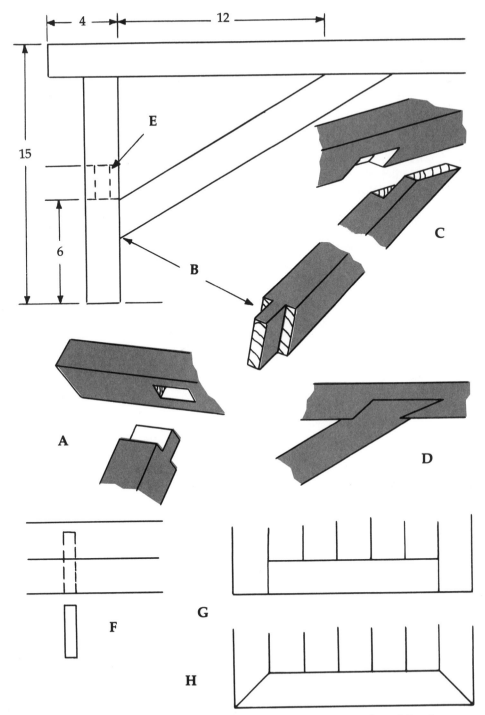

Fig. 9-8. Sizes and methods of constructing the Hardwood Bench.

a permanent situation. If the table is to be used for outdoor hobbies, then a stiff solid top would be an advantage. For the more common outdoor use of a table, it would be better to lighten construction, while retaining the typical butcher-block appearance, so it could partner forms or chairs made the same way.

The table shown in FIG. 9-9 is of a moderate size, with the usual sturdy butcher-block appearance, but with a top that is not as heavy as it appears. The sizes given in FIG. 9-10 and TABLE 9-1 are suggestions. They can be varied according to needs and available wood. Most of the parts are 2-inch-square and 1-×-2-inch sections. They are shown without allowance for planing, but the wood should be planed all around. The final sizes will be less than shown.

It is the central area of the top that controls other sizes. Make this part first. If you work the other way and need to fit the top into a frame, you will need to cut the width of one strip. Join enough strips together (FIG. 9-11A). It might be sufficient to rely on glue only. If so, assemble all the parts of the top face downward on a flat surface covered with paper to prevent glue sticking to it. Pull them together with bar clamps. You will need to put weights on the assembly to prevent it from buckling. A safer way of keeping it flat is to assemble the strips in groups of two or three that have their tops planed true, before joining them to other groups.

You could use nails between the parts in predrilled holes or dowels across in a similar way. Three along each joint should be enough. Have all the pieces too long at this stage so that you can trim the whole assembly as if it is a single board. The way you deal with the ends depends on your equipment. The best way is to rabbet across so that a tongue goes into a plowed groove in the frame (FIG. 9-11B). For this task, you could use a router, two passes on a table saw, or a hand fillester plane.

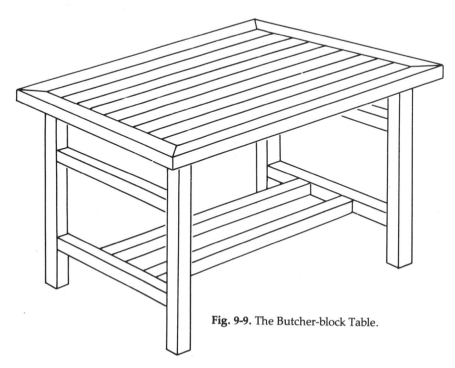

Fig. 9-9. The Butcher-block Table.

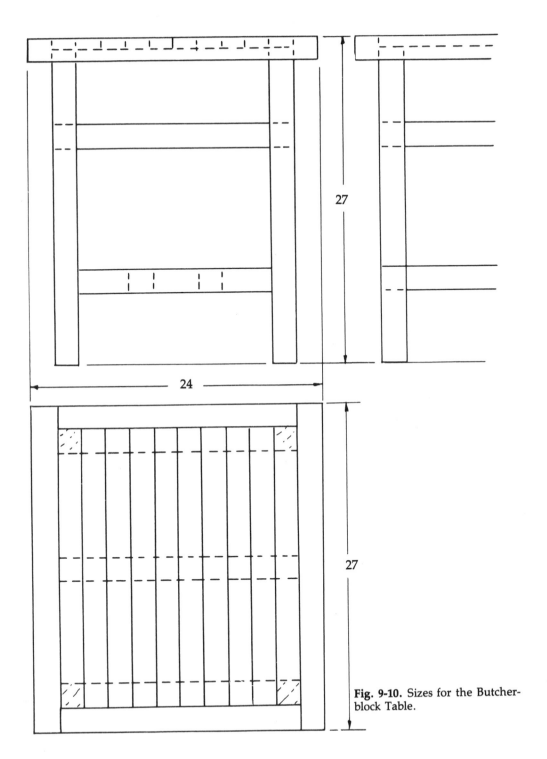

Fig. 9-10. Sizes for the Butcher-block Table.

Table 9-1. Materials List for Butcher-block Table.

10 tops	$2 \times 24 \times 1$
2 tops	$2 \times 28 \times 2$
2 tops	$2 \times 21 \times 2$
1 top stiffener	$2 \times 21 \times 1$
4 legs	$2 \times 27 \times 2$
4 rails	$2 \times 20 \times 2$
4 rails	$2 \times 24 \times 2$
2 rails	$2 \times 20 \times 1$

Alternatively, you can use dowels in square-cut ends (FIG. 9-11C). At the sides, you can glue the joints or use a few dowels there. In the 1-inch thickness, the dowels could be ¾ inch in diameter.

There are three ways of making the frame. You can make the ends go right across with the sides taken into the same plowed grooves (FIG. 9-12A). You could carry the sides through so that the ends are covered, and use dowels in the joint (FIG. 9-12B), going either partly into the sides or taken through. (Exposed dowel ends can be regarded as a design feature in this type of construction.) You also could miter the corners and take dowels through diagonally (FIG. 9-12C).

The top could be stiff enough as it is, but you also could place a piece across under the center, tenoning it into the sides (FIG. 9-11D). Complete the top before you start on the framing. Clean off surplus glue where the legs and their top bars will come underneath.

The legs and rails are all square to match the solid appearance of the top. Four rails go around the table a short distance down from the top. Then there are two rails between the legs at the ends and lengthwise rails between them. At the tops of the legs, there are rails across to take screws upward into the tabletop.

Mark out the legs (FIG. 9-11E). Use mortise-and-tenon joints for the rails. The tenons can go about halfway through the legs. You will need to miter the lower ones where they meet. You could use doweled joints if you prefer, but tenons are more appropriate. You can tenon the thinner top rails to take screws, but they are better dovetailed into the tops of the legs (FIG. 9-11F). Drill for screws before assembly, but angle them slightly so that there is clearance for your screwdriver past the main rail. Make the rails of a length that allows the legs to come closely inside the top frame.

Make up the two end leg and rail assemblies. See that they are square, flat, and match as a pair. Join them with the rails the other way and fit the framework to the tabletop.

RADIAL TABLETOPS

Butcher-block tops do not need to be just parallel strips. You can make interesting tables with the tops divided into segments that are all in the same wood or in alternating colors of woods. You can show your skill by making tops using narrow strips and a large number of segments. For the usual purposes of an outdoor table, however, a more simple arrangement would be appreciated just as much. It will usually be sufficient to divide the top into four segments.

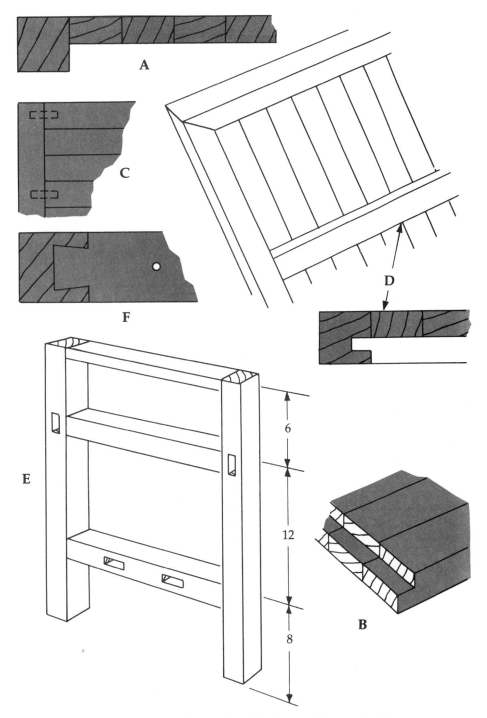

Fig. 9-11. Assembly details of the top and leg construction.

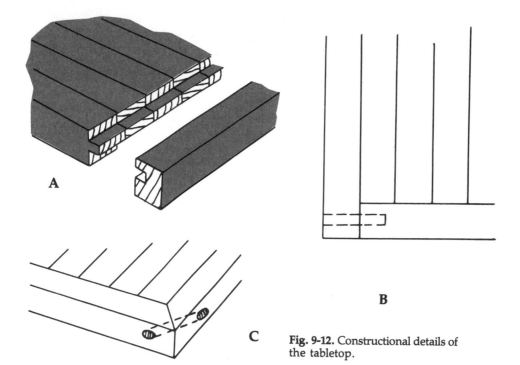

Fig. 9-12. Constructional details of the tabletop.

An example is a square top with or without a border (FIG. 9-13A). This is shown with 2-×-4-inch pieces, with the greater width on the top, but you could also use 2-inch-square pieces or even narrower ones. Join enough pieces to make up the width of a side, with the outside edge cut squarely, but extended enough to mark the miter (FIG. 9-13B). The safest way to get an accurate shape is to set out the final square, with diagonals, full size on a piece of scrap plywood or hardboard, then cut and plane the miter edges to that shape. In any case, you will need to do some careful planing for final close fitting. Mark adjoining surfaces so that they go back in the same place, then drill for a few dowels.

Exposed ends of hardwood look attractive with their different grain patterns, particularly if woods are mixed and the ends are sealed with varnish. Softwoods are better covered. You can make a border (FIG. 9-13C) with mitered or lapped corners. You can attach the top to legs and framing made in the way described for the previous table.

A very similar top is easily converted to round (FIG. 9-13D). This is shown with square strips. The best plan to get a good shape is to start with the outline of a square table and draw the circle when the parts are joined. You could draw curves on each segment, but cut oversize so there can be a final trimming to a true circle later.

The strips used do not all need to have the same widths. You can obtain an interesting effect by using random widths. This is a way of using up oddments left from other work. You can alternate wide and narrow pieces. Dark narrow pieces between lighter colored ones can be very attractive. An example is shown with an octagonal outline (FIG. 9-13E), but you could use the design in other shapes.

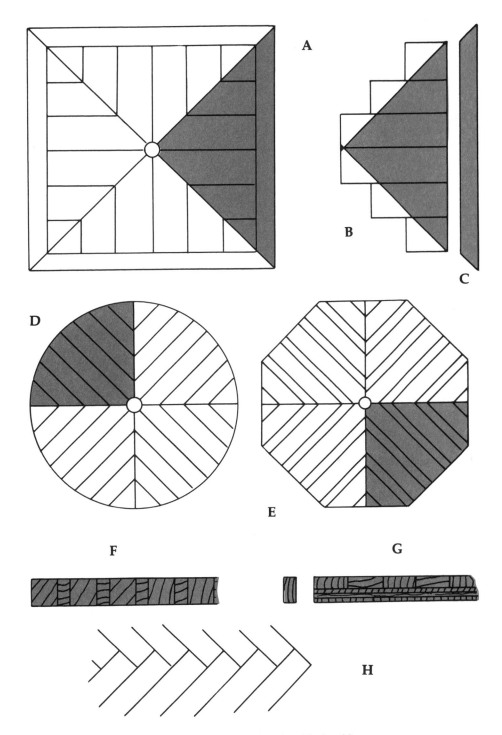

Fig. 9-13. Suggestions for radial butcher-block tabletops.

You can border any top having straight edges with strips glued and nailed or screwed on. An alternative to a square, unbordered edge is to make it semicircular or to bevel around top and bottom edges.

The usual assembly is with pieces to the full thickness of the top (FIG. 9-13F), but there is an alternative way of getting a similar top appearance using thinner wood. For the base, mark or cut a piece of stout exterior-grade plywood to the shape the table is to be. On the plywood, place thinner strips of wood to make up any pattern you prefer (FIG. 9-13G). You can use any of the patterns suitable for solid wood, but in this case you can put the pieces in place over a penciled pattern on the plywood. You can glue the parts or drive screws from below as well. Glue is advisable, in any case, because it seals the gaps and prevents water from becoming trapped between and under the strips.

A variation in pattern that would be difficult with solid pieces but that is easier to do on a plywood base, is to arrange the meeting pieces in a herringbone pattern (FIG. 9-13H) instead of straight miters. Add a border, bedded in glue, to prevent moisture from being absorbed by the exposed end grain of the plywood veneers.

FLAT-SEAT CHAIR

Chairs to match other butcher-block furniture can have their seats and backs made in the typical manner, but otherwise they follow the usual construction. This project is a plain chair with a flat, sloping seat and a similar back (FIG. 9-14). The butcher-block parts are made up from strips 1⅜ inches square (FIG. 9-15). The

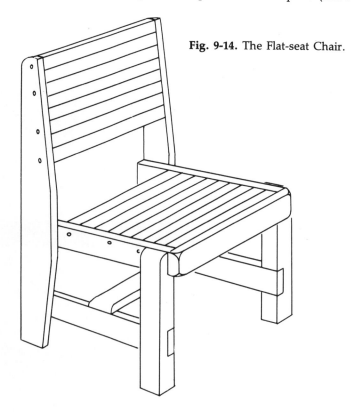

Fig. 9-14. The Flat-seat Chair.

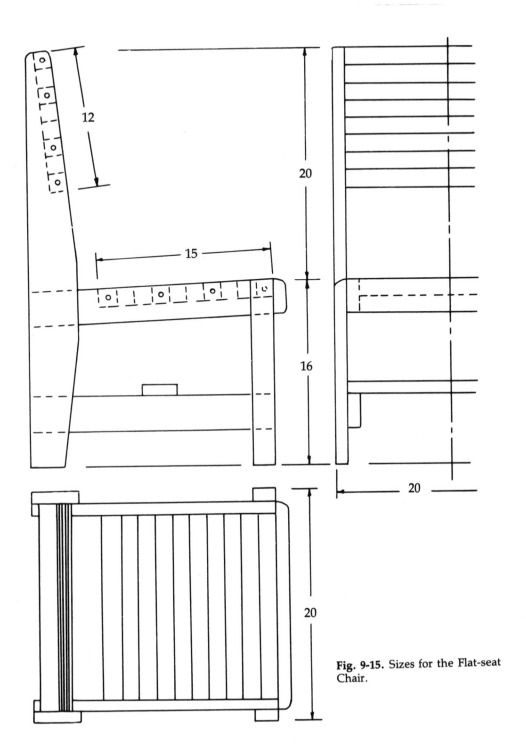

Fig. 9-15. Sizes for the Flat-seat Chair.

Table 9-2. Materials List for Flat-Seat Chair.

10 seats	1½ × 17 × 1½
8 backs	1½ × 19 × 1½
2 legs	4 × 37 × 1
2 legs	2 × 17 × 1
2 seat sides	3 × 22 × 1
1 seat front	3 × 21 × 1
2 bottom rails	3 × 22 × 1
1 bottom rail	3 × 20 × 1

design is intended for hardwood that will match a table. Like other assemblies, you can use a mixture of woods that will look good when varnished.

The butcher-block parts control some of the other sizes. Start with the seat. Make up enough pieces to give a total width of about 15 inches. You could use glue only or nail or dowel through as you add each piece (as described for some of the benches). Square the ends to length. Round what will be the rear edge, but leave the front square because it will receive a cover strip.

Join the ends of the seat to the sides with dowels (FIG. 9-16A). For accurate drilling, mark where the holes will come in the sides and drill through both together. Then put a side against an end and use its holes as a guide to drill into

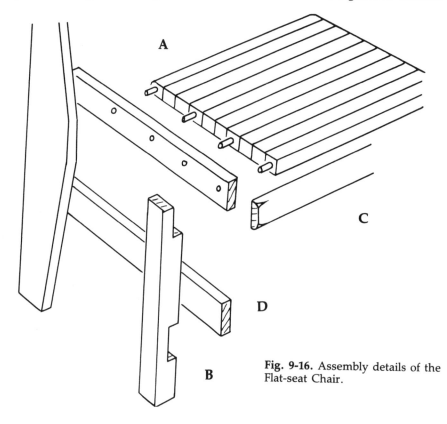

Fig. 9-16. Assembly details of the Flat-seat Chair.

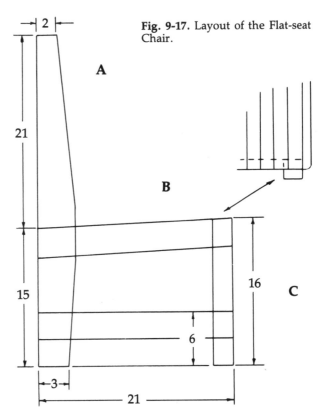

Fig. 9-17. Layout of the Flat-seat Chair.

the end grain. Have the front end of each side square with the seat, but leave the rear end too long at this stage. Cut it against the rear leg later. Join the seat and sides. Trim the dowel ends later.

The length of the back is the same as the distance across the seat and its sides. Make the butcher-block back and mark where its dowels will come.

Make the back legs (FIG. 9-17A), tapering them to the ends, but keeping them parallel where the seat sides will be attached. Give the seat a slope back. Set this out full size to get the position and angle of the seat side on the legs (FIG. 9-17B). Make the front legs (FIG. 9-17C) square, but notched to take the seat sides and the lower rails (FIG. 9-16B).

Fit the butcher-block back between the rear legs in the same way as the seat is doweled to its sides. Use your full-size setting out as a guide to the position and angle of the seat sides on the rear legs. Then join with glue and screws driven from inside. Fit the front legs and see that they are parallel to the straight edges of the rear legs. Well-round the exposed edges at the tops of the front legs.

Add the seat front (FIG. 9-16C) and well-round its edges and ends. Fit the lower rails at the sides into the front leg notches (FIG. 9-16D) and screw them inside to the legs parallel to the floor. Add a rail across between their centers to help rigidity. Take off sharpness of edges and remove surplus glue before varnishing.

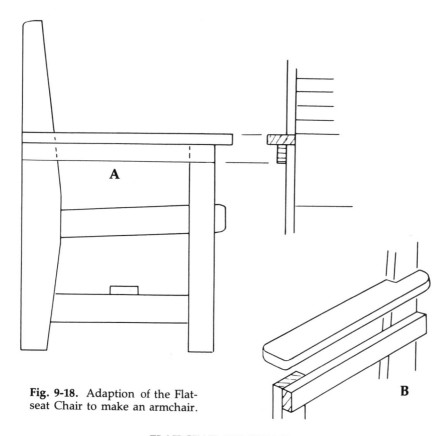

Fig. 9-18. Adaption of the Flat-seat Chair to make an armchair.

FLAT-SEAT ARMCHAIR

The open seat of the previous design can be converted to an armchair during construction. Sizes can remain the same or you can increase the seat area by 1 or 2 inches in both directions.

The general design remains the same, but carry the front legs up to hold the arms (FIG. 9-18). Instead of square front legs, use a 1-×-3-inch section screwed to the outsides of the seat sides in the same way as the rear legs. At the tops of the front legs, arrange a 1-×-2-inch rail to the back legs (FIG. 9-18A). Screw it outside both legs and parallel with the floor—not with the sloping seat.

The 1-×-3-inch arms go above these strips. Notch them around the rear legs. You could curve the outline of an arm, but for the solid butcher-block appearance they are better straight (FIG. 9-18B) with rounded edges and corners. Screw downward and into the back legs, preferably with the screw heads counterbored and plugged. If you screw outward from the rear legs, the heads will not be very obvious.

SHAPED-SEAT CHAIR

If a chair is to be comfortable for long use without padding, it needs some shaping. Ideally, there should be compound curvature in the seat, but that is almost impossible to produce in wood without considerable, careful work. The most

Table 9-3. Materials List for Shaped-Seat Chair.

2 legs	4 × 35 × 1½
2 legs	3 × 16 × 1½
2 sides	3 × 20 × 1½
1 front rail	3 × 20 × 1½
9 seats	1½ × 21 × 1
12 backs	1½ × 16 × 1
2 back supports	
	from 6 × 20 × 1

important need is shaping from front to back. This can be arranged fairly easily with the butcher-block technique. It helps to have some curve across the chair back, and that is also fairly easy to make. (See TABLE 9-3.)

The chair shown in FIG. 9-19 is intended to be rather more advanced than hammer-and-nail construction, or even dowel construction. It is an example of cabinetwork taken outdoors. The finished chair can have uses in the house, as well as outside, if it is given a good finish. If made of hardwoods—probably of mixed colors—and finished with clear varnish, it becomes a very attractive piece of furniture for use anywhere. FIGURE 9-20 shows a chair of fairly roomy proportions. Sizes could be reduced slightly if it is to be used indoors with other smaller chairs, but outdoors a large size will often be appreciated.

Fig. 9-19. The Shaped-seat Chair.

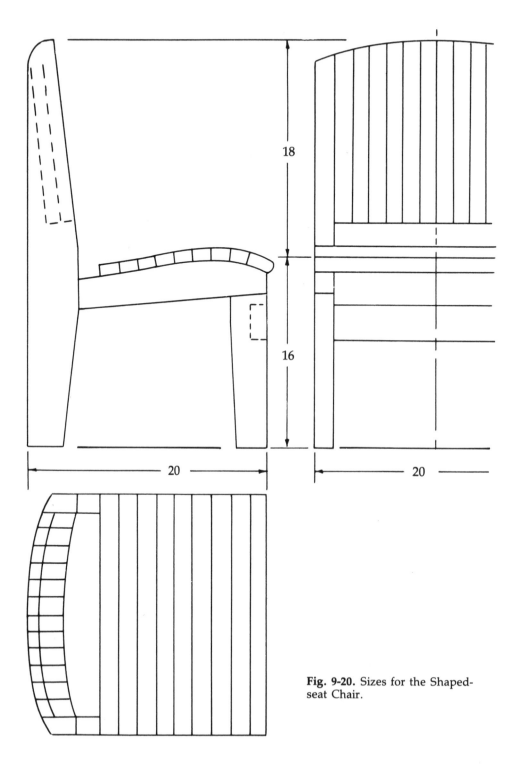

Fig. 9-20. Sizes for the Shaped-seat Chair.

The rails that support the seat slope back for economy in cutting the curve. Make a full-size outline drawing of a side view (FIG. 9-21A). From this, get the shape of a rail and mark on it the angles of the cuts and joints. Then draw the curve of the top edge. Use the pattern of 1½-inch squares as a guide (FIG. 9-21B). Cut the curve on the two matching sides.

Mark out the front legs so that you can cut the joints between them and the seat sides. To make these joints, it is best to use double tenons cut back about ½ inch from the front (FIG. 9-21C). They go about 1¼ inches into the seat sides. Cut the mortises in the seat sides before you cut the wood to length in order to reduce the risk of short grain breaking out.

The curving of the top edge reduces the rear end of the sides to about 2½ inches. Make a mortise-and-tenon joint there to the leg, with double tenons similar to those on the front legs, but there is no need to cut back from either edge. Cut the tenons on the sides. You can leave the matching mortises until later.

With the two sides prepared, have ready the pieces that will make the seat. Because of the varying curve, you must plane their edges to meet as you fit each one in turn. This is not as difficult as you might think because one edge of each piece is always square in section. You will start at the front and work back. Take care to keep the assembly square. Although the joints will be glued, it helps in assembly to put one screw in the end of each piece you fit it. In the finished chair, the seat will look good with plugs over counterbored screw heads. At this stage, it will be simplest to use thin temporary screws. When the seat is fully assembled and the glue set, you can remove the screws, and drill and counterbore the holes for larger screws and plugs.

Start at the front, with one piece having both edges square (FIG. 9-22A). Plane the edge of the next piece to fit against it closely. Leave its other edge square (FIG. 9-22B), then glue and screw it in place. Do the same with the next one, and so on until you have made up enough for the seat. Later you can plane and sand the top surface to a smooth curve, if you prefer, but the series of narrow flats will not be noticed when sitting and they help to give the butcher-block appearance. Level the outer ends of the strips and round the top edges. Well-round the front edge of the seat.

Make the back legs (FIG. 9-21D). Cut the mortises for the seat sides, but leave preparation for the back until you make up that piece. The butcher-block back must fit between the back legs, which will be the same distance apart as the sides of the seat, so use them as a gauge for the overall width.

In the finished chair, there are two curved pieces behind the back tenoned into the back legs (FIG. 9-21E). In order to get the curve of the butcher-block back true, make these pieces too wide at first. You can use them as cradles in which to assemble the back. If made too narrow, they could buckle during assembly. They are shown about 6 inches wide, but exact width is not important. Mark on these pieces their final shapes and the tenons which you will need to cut after you have glued on all the strips.

Arrange one piece at what will be the bottom edge of the back and the other far enough down to allow for its curved top edge. Then put on the central strip (FIG. 9-22C). This has both edges square and must be square to the supports. Glue and screw it in the same way as the seat strips. Work outward from that and keep the bottom ends level. Plane the next pieces to match it, but leave their other edges square. Fit them in turn on opposite sides so that the width increases symmetrically about the center. When you reach the outside, you will need to

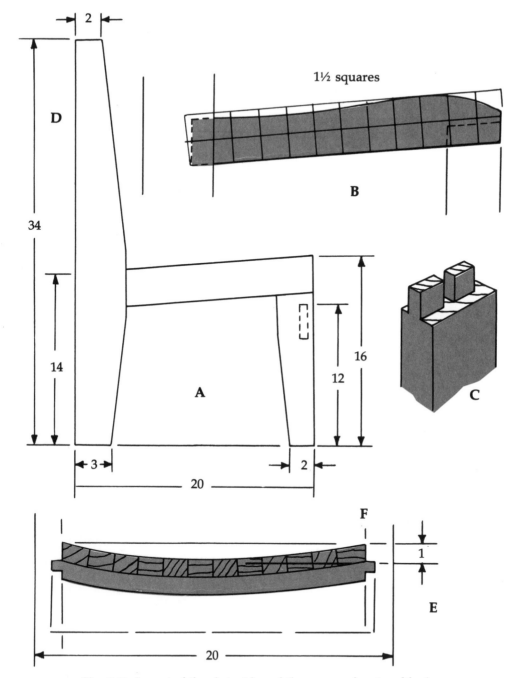

Fig. 9-21. Layout of the chair side and the curves of seat and back.

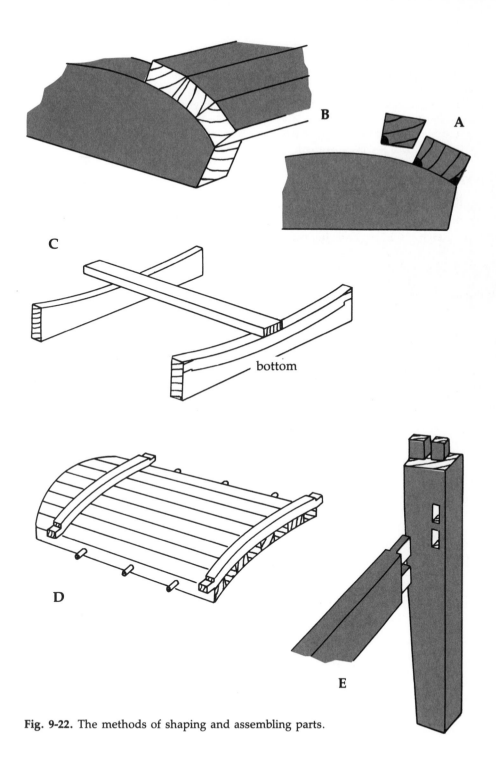

Fig. 9-22. The methods of shaping and assembling parts.

plane the edges to size and to the angle that will fit them between the legs (FIG. 9-21F).

Cut off the surplus wood from the supports at the back. Trim them to a neat curve and round their exposed edges. Draw a curve over the tops of the strips and cut the curve. You can make it resemble anything you like, but keep it symmetrical and about 2 inches lower at the sides than at the center. In addition to the tenons and glue between the back and the legs, there should be some dowels (FIG. 9-22D). Use the back to mark where mortises and dowel holes are to come on the legs. Shape the tops of the legs to follow on the curve of the back, and round the outer corners.

Complete the front legs. Make the front rail (FIG. 9-22E), which crosses far enough below the seat to avoid its joints and provides crosswise stiffness without interfering with a sitter's legs.

Assembly is best done in one process, instead of in two steps as with many chairs. Fit the rail between the front legs and join them to the seat. Check squareness in the front view by measuring diagonals. Check the angle in side view by comparing with your full-size drawing. Assemble the back to the rear legs, preferably pulling tight with bar clamps, and then bring the rear legs to the seat. As you close those joints, check that the rear edges of the back legs are parallel with the front edges of the front legs.

Stand the chair on a level surface and look at it from all directions to see that it is true. You can make adjustments before the glue starts to set. If any tenoned joints are not as good a fit as they should be, you can strengthen them by drilling across for ¼-inch dowels. Their exposed ends will form part of the pattern made by the plugs over screws in the seat and back.

Index

Other Books in The TAB Furniture Woodshop Series

Do-It-Yourselfer's Guide to Furniture Repair and Refinishing—2nd Edition

Brush up on the latest woodworking techniques and applications.
Restore furniture to its original character and beauty—even make it better than it was! Precise directions cover everything from selecting a finish to using stains and fillers, from striping the old varnish to applying the new, even restoring cane, metal, and bamboo furniture. Almost 200 two-color illustrations show you how to: make inlays . . . turn wood . . . rebuild panels . . . reupholster . . . reinforce joints . . . replace veneers . . . remove blemishes . . . imitate grains . . . "antique" surfaces . . . and much, much more!

Designing and Building Colonial and Early American Furniture, with 47 Projects—2nd Edition

Capture the spirit and style of authentic Colonial and Early American craftsmanship!
Build your own Shaker, Pennsylvania Dutch, and other Colonial and Early American style furniture for a fraction of what you'd pay for authentic antiques or even store-bought reproductions! Blandford provides expert guidance in such traditional woodworking techniques as joining, veneering, carving, turning, and molding. He also shows you how to recognize good furniture design, how to solve specific design problems, how to use power tools to save time without sacrificing design integrity, and much more.

Designing and Building Children's Furniture with 61 Projects—2nd Edition

A step-by-step guide to making all kinds of children's furniture and toys, from cribs, cradles, and desks, to a rocking horse, play house, and toy box.
Devoted entirely to children's furniture, this book shows you how to turn inexpensive materials into useful furnishings children will enjoy. You'll learn the basics of furniture making, along with some important woodworking tips and techniques. Packed with two-color illustrations and easy-to-follow instructions, this revised edition provides everything you need to construct useful, sturdy furniture that is as much fun to make as as it is to use.

Designing and Building Space-Saving Furniture, with 28 Projects—2nd Edition

Unique ideas for saving money and space with built-in furniture you create!
Step-by-step directions, exploded drawings, detailed materials lists, and plenty of suggestions for project variations explain every aspect of making space-saving furniture. An excellent guide to designing and constructing built-in furniture, this book provides the novice craftsman with a complete course in measuring, marking, designing, and building furniture to meet specific space restrictions. Projects include complete instructions for building corner and hanging cabinets, room dividers, and units for kitchens, bedrooms, and other household areas.